macromedia®
FLASH® 8
Training from the Source

James English

macromedia®
PRESS

Macromedia® Flash® 8
Training from the Source
James English

 Macromedia Press books are published by:

Peachpit

1249 Eighth Street
Berkeley, CA 94710
510/524-2178
800/283-9444
510/524-2221 (fax)
Find us on the World Wide Web at:
www.peachpit.com
www.macromedia.com

To report errors, please send a note to errata@peachpit.com

Printed and bound in the United States of America

ISBN 0-321-33629-1

9 8 7 6 5 4 3 2 1

Credits

Author
James English

Macromedia Press Editor
Angela C. Kozlowski

Editor
Robyn G. Thomas

Technical Editor
Demian A. Holmberg

Production Coordinator
Simmy Cover

Copy Editor
Nancy Sixsmith

Indexer
Joy Dean Lee

Cover Production
Ellen Reilly

Compositor
Jerry Ballew

Bio

A Macromedia Certified Instructor, James English can be found in New York helping people discover Macromedia Flash, Dreamweaver, and Fireworks. He works for a company called Motion Over Time, which for five years now has put up with his various eccentricities. Depending on with whom you speak, he absolutely despises talking about himself, enjoys teaching people how to do stuff, is a dreadful bore, and is entirely too big for his britches. Oh, and he's probably one of the few people left who still doesn't have his own website. Shame, shame on him.

Dedication

This book is dedicated to my family, without whom what little sanity I have would have long since flittered away, and to those whom I am proud to count among my friends. You know who you are.

Acknowledgments

This book is the result of the hard work of many people. It is also an update of Jen deHaan's previous and exceptional work. In fact, much of Jen's original writing is still found in the update, which is a testament to her skill and ability. I owe you one also for hosting the ColdFusion scripts used to process the forms in this book! Thank you very much Jen, and I hope this update is a credit to you. You're the cat's whiskers!

Thank you also to Byron Regej, who took care of the artwork you see through the book; his hard work saved me more time than he can possibly imagine. He even sacrificed precious moments from his vacation with his father to help me out! A better friend and a more professional guy you could hardly hope to find.

Special thanks goes to the very kind, very patient Robyn Thomas and Angela Kozlowski; to Nancy Sixsmith and Demian A. Holmberg for keeping me honest; to Nilson Neuschotz, my employer and friend at Motion Over Time; and to everyone who lent their expertise to this project. None of this work could have been done without you.

And last but not least, thank you to my family, woefully neglected through the summer.

My thanks again to all of you, and anyone whom I may have missed. You are all wonderful people and I'm thankful to know you all.

Table of Contents

Prerequisites

To make the most of this course, you should at the very least understand web terminology. This book isn't designed to teach you anything more than Flash 8 Basic, so the more you understand the World Wide Web, the better off you'll be. Other than that, as long as you can turn a computer on and off, you'll be a great candidate for this book.

Outline

As you'll soon discover, this book mirrors real-world practices as much as possible. Although certain sections of the book depart from what would be considered a real-world practice, every attempt has been made to inform you. The exercises are designed to get you using the tools and the interface quickly so that you can begin to work on projects of your own with as smooth a transition as possible.

This curriculum should take approximately 16–20 hours to complete and includes the following lessons:

Lesson 1: Learning the Basics

Lesson 2: Creating Graphics

Lesson 3: Using Text

Lesson 4: Creating and Editing Symbols

Lesson 5: Creating Animations

Lesson 6: Adding Basic Interactivity

Lesson 7: Adding Sound and Video

Lesson 8: Creating Forms Using Components

Lesson 9: Learning ActionScript Basics

Lesson 10: Loading and Optimizing Flash Content

Lesson 11: Publishing Flash Documents

The Project Application

Macromedia Flash 8: Training from the Source includes a vast number of comprehensive tutorials aimed at showing you how to create a complete application using Flash 8 Basic. You will create an "online bookstore" application (without a shopping cart) that loads text, images, and a video presentation into the website, which serves as a tour for the website. It also contains a couple of feedback forms that connect to a server script, some audio, and even a partially animated map providing directions to the fictitious store.

By the end of 11 hands-on lessons, you will complete building an entire website using Flash. You will begin by creating the graphical user interface, which includes imported graphics, drawings you create right in Flash, as well as different kinds of animations. You import a video into a Flash Timeline and publish SWFs with the embedded video you imported. Then you will create an interactive presentation that uses those SWFs using ActionScript and the Timeline, which will be loaded at a different point into the main application.

This project includes learning the fundamentals of ActionScript: from the meaning of the scripting terminology to some of the better practices for completing a task and working with code. Even if you are uneasy with writing scripts or any kind of code in general, you will probably find the coding examples that are used both easy and intuitive. Finally, you will optimize your application so it is appropriate for the web and then publish the files so they can be uploaded and placed online.

Standard Elements in the Book

Each lesson in this book begins by outlining the major focus of the lesson at hand and introducing new features. Learning objectives and the approximate time needed to complete all the exercises are also listed at the beginning of each lesson. The projects are divided into short exercises that explain the importance of each skill you learn. Every lesson will build on the concepts and techniques used in the previous lessons.

Tips: Alternative ways to perform tasks and suggestions to consider when applying the skills you are learning.

Notes: Additional background information to expand your knowledge, as well as advanced techniques you can explore in order to further develop your skills.

Boldface text: Text that you must type while working through the steps in the lessons.

Code in text: Code keywords appear in slightly different form from the rest of the text so you can identify them.

Italicized text: New vocabulary that is introduced and emphasized in each lesson.

Menu commands and keyboard shortcuts: There are often multiple ways to perform the same task in Flash. The different options will be pointed out in each lesson. Menu commands are shown with angle brackets between the menu names and commands: Menu > Command > Subcommand. Keyboard shortcuts are shown with a plus sign between the names of keys to indicate that you should press the keys simultaneously; for example, Shift+Tab means that you should press the Shift and Tab keys at the same time.

Appendixes: This book includes three appendixes. Appendix A, "Installing Extensions," includes information on how to install and use the Macromedia Extension Manager and where to find extensions. Appendix B, "Resources," contains links to valuable online resources. Appendix C, "Keyboard Shortcuts," lists shortcuts in Flash 8 Basic.

CD-ROM: The CD-ROM included with the book includes a trial version of Macromedia Flash 8, all the media files, starting files, incremental project files, and completed projects for each of the lessons in the book. Any time you want to reference one of the files being built in a lesson to verify that you are correctly executing the steps in the exercises, you will find the files organized on the CD-ROM under the corresponding lesson. For example, the files for Lesson 4 are located on the CD-ROM in the lesson04 folder.

The directory structure of the lessons you will be working with is as follows:

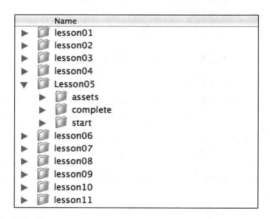

For additional practice with the skills you will learn in each lesson, try re-creating the starting files that have been provided for you in the lesson files.

Macromedia *Training from the Source*

The Macromedia *Training from the Source* and *Advanced Training from the Source* series are developed in association with Macromedia, and reviewed by the product support teams. Ideal for active learners, the books in the *Training from the Source* series offer hands-on instruction designed to provide you with a solid grounding in the program's fundamentals. If you learn best by doing, this is the series for you. Each *Training from the Source* title contains hours of instruction on Macromedia software products. They are designed to teach the techniques that you need to create sophisticated professional-level projects. Each book includes a CD-ROM that contains all the files used in the lessons, completed projects for comparison and more.

Macromedia Authorized Training and Certification

This book is geared to enable you to study at your own pace with content from the source. Other training options exist through the Macromedia Authorized Training Partner program. Get up to speed in a matter of days with task-oriented courses taught by Macromedia Certified Instructors. Or learn on your own with interactive online training from Macromedia University. All these sources of training will prepare you to become a Macromedia Certified Developer.

For more information about authorized training and certification, check out `www.macromedia.com/go/training1`.

What You Will Learn

You will develop the skills you need to create and maintain your own websites as you work through these lessons.

By the end of the course, you will be able to:

- Navigate and use the toolset found in the Flash authoring environment
- Use assets to create an engaging user interface
- Create animation using several different animating techniques
- Import media such as PNG and video files
- Use the built-in component set to create forms to capture data from a visitor
- Use Script Assist to add interactivity to your Flash Application
- Use behaviors to instantly add ActionScript to a document
- Understand how ActionScript works with your Flash documents and make components work
- Use ActionScript to send information out of Flash
- Load external content at run
- Add metadata to your Flash documents for better search engine visibility
- Organize your FLA files so you can optimize and publish your Flash files

Minimum System Requirements

Windows

- 800 MHz Intel Pentium III processor (or equivalent) and later
- Windows 2000, Windows XP
- 256 MB RAM (1 GB recommended to run more than one Studio 8 product simultaneously)
- 1024 x 768, 16-bit display (32-bit recommended)
- 710 MB available disk space

Macintosh

- 600 MHz PowerPC G3 and later
- Mac OS X 10.3, 10.4
- 256 MB RAM (1 GB recommended to run more than one Studio 8 product simultaneously)
- 1024 x 768, thousands of colors display (millions of colors recommended)
- 360 MB available disk space

* Some features require QuickTime 6.3 or QuickTime Pro 6.3 or higher.

* Flash 8 will require product activation over the Internet or by phone.

The Studio 8 line of products is extremely exciting, and we're waiting to be amazed by what you will do with it. With a strong foundation in Flash, you can grow and expand your skillset quickly. Flash is really not too difficult to use, no matter what your background might be. With a little bit of initiative and effort, you can fly through the following lessons and be building your own custom applications and sites in no time.

1 Learning the Basics

So you want to learn how to use Flash 8 Basic or Flash 8 Professional? No problem. You probably already know what these tools do, but here's the breakdown: Flash gives you the ability to create applications, animations, games, or applications for mobile devices such as cell phones. You can deploy all these things on the web, on CD-ROM, and over a network, or you can run them on desktops or laptops. Because of the ubiquity of Flash Player, using Flash to produce websites is ideal because Flash isn't burdened by the restrictions of HTML. You can use it to create desktop-like applications delivered via the web!

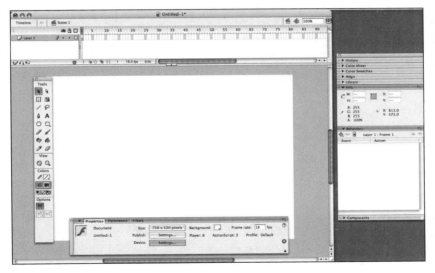

The Flash interface

In this first lesson, you'll learn what is probably the most important concept: how to navigate through the Flash interface and use its tools to produce the advanced websites that you want (and have wanted since you first launched your first browser). You'll learn about the workspace, the panels, the tools, and of course how to publish a SWF file (although the complexity of publishing isn't covered until Lesson 11). At the very end of this lesson, you'll look at the application you'll build throughout the rest of the course.

What You Will Learn

In this lesson, you will:

- Explore the Flash workspace
- Create and save a new Flash document
- Use panels, menus, the Stage
- Use the Timeline and frames
- Change document settings and preferences
- Test a SWF file
- Learn how to find help
- Explore the final project

Approximate Time

This lesson takes approximately one hour to complete.

Lesson Files

Media Files:
None

Starting Files:
None

Completed Files:
lesson01/complete/bookstore3.fla

Introducing Flash 8

Macromedia Flash is a fusion of design and development tools used to produce everything from websites to computer-based training modules. It has a set of richly featured drawing tools and an object-oriented scripting language that when combined can be used to create attractive interfaces with V8 engines (so to speak). What's more, with the introduction of the Flash Lite Player, Flash can be used to create software for mobile devices.

Flash is actually broken up into two separate pieces of software. First is the editing environment, which you use to produce your own software. The second is Flash Player, which interprets, displays, and executes applications distributed as SWF files. (*SWF* stands for *small web file*, and although the format is primarily used for delivering web-based applications, it is by no means limited to that.) Whichever way you distribute it, the SWF file format can be viewed only if the end user has Flash Player involved.

> **Tip** *Flash 8 Basic and Flash 8 Professional allow you to publish your applications for previous versions of Flash Player, as well as for Flash Lite (for mobile platforms).*

So why should you care about Flash? Well, for starters, it's very flexible, and (in fact) extensible, so what it doesn't do out-of-the-box, you can make it do on your own. Better yet, other people have written extensions that you can download and install directly from the Macromedia website. For another, Flash Player is practically ubiquitous, being installed on roughly 97% of web browsing computers worldwide. Flash Player is small, quick and easy to install and update, and freely distributed. Finally, the Flash product is integrated with other Macromedia software, such as Fireworks and Dreaweaver, and other third-party software to streamline your workflow.

> **Tip** *For extensions to Flash, go to www.macromedia.com/exchange, and browse the Flash category. Some extensions are free, some you have to buy, and hardly any of them are made by Macromedia. Be sure to check the ratings before you decide to download anything.*

Finally, you should care about Flash because of ActionScript. Aptly named, ActionScript is the engine that makes your applications go. It is an object-oriented scripting language, based on the same standard as JavaScript and Rhino, and is altogether a nifty tool to help you make your Flash-based applications small, powerful, and a joy to use.

There are numerous other reasons to use and care about Flash, all of which you will explore as you move through this training book. So don't panic; those other things you've heard of (such as sharing assets across SWF files and preloading and all that other industry jargon) will be covered.

Looking at the Flash Workspace

When you open Flash 8 for the first time, regardless of which version you are using, the first thing you will see is the Start menu, which is actually a SWF file split into several categories: Open Recent Item > Create New > Templates at the top; a section displays at the bottom that contains links to various tutorials, and a section displays that either shows updates to Flash or displays a link to Macromedia if there are no updates available.

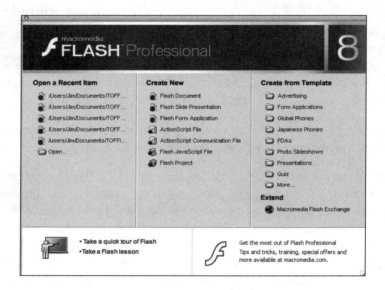

Tip *The Start page does need an active Internet connection to check for updates to Flash 8. If you have no Internet connection, things might slow down a bit; press the Do Not Show Again button at the lower left of the start screen to disable it. You can also disable it in Edit › Preferences for Windows or Flash 8 › Preferences on the Mac, in the General tab.*

The Flash workspace, also known as the *authoring environment*, has a series of panels situated around a Stage. Flash files are based on Timelines, which is where all your visual assets and ActionScripts are organized into layers. A playhead moves along these Timelines when a file with more than one frame plays in Flash Player. Frames represent positions in time and serve much the same purpose as frames in a cinema film, which is to produce the appearance of motion. Following are screen shots for Flash 8 on both the Mac and Windows platforms. You will learn more about how each part of the workspace functions later in this lesson and throughout the book. Many options will be dimmed or not visible until you create a new document of some sort.

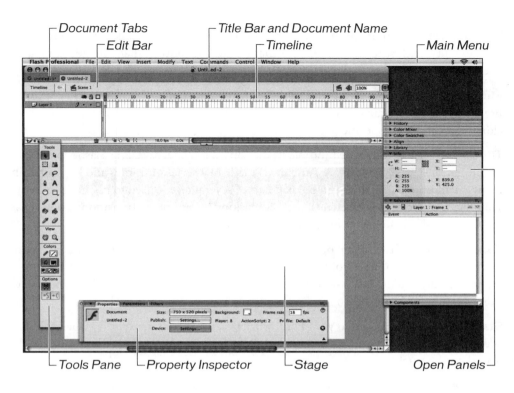

Document Tabs · Edit Bar · Title Bar and Document Name · Timeline · Main Menu

Tools Pane · Property Inspector · Stage · Open Panels

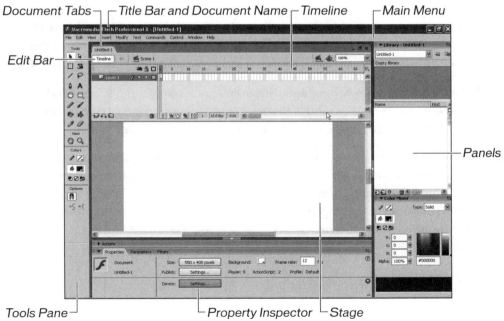

Document Tabs · Title Bar and Document Name · Timeline · Main Menu

Edit Bar

Panels

Tools Pane · Property Inspector · Stage

The authoring environment can be divided into several large sections, based on their functionality. Each section also contains many different controls that you will learn about later on in the book.

Menus: Menus in Flash are much like the menus in most other software packages you use. Flash menus contain common commands—such as Save, Copy, Paste, and Help—alongside commands specific to the software.

Timeline: SWF files can have multiple frames on a Timeline, revealing Flash's history as an animation-based program. A Timeline is made of a series of frames and keyframes in a row. In addition, Timelines can be made up of several layers, used to organize content spatially or to create special effects, such as masking for animated transitions. A playhead moves along the Timeline to produce the appearance of animation.

Panels: Panels in Flash contain options used to control nearly every aspect of any application you produce in Flash. They contain options to add ActionScript behaviors and colors, create your own colors, align objects, or store assets. All the panels in Flash can be opened from the Window drop-down list.

Stage: The Stage is critical to your Flash work because it contains all the visual objects you intend to display. Items such as buttons, text, form elements, and animations are all placed on the Stage.

Document tabs and the edit bar: For every open document in Flash, a document tab is produced that gives a designer or developer a quick way to move between open files. The edit bar, located directly below the document tabs, lets you know what things you're actively editing, such as scenes, screens, symbols, or grouped items. The edit bar also has a drop-down list with a number of fixed zoom options to quickly alter the magnification of the Stage.

Tip   *Document tabs are not visible unless the Stage is maximized. When minimized, all the documents float around in the workspace. Pressing the Maximize button on the Stage title bar snaps everything back into a nice neat tab menu.*

Property inspector: The Property inspector is a context-sensitive panel that displays information about whatever object is currently selected, be it the Stage, text, button, or what-have-you. What's more, it allows you to actually alter many of those properties, such as the x and y location in the Stage, width and height, and, in the case of symbols and components, the names of the instances arranged in your document.

Creating Your First Flash 8 Document

There are several different kinds of documents you can build using flash. You can create media documents, such as the SWF files you see with animation and video. You can also create documents that contain only ActionScript code to be used as either *includes* or *classes*. Terrifying words to the uninitiated developer, they simply provide a way to encapsulate ActionScript externally so that it can be used with many things. Kind of like posting a cake recipe online. Anyone who wants to bake a cake can follow the instructions posted online. One just needs to know where the instructions are, and boom, we have a million bakers sharing the same set of steps to make the perfect cake. Hungry yet?

In this exercise, you will create a new FLA document that eventually serves as the main document for the rest of the application. It will become the container for all the rest of the content that will be loaded in to it (for example, text, graphics, video, and other SWF files).

Note *The FLA file is the editable format of your Flash application and cannot be viewed over the web or used as a functioning application for an end user. You must publish at least a SWF file for an end user to interact with your application, although there are other formats available to you. See Lesson 11 for more information.*

1. Open Flash from your operating system's application launching method.

On Windows, the Flash application can usually be launched from Start > All Programs > Macromedia > Macromedia Flash 8. On OS X, you can launch from the Finder's Applications Directory under Macromedia Flash 8. Simply double-click the icon to launch.

Note *If you just installed Flash on your computer and you are opening it for the first time, you need to activate the software. This simple process requires you only to follow detailed steps displayed in a dialog box. For more information on software activation, refer to Macromedia's information at www.macromedia.com/software/activation.*

Flash launches with the Start screen open by default. The Start screen is where you can choose to create a new Flash document or open a new document from a template. After you create a Flash document, you can open a file you have recently worked on using the Start screen.

2. Create a new Flash document by clicking the Flash Document link under the Create New heading.

When you create any new Flash documents, the document opens with the default settings. You can change these settings and make them the default so that every new document opens with your own custom preferences. More on that later in this lesson.

3. With your new document open, click the background; change the Stage size to **780** pixels by **520** pixels in the Document Properties dialog box.

Here's where the Property inspector comes in. Click once on the Stage and then look at your Property inspector. You should see a Size button. Press that button to pull up the Document Properties dialog box.

In the dialog box, set the width to **780** pixels and the height to **520** pixels. In the Title field, type **Tech Bookstore Home**. In the Description field, type a brief, relevant description such as the following: **The Tech Bookstore provides self-paced instructional guides and references books for any field related to Information Technology**.

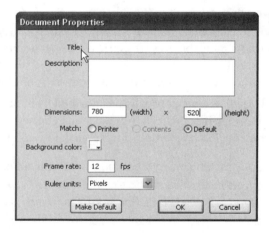

The Title and Description fields, which are used as *metadata*, serve the same purpose as metatags in HTML. That is, they are used to ensure that your website, Flash SWF files and all, holds information likely to increase your listing on a search engine.

Click OK to close the dialog box.

4. Change the document frame rate to **21** frames per second (fps) on the Property inspector.

Yes, you're right. You could have done this in the Document Properties dialog box as well, in the Frame Rate box, but then you wouldn't have gotten to use the Property inspector!

The frame rate controls the display of any given frame. The higher the frame rate, the more smoothly the animation plays. But you must also keep in mind that higher frame rates will also consume more CPU on the end user's computer, so you don't want to go overboard.

Note *The default frame rate is 12 fps. 10 fps is the lowest frame rate you can choose that the eye will register as natural motion. 21 fps has been chosen simply to make later animations play more smoothly. You could have just as easily chosen 18, 24, or 29 to achieve the same effect.*

Also on the Property inspector for document properties, you can change your background color, the Flash Player version you are publishing for, or settings for Flash Lite, the mobile version of Flash Player for handheld devices such as cell phones and PDAs.

Tip *The Devices settings button will be dimmed unless the Flash Player version has been changed in Publish Settings to Flash Lite 1.0 or Flash Lite 1.1. You'll learn more about Publish Settings later.*

Tip *If you will publish for a Flash Player version earlier than Flash 8, press the Publish Settings button and change the Flash Player version right away, before you start adding content to your document. This prevents you from accidentally adding Flash Player 8-specific features that are not supported in earlier versions of Flash.*

5. Select File > Save As and save the file as bookstore1.fla.

Before you save the file, create a folder on your desktop called TechBookstore. You will save all your files in this folder. Save this file as **bookstore1.fla**; you will be versioning the file up any time you make a significant change, hence the number in the name.

6. Select File > Close to close the document you just saved.

If you plan to move immediately ahead to the next set of exercises, this step is not necessary.

Working with Panels

In the previous exercise, you learned what panels are and you even used the Property inspector—which is a panel—to change the size of the Stage and the frame rate of your document. Taking a look at the features and parts of panels found in the authoring environment is important, so you can learn all about what you can create and manipulate in Flash. However, first you need to learn how to open, move, and use the panels that you need. In this exercise, you learn more about how to open, arrange, and use panels in the workspace. In the following lessons, you will use different panels to modify your work.

1. Select File > Open and open the bookstore1.fla document from your hard drive.

If the bookstore1.fla file from the previous exercise is still open, this step is unnecessary.

> **Tip** *If you are opening a file in Flash 8 Basic that was previously edited using Flash 8 Professional features, you will not be able to edit the file using Flash 8 Professional features. It's best to edit the file in the version of Flash 8 that created it.*

2. Select File > Save As to save a new version of bookstore1.fla as bookstore2.fla.

Because we will make some significant changes, it's a good idea to save the file as a different version. This is a standard practice, and it is used to ensure that you always have an earlier version of the file to go back to in case you need it.

3. Open the History panel from the Window drop-down list.

Flash 8 opens with a default panel layout. Not included is the very useful History panel, which is keeping track of the edits that you make. How many edits it keeps track of is based on your preferences, which you will set later on in this lesson.

Select Window > Other Panels > History to open the panel. Note that there are many other panels to use in the Window drop-down list, some of which are condensed in an Other Panels category, which contains very useful panels that are used from time to time.

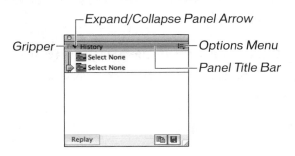

When you open a panel from the Window menu, chances are it is floating over your workspace and not docked with the other panels. To dock a panel, you have to press on the gripper, which is a series of small dots to the far left of the panel's title bar, and drag the panel into the position you want to dock it in. You know you're in a dockable area because you see a black highlight appear, indicating that the panel can be docked there. Panels can also be expanded or collapsed with the expand/collapse arrow, and all panels have an Options menu at the far right of their title bars when expanded. The options menu contains different things for different panels.

4. **Dock the panel with your other panels to the right using the gripper.**

When you mouse over the gripper, you will see a four-way arrow, indicating that you can now drag the panel into the position you want. You can also change the order of docked panels with the gripper.

5. **Minimize the History panel.**

You can minimize and maximize panels by clicking the name or the expand/collapse arrow.

| Tip | *You can also minimize panels by double-clicking anywhere on the panel's title bar.*

6. **Select Window › Components to open the Components panel and then dock it.**

Notice that panels can often be opened using keyboard shortcuts. In the case of the Components panel, the keyboard shortcut is Ctrl+F7 on Windows platforms; on OS X, it is Cmd+F7.

7. Click the Components panel's Options menu.

Every panel has an Options menu. If you click the Options menus of different panels, you'll see different options, depending on which panel you selected. All have Help, Maximize Panel, and Close Panel options in their menus.

8. From the Components panel, expand the User Interface category and drag an instance of the Button component onto the Stage.

Components are pre-built and self-contained Flash elements that you can use for rapid development. Each component does something different, and although you won't learn much about them right here, you do look at them in detail in Lesson 8. Right now, you just want something on the Stage that you can affect with a different panel.

9. Open the Align panel from the Window drop-down list and dock it. Use the Selection tool (black arrow) to make sure that the button is selected on the Stage and use the Align panel to center the button on the Stage.

The Align panel can line things up with respect to each other or line things up with respect to the Stage. To align items on the Stage, make sure that the To Stage button in the Align panel is highlighted. Use the top row of buttons to align.

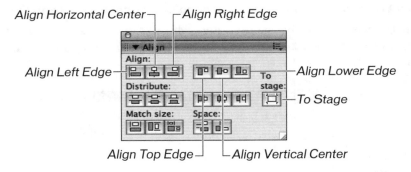

To align your button, press the Align Horizontal Center button; then press the Align Vertical Center button, which places your button at the center of the Stage.

10. Open more panels to author with from the Window menu.

Throughout the book, you will need to use the Actions panel (open it if it isn't already open).

Dock all these panels wherever you like them. In the next step, you will save your layout to be retrieved easily whenever you need it.

11. Save the panel layout as a new panel set by choosing Window > Workspace Layout > Save Current.

The Save Panel Layout dialog box opens. Name the panel set **TechBookstore** in the Name field and click OK. This procedure saves your workspace with all the additional panels you just opened. If you return to the default layout, you can change to the TechBookstore layout at any time by choosing Window > Workspace Layout > TechBookstore. If you change the panel layout, you can overwrite it by saving it as the same name.

Tip · *You can also delete or rename panel layouts by choosing Window > Workspace Layout > Manage. The Manage Workspace Layouts dialog box appears, which displays all your user-created workspace with options to rename or to delete.*

In the next exercise, you will work with the Timeline and with frames. Be sure to save your work.

Using the Timeline and Frames

All the content you work with in a SWF file is placed and organized somewhere on a Timeline. Timelines are used to display content over time (hence their name), although you can have a Timeline with only one frame easily enough. Timelines contain frames and keyframes that produce the appearance of animation or other changes and transitions; to achieve this appearance, a playhead moves along a Timeline to display the content of frames for whatever duration your frame rate designates. For instance, at 12 frames per second (fps), each frame is displayed for one-twelfth of a second before the playhead moves to the next. It's a little like feeding film through a projector.

Layers are also used in the Timeline to organize content spatially. Layers stack one on top of the other, and can contain differing amounts of frames without regard to other layers in the same Timeline. You'll learn more about layers in the next exercise.

Keyframes are where changes occur on a Timeline. You might have new content in a keyframe or change part of an animation. A keyframe can also hold ActionScript and sounds. Frames are used between keyframes to fill in parts of an animation or the Timeline and are effectively placeholders. You do not define changes in frames, or else they are turned into keyframes.

Most Flash documents have more than one Timeline. Just as there are many frames, there can be many Timelines in mini-movies that you create within the Flash document. You will find out more about how there can be more than one Timeline nested within another in Lesson 4.

In this exercise, you learn how to use the Timeline and select, move, and delete frames. You can continue using bookstore2.fla for this exercise.

1. If the Timeline is not already open, select Window > Timeline.

The Timeline panel should already be open. It is located at the top of your document, just below the edit bar. If it is collapsed, choosing Window > Timeline will expand it. You can simply click on the Timeline button to expand and collapse the Timeline as well.

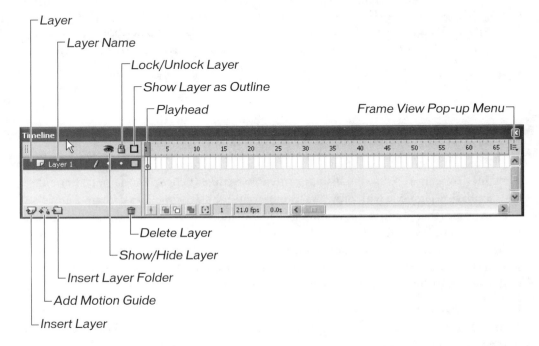

The Timeline is made up of two different panes: the Layers pane, which you use to organize content spatially, and the Timeline itself, made of frames and layers. When you first create a Flash document, one layer is created in the Layers pane and given the default name of Layer 1, and one keyframe is inserted in the Timeline for that layer.

The red playhead is located at Frame position 1 because there are no other frames that follow it. The row numbers running along the top of the Timeline represents the frame numbers along the Timeline itself. Frames can be referenced by number or by name using frame labels, which you will create in the next task.

2. Lengthen the area to view the layer names by resizing the Timeline.

Drag the bar separating the layer names and frames to resize the area for viewing layer names. When you mouse over the bar, a double-ended arrow cursor appears. When this appears, you can click the bar and drag it to the right to make the layer name area larger, so you can read the entire layer name.

Tip *As you add more layers, your Layers pane will become scrollable. You can increase the height of the Timeline by dragging the bar separating the Timeline from the application window vertically if the panel is docked. Otherwise, you can use the lower-right corner of the Timeline to resize the panel. That way, you can see more layers in the pane without having to scroll.*

3. Select a different frame view from the Timeline's frame view pop-up menu, or leave the default view you have been working with.

You can change the way you view frames in the Timeline. Select the frame view pop-up menu in the upper-right corner of the Timeline.

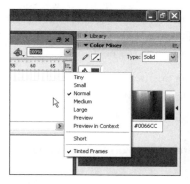

The menu allows you to change the size and appearance of frames in the Timeline. Change the width of frames by selecting Tiny, Small, Normal, Medium, or Large. Selecting or deselecting the Short option changes frame height. The grey shading you see on some frames can be turned off by selecting or deselecting Tinted Frames.

You can even preview content that you have in frames. Preview will display the content of each frame within the Timeline. If you want to display thumbnails of each filled and empty frame, select Preview in Context. This feature is useful when you are creating animations because you can view how the animation progresses over time.

For this project, you will use the default settings of normal sized frames and leave Tinted Frames selected.

4. Create a new keyframe and a frame on Layer 1 by choosing Insert > Timeline > Keyframe.

A new document has an empty keyframe in Frame 1 of Layer 1. When you added the Button component to the Stage in the previous exercise, the empty keyframe (hollow dot) turned into a keyframe (filled dot).

Note *You can add content to the Timeline only if a frame or keyframe is selected and its layer is unlocked. If there are no frames on the layer you have selected, you must first create a keyframe to add content to.*

Tip *You can create frames and keyframes using menu commands or keyboard shortcuts. If you Right-click or Control-click on a frame position, you can choose to insert Keyframes, Blank Keyframes, or Frames from the context menu. The keyboard shortcut F6 adds a keyframe, F7 adds a blank keyframe, and F5 adds a normal frame.*

When you used the Insert menu to insert a keyframe, it placed the new keyframe in Frame position 2 of Layer 1. It also copied the graphic from the previous keyframe. Even though these keyframes are on the same layer, they are apart from each other. If you edit keyframe 2, the contents of keyframe 1 will be unaffected. When you insert a blank keyframe, the graphics are not copied from one keyframe to the next.

To insert a frame, select Frame position 3 of Layer 1 and use the keyboard shortcut F5. This extends the content in time, but you cannot change the content in a frame. It's a placeholder only.

5. Select, move, and delete frames on the Timeline by using your mouse and the Shift key.

You have already selected a frame in Step 4 by clicking on the frame. You can select multiple frames in a row by clicking the first frame, holding down the Shift key, and then clicking on the last frame. If you don't want to select continuous frames, hold down the Ctrl or Command keys while clicking individual frames. To select all the frames on the Timeline, Right- or Control-click and select Select All Frames from the context menu.

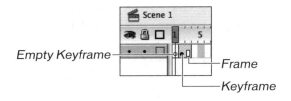

Select Frames 2 and 3 of Layer 1 (but not Frame 1) and then drag the selection to Frames 4 and 5. You are moving these two frames to a new location (or position in time).

Notice that Frame 1 now extends to Frame 3. If you want to copy and then move a keyframe instead, simply hold down the Alt or Option keys while dragging the selected keyframe to a new frame.

Note *If you select a keyframe on the Timeline, everything on that keyframe is selected on the Stage. If you select an element on the Stage, it highlights the keyframe that it is in on the Timeline.*

6. Delete the Button component and frames.

Because you don't need a button yet, delete the component from the Stage by selecting it with the Selection tool (black arrow) and by pressing either Backspace or Delete on your keyboard. You can also remove things from the Stage by Right- or Control-clicking the item and choosing Cut from the context menu.

Note *Choosing Cut moves the item to the Clipboard, so that it can be pasted somewhere else. If you cut another item right after it, whatever was in your operating system's Clipboard will be purged and replaced with the new item. Deleting something is permanent; you can't paste a deleted item anywhere, but you can always undo to get it back by choosing Edit > Undo or using the keyboard shortcuts control or command+Z, whichever is relevant to your OS.*

To delete frames, Delete and Backspace won't work. Using them deletes the contents of frames and keyframes, but not the frames and keyframes themselves. Select all the empty frames on the Timeline except for Frame 1; then Right- or Control-click on the selection and select Remove Frames from the context menu. You can also select Edit > Timeline > Remove Frames or the keyboard shortcut Shift + F5.

7. Save the changes you made to the document.

Working with Layers

Now that you've worked with the document Timeline a little, you should learn more about how to use layers. As you've seen, layers are in the Timeline and can be stacked on top of one another. You can create new layers by using the Insert Layer button in the Timeline or by using Insert > Timeline > Layer.

Layers are really an organizational tool for the various assets you will use in any document you produce. In Flash, layers are used to do everything to create the illusion of depth and perspective to storing sounds and ActionScript in keyframes. It is considered a best practice to organize like content into aptly named layers; all your static text would go into a layer named something like Static Text, as opposed to Layer 15, which doesn't mean anything. This brings you to your next best practice: Layers should be named descriptive of their content wherever possible.

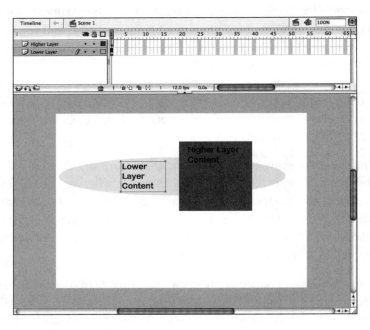

Note *Layer names don't mean anything to Flash in the published version of the file, apart from defining a stacking order. Layer names are for human types.*

One of the interesting things about Flash is that layers can have special properties. We have normal layers, which we use for general display of content; guide layers, which you would use for tracing (among other things); motion guide layers, which cause an animation to follow a path; and mask layers, which can be used to do very cool things like transitions. Guide layers don't publish with the SWF file, and motion guides are invisible when published. What's more, all these layers can be organized into layer folders to conserve screen space in the Layers pane.

In the next exercise, you will learn how to add and name new layers and change their properties. You will also learn how to organize layers into layer folders. You should still be using bookstore2.fla for this exercise.

1. If the Timeline is not already open, select Window › Timeline from the main menu or click the Timeline button in the upper-right corner of the document window.

2. Rename Layer 1 by double-clicking the layer's name and typing in background.

After you double-click the layer name, the name becomes editable and you can type in a new name for the layer. Press Enter after you finish typing **background** as the new name for Layer 1.

> **Tip** *You can also double-click the layer's type icon, which opens up the Layer Properties dialog box, in which you not only change the name but also what kind of layer it is. The Layer Type icon is the little thumbnail immediately to the left of the layer name.*

3. Add a new layer by clicking the Insert Layer button and rename the layer labels.

When you add a new layer, Flash automatically names the layer something like Layer 2. The number is indicative only of how many layers have thus far been created in the document; it has no meaning otherwise. It's a good idea to rename the layer right away.

Double-click the layer name and rename it **labels**. This layer is now active because you selected it in the Layers pane. Anything created or dragged on to the Stage is placed in the active layer. When you select a layer with content in the Layers pane, all the content in the layer is likewise selected.

The active layer has a small pencil icon next to its name. Click the background layer now. If anything is created or dragged onto the Stage, it is placed on the active layer. Any edits you make to a layer are made to the active layer.

4. Add a frame label to the new labels layer.

Frame labels are used to name a particular frame number so it can be referred to with ActionScript. There are a number of advantages to specifying frame labels over frame numbers in ActionScript, because they can be moved around in the Timeline.

First, only keyframes can be labeled, so anywhere you need to add a frame label, you must have a keyframe. To label the keyframe, select it in the Timeline. In the upper-left corner of the Property inspector is a field with dimmed text in it that says <Frame Label>. Enter **home** into that field and hit Enter.

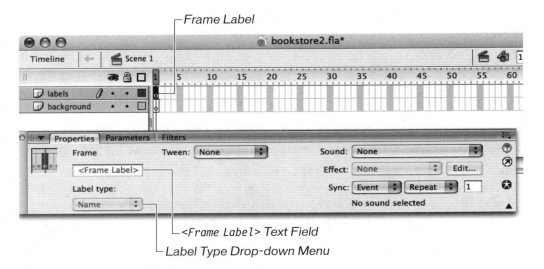

Frame Label

<Frame Label> Text Field

Label Type Drop-down Menu

Note _There are three frame label types: name (which you just created), comment (which is used just to store information about the frame), and anchor. As of this writing, anchor works only with Internet Explorer and is implemented so that users can bookmark these frames and click the Back and Forward buttons on their browser to navigate through your Flash SWF file._

5. Lock the label layer by clicking the Lock Layer button.

Click the dot that is under the lock layer icon, and a small icon of a lock replaces it. Clicking the dot locks the label layer so you cannot add anything to the Stage on that layer. Clicking the button again will unlock it.

If you Right-click a layer, you can select Lock Others from the context menu, so that every layer except the one you are actively editing is locked.

Locking layers is very useful when you want to control your selections and avoid accidentally placing elements on the Stage in the wrong layer (which can break an animation). You can also change the visibility of a layer by using the small dot under the Show/Hide layer icon that looks like an eye. When a layer is hidden, it cannot be edited, and an *X* replaces the dot in the Layers pane.

6. Create a layer folder by clicking the New Layer Folder button.

Folders help you organize layers into related content. Select the background layer and then click the New Layer Folder button, which is the third button from the left in the lower-left corner of the Layers pane. A layer folder, called Folder 1 by default, is created above the background layer. Double-click the layer folder name and change it to **graphics**.

The folder doesn't have any contents. Drag the background layer into the layer folder; it indents to indicate that it is now in the folder, and the folder itself can be expanded or collapsed. Click the arrow to the left of the layer folder name to expand and collapse the layer folder.

7. Create a new layer and then create a shape on the Stage using the Rectangle tool.

Select the background layer; then click the New Layer icon to create a new layer above it. Name the new layer **temp**.

We haven't covered drawing yet; we'll do that in Lesson 2. For now, verify that the Tools panel is open. If not, select Window > Tools to open it. Select the Rectangle tool from the Tools panel and draw a rectangle of any size or shape in the new layer. To draw a rectangle, click and drag the cursor diagonally anywhere on the Stage with the tool selected. While you're dragging, you see an outline of what the rectangle will look like when it's created. When you have a shape that you like, release the mouse button to create the rectangle.

Oval Tool —————— 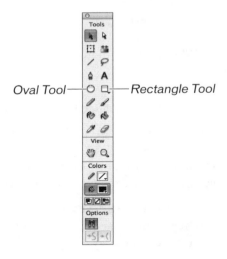 —————— Rectangle Tool

8. Create an oval shape in the background layer.

Highlight the background layer, select the Oval tool, and click and drag diagonally across the Stage to draw the oval. Notice that the rectangle is layered on top of the oval because the oval is in a lower layer.

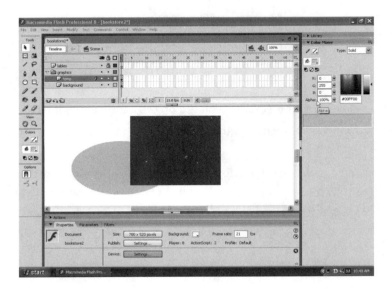

9. Change the order in which the background and temp layers are stacked.

To change layer order, simply click and drag layers up or down in the Layers pane. To change the order of the background and temp layers, click the temp layer and drag it below the background layer. When you see a thick line underneath the background layer, you can let go of the mouse because the temp layer is now in position.

Notice now that the stacking order of the rectangle and the oval is reversed. This demonstrates layer stacking order and how layers can be used to spatially organize content. Because you won't actually be using these graphics throughout the project, delete them.

To delete the graphic in the background layer, select Frame 1 of the background layer; this selects all the background layer's contents. Press Backspace or Delete to remove the graphic.

10. Delete the temp layer.

To delete a layer, select it first in the Layers pane; then click the trash can icon in the pane's lower-right corner.

Highlight the temp layer; then click the trash can icon. This removes all contents of the layer, as well as the layer itself.

> **Tip** *You can also Right- or Control-click the layer name and select Delete Layer from the context menu.*

11. Save your changes.

Setting Your Preferences

Preferences allow you to control many parts of Flash, from general editing to vector graphics to ActionScript settings. Those settings are made in the Preferences dialog box, in which you change your Flash 8 preferences (the next exercise shows you how).

1. On Windows, select Edit > Preferences to open the Preferences dialog box. On OS X, select Flash 8 > Preferences.

The Preferences dialog box is separated into two sections. On the left are the different categories of settings. On the right are the settings for each selected category. The General category, which shows by default, sets basic controls for authoring files, including two different types of Undo. The ActionScript category is used to set the ActionScript window font and font size, as well as to change indent space and syntax coloring. The Auto Format category is also used with ActionScript. As a developer types code, the ActionScript window can automatically change the appearance of the code to make it easier to read; it does so based on the settings in the Auto Format category. Tool settings for drawing vector objects are in the Drawing category, and items such as font mapping and text flow defaults are in the Text category. Lastly, the Warnings category allows you to select which warnings appear in Flash when something is about to go awry.

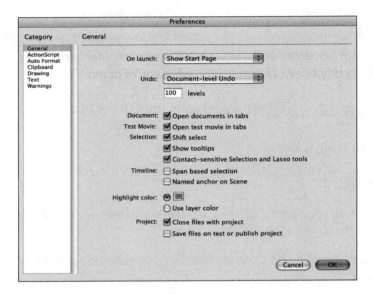

Click each category and explore some of the settings that you can change using this dialog box.

2. Change the number of Undo values to 150 in the General category for document-level undos.

There are two different types of undo levels in Flash 8 Basic and Flash 8 Professional. First is the *document-level* undo, which keeps track of all the changes being made to the document as a whole in a single history list, including selections. Next is *object-level* undo, which keeps separate history lists for each object you edit. The advantage of the object-level undo is that it gives you a way to step back on a single object without having to affect any other object on the Stage.

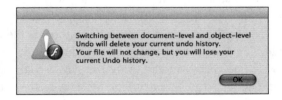

When you switch between the two, you see an alert box, telling you that any history steps tracked up to that point will be deleted, although your file will be unaffected. Switchers beware—now you can't say that you haven't been warned.

Tip *150 undo levels is a little on the high side for many designers or developers. How high your undo levels should be is really a matter of personal preference. The one thing to bear in mind though is that the more undo levels you have, the more system resources are consumed on your computer, which can slow things down pretty drastically, depending on what you're doing.*

3. In the On Launch drop-down list, change from Show Start Page to Last Documents Open.

This preference opens the last documents you worked on in Flash by default the next time you open Flash 8. If you are sharing a computer with someone, this isn't a prudent choice, but it's there for you if you want it. Step 3 is not absolutely necessary, so if you prefer to show the Start Page by default, leave that option selected.

For now, leave your other Preferences set to the defaults and click OK.

4. Select Edit > Customize Tools Panel on Windows and Flash 8 > Customize Tools Panel on OS X.

From time to time, you might install extensions in Flash that add to your tool set, or you might want to alter in some way the default tool arrangement that comes with Flash. Choosing to edit your Tools panel gives you those options.

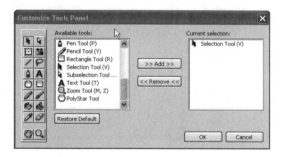

By default, all the tools that come with Flash already show on the Tools panel. You can leave the default settings for ease of use, but in your everyday project life, this is the dialog box you use to change your Tools panel around, add new tools to the Tools panel, or remove tools from it that you never use.

Testing an FLA File

A Flash document cannot be shared online without publishing it into a format that can be viewed using Flash Player (although there are other formats available). Before you publish a file for uploading, you probably will want to test it pretty extensively first to see whether the features you added actually work. Although Lesson 11 covers publishing in detail, you will walk through the basics in this lesson. You should still be working on bookstore2.fla.

1. Select File > Save As and save bookstore2.fla as **bookstore3.fla**.

Make sure that you save this file in the TechBookstore directory on your hard drive.

2. Select the background layer and then drag a Button component from the Components panel to the Stage.

Drop a Button component on the background layer anywhere on the Stage. You simply need something on the Stage so you don't have to test an empty document.

3. Select Control > Test Movie from the main menu to test the FLA file.

The testing environment opens, and your file displays as a SWF file. Flash actually publishes the SWF file specifically so it can be tested, and the SWF file is playing in the integrated Flash Player.

This is the way your SWF file generally appears online when it's playing in Flash Player.

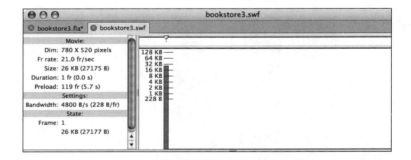

4. Close out of the testing environment by clicking the X on the document tab.

You can also select File > Close to close the testing environment. The test SWF file closes, and you are taken back to the authoring environment. If you look in your TechBookstore folder, you can see a SWF version of your file.

5. Select File > Publish Preview > Default to preview your Flash work in a browser.

By default, Publish Preview produces both an HTML file and a Flash SWF file, so you can see whether the file works in a browser. The HTML file is actually published to your hard drive, just like the SWF file.

In your browser window, select View > Page Source to view the source code that Flash has produced. Notice that the SWF file is referenced in the HTML file with both OBJECT and EMBED tags and that Flash filled out all the appropriate parameters for you.

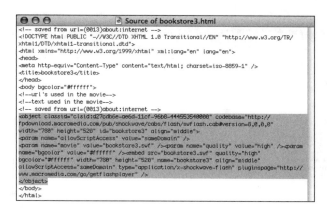

6. Return to Flash and delete the component from the background layer.

Select the Button component on the stage and press Backspace or Delete to remove it from the Stage.

7. Save the changes you made to the file.

Finding Help

Flash has a very sophisticated help system. The Help panel has a search feature, a drop-down list of categories, expandable/collapsible categories, and a pane to display all the information you have requested. You can also check for updates by clicking the Update button at the upper-right of the panel. Most people forget about documentation, but here you're reminded about it because the documentation often has the answers to many of your questions.

Flash Help is extracted from a number of "books" that come with the program, including the following:

- Features
- Tutorials & Samples
- ActionScript 2.0
- Components

- Extending
- Language Reference (ActionScript and Components)
- Flash Lite
- 3rd Party

1. Select Help > Flash Help to open the Help panel.

Take a moment to explore the different categories of the Flash help system.

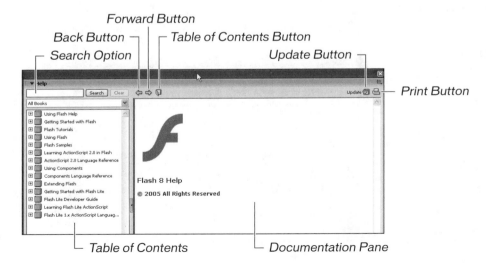

2. Click the Update button to check for documentation updates.

This works only if you have a live connection to the Internet. Flash will communicate with Macromedia's servers to see whether there have been any updates to the Flash documentation set. If so, you are prompted to download and install any updates.

Tip *It's a good idea to check for documentation updates on a regular basis.*

3. Enter a term in the search field, such as brush, and click Search to view the results.

Flash searches its documentation for entries related to your search string and displays them in the Table of Contents area. Click any of the results to view the documentation related to your search.

4. From the Help drop-down list, select Flash Support Center.

This opens a browser to Macromedia's online Flash support page, in which you can find articles, tips, and FAQs related to Flash. When you can't find what you want in the documentation, don't forget to look onlinew (in particular, the Macromedia website).

Exploring the Project

You will create a fully working website by the end of this book. The techniques you learn can be applied to any website or project you build in Flash. Many parts of this site can be recycled into your own projects.

You can see the finished website online at http://flash.TrainingFromTheSource.com/.

The website is a SWF file that is embedded in an HTML page. The HTML page has some modification, so it is centered on the page with a custom background pattern. Click the three buttons near the top to explore the various amounts of dynamic data loaded into many of the different components that ship with Flash 8 and Flash 8 Professional. Notice all the graphic, animation, presentation, video, dynamic, and sound elements within this single website.

Because these components use some of the features specific to Flash Player 8, anyone viewing the site needs that player version (or greater) to view the website. If you don't have Flash Player 8 or greater, download and install the latest player from www.macromedia. com/go/getflashplayer.

What You Have Learned

In this lesson, you have:

- Explored the Flash authoring environment (pages 4–6)
- Learned how to create and save Flash documents (pages 7–9)
- Worked with panels (pages 10–13)
- Used and modified frames and layers on the Timeline (pages 13–17)
- Used layers to organize content (pages 17–23)
- Set and customized your own preferences (pages 23–25)
- Tested your FLA file (pages 26–28)
- Found out how to solve problems using the Help panel (pages 28–29)
- Explored the project you will be building (pages 29–30)

2 Creating Graphics

What good is an application or a document without graphics? Graphics serve so many purposes in any interface, from providing users visual cues, to interacting with the application, to evoking moods or sensations or other emotional states. And although it's true that you don't need graphics to develop an application in Macromedia Flash, it's just as true that your application lacks life without graphics. Human beings are visual by nature, after all.

In this lesson, you will use the Flash drawing tools to produce graphics of your own. You will also import and optimize bitmaps that were already created for you. All the graphics that you create and import in this lesson will be used for the main layout, logo animation, and menu system for the project that you will be building though the course. You will also learn how to use Flash tools and panels to manipulate graphics and make use of layers to create a mask effect. Finally, you will use the Library panel to organize your assets.

The finished background

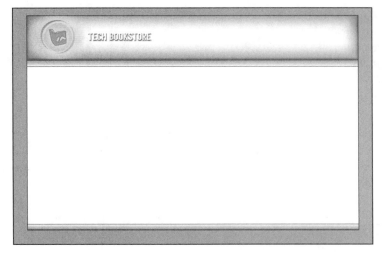

What You Will Learn

In this lesson, you will:

- Use the Tools panel
- Use fills and strokes
- Use the Object Drawing model
- Use the drawing tools to create graphics
- Use guides and snapping
- Create and manipulate graphics
- Create and use a mask layer
- Use strokes
- Learn about the library and assets
- Import and optimize bitmaps
- Import vector drawings
- Work with colors, fill, and blend modes

Approximate Time

This lesson takes approximately 1 hour and 30 minutes to complete.

Lesson Files

Media Files:

lesson02/assets/company_down.png
lesson02/assets/company_up.png
lesson02/assets/contact_down.png
lesson02/assets/contact_up.png
lesson02/assets/products_down.png
lesson02/assets/products_up.png
lesson02/assets/title.png
lesson02/assets/logo.png
lesson02/assets/map.FH11

Starting Files:

lesson02/start/bookstore3.fla

Completed Files:

lesson02/complete/bookstore6.fla
lesson02/complete/ma.fla

Using the Tools Panel

You have already used a few tools from the Tools panel in Lesson 1. In this lesson, you will learn more about what you can do with the drawing tools. There are four main parts of the Tools panel: tools area, view area, colors area, and options area. Each section contains buttons that do a task, but the buttons themselves are not labeled. However, if you hover over the tools with the mouse, a tooltip appears that tells you the name of the tool. A button can also have a menu attached to it. If so, there is a small black arrow at the lower right of the button. Click and hold the button to display the menu.

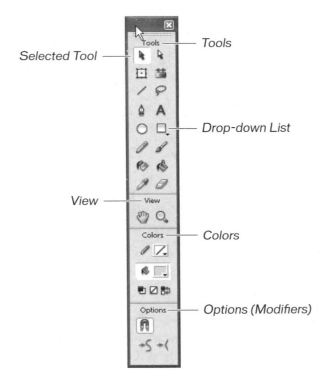

Selected Tool

Tools

Drop-down List

View

Colors

Options (Modifiers)

The tools in the Tools panel are used for creating, selecting, and manipulating graphics. They are also used for changing the view on the Stage, or the position of the Stage and its contents in the document window. Some tools have additional options, which display in the options area of the Tools panel when the tool is selected.

When you select a tool in the Tools panel, the contents of the Property inspector will change to reflect what the tool is being used to do. For instance, if you select the Text tool, the

Property inspector switches to display the text properties you can edit, such as text type, font, and justification. When you have a drawing tool selected, stroke and fill options show on the Property inspector.

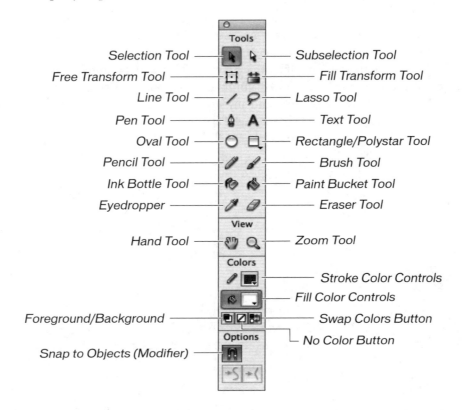

The Selection, Subselection, and Lasso tools are used to select elements on the Stage. The Line, Pen, Text, Oval, Rectangle, Polystar, Pencil, and Brush tools are used to create graphics. The Free Transform, Fill Transform, Ink Bottle, Paint Bucket, Eyedropper, and Eraser tools are for modifying graphics. In the view area, the Hand tool and Zoom tool are used to move the Stage around or magnify and minimize the Stage, respectively. The colors area is used to select stroke or fill colors when you create shapes. Remember that there are additional settings for each tool in the options area and/or Property inspector.

Learning About Fills and Strokes

In Flash 8, you can create strokes and fills separately or together using one of the shape drawing tools. Tools like the Line and the Pencil tool draw only strokes, which essentially is just a line. Strokes can have different styles and thicknesses, as well as different colors. Strokes can be drawn independently of shapes; besides drawing freehand with the Pencil or Line tool, you can select a shape tool, shut off the fill color, set a stroke color, and draw the outline of a shape. You can use the Ink Bottle tool to change strokes that have already been drawn by selecting the tool, changing its settings in the Property inspector, and clicking a stroke with the tool. Presto! The stroke is now different.

The Brush tool draws areas of fill. A fill, which is the area inside of a closed or open shape, can be a solid, linear or radial gradient, or a bitmap image. Shapes with gaps can contain fills, as long as the gaps aren't too large, and any stroke that creates a shape can be filled in with the Paint Bucket tool. When you use one of the shape tools, be it Oval, Rectangle, or Polystar, Flash will by default draw a shape with both a stroke *and* a fill. You can prevent the stroke from being drawn by selecting the stroke control color in the colors area of the Tools panel and clicking the No Color button. You can add strokes to fills that have none by clicking them with the Ink Bottle tool.

When you draw a shape or a stroke on the Stage, you have two drawing models to select from: the Merge Drawing model (default) and the Object Drawing model.

In the Merge Drawing model, when you draw an object on the Stage with both stroke and fill, the stroke and fill are treated as two separate objects. If you click and drag in the center of the shape, the fill is dragged away from the stroke when you let go of the mouse cursor. To select both the stroke and fill at the same time, you must double-click the object. What's more, if two objects of differing colors touch, the shape in the lower stacking order is merged with the shape in the higher stacking order. If you click and draw the shapes apart, the merged shape will be permanently altered. The effect makes it look as if the object in the lower layer has been "punched out." Same color shapes are treated as a single object where they touch.

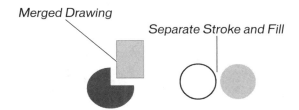

This whole merging thing seems like a real drag at first, and it can be difficult to get used to the independent strokes and fills. After you work with it for a while, however, you'll see that it really allows you to create more interesting shapes and effects that you couldn't otherwise do. Still, you have a few options to prevent punch out from happening: Group the shapes (which has the added advantage of putting the stroke and fill into one "box"), draw your graphics on different layers, or use the Object Drawing model.

In the Object Drawing model, shapes are drawn as separate objects. If they overlap, they won't merge because the shapes are essentially grouped when drawn. To toggle on or off the Object Drawing model, click the Object Drawing button in the options area of the Tools panel with a shape tool selected.

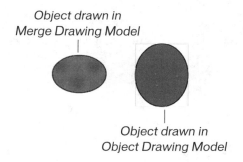

Object drawn in Merge Drawing Model

Object drawn in Object Drawing Model

Using Vector and Bitmap Images

The drawings that you create in Flash are made up of vectors, which is the native graphics format in Flash. Vector graphics are made up of lines and curves that are defined by mathematical calculations. Bitmaps, on the other hand, are made up of pixels on a fixed-width grid. Usually, vector graphics tend to be a bit smaller because they're really just math; however, the more complex your drawing is, the bigger your file size will be, so that's where the bitmap comes in. Complex graphics with lots of tonality, gradients, and shading sometimes are better off as bitmaps because they will have a smaller file size burden. Images such as photographs should be bitmaps by default, although they can be converted from one format to another.

The real advantage of vector artwork is in scaling up or down. When you resize a vector graphic, you're merely modifying the equation that drew it, so no matter which direction you're going in, you don't lose resolution. Bitmaps don't have that advantage because they're on a grid. When you make the grid bigger, the pixel definitions maintain their ratios, so the image, scaling up, looks like a big, giant, ugly honeycomb mess. The pixels are resizing, thus losing their quality. Sometimes, pixels don't look so good when you scale down, too.

Using Color

Color in Flash relies on palettes that contain swatches. There are different kinds of palettes available for you to use, or you can create and save your own palettes by using the Color Swatches panel. For the Tech Bookstore website you're creating, you will select colors from the default Web Safe palette that contains 216 colors. This palette contains only the colors that can be successfully viewed on most people's monitors. It is possible to add a custom color to the palette using the Color Mixer. All you need to do is select a pixel color anywhere in Flash or on the desktop from a bitmap image (or by using the Eyedropper tool), and then select Add Swatch from the Options menu. The selected color is added as a swatch to the button row of the palette you have open.

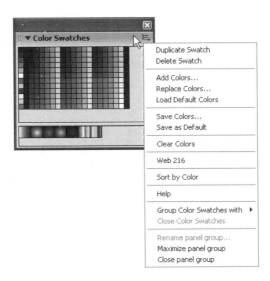

The Web 216 or Web Safe color palette was developed back when monitors supported only 256 colors. Because Mac and PC used different color palettes for their systems, only 216 colors were common between them. These days, however, very nearly every device is capable of supporting and displaying well in excess of 256 colors, including mobile phones and PDAs. So it's okay to use any color that tickles your fancy, unless you're unfortunate enough to have to design for a very primitive device.

Tip *You can also read in colors from a GIF image by selecting Add Colors from the Color Swatches panel Options menu and then navigating to the image that contains the colors you want to use.*

You can use the swatch colors from the palettes to select colors for filling shapes, drawing, applying to strokes, or changing the background color of the Stage. Colors can be defined in several different ways: You can select or change colors using RGB (red, green, blue), HSB (hue, saturation, brightness), or standard hexadecimal. These color modes simply have different ways of representing color, and you can switch between RGB and HSB freely at any time. You always have the option of using hexadecimal for color designation. RGB mode adds three numerical values to define a color, whereas HSB mode uses a value for the degree of rotation on the color wheel, and percentages for saturation and brightness, to define the color. Hexadecimal colors use a base-16 system that uses a combination of six numbers and letters to define a color. You might be familiar with this color mode if you have written HTML because that is the standard color mode used on the web. This lesson and book will provide hexadecimal values for colors, but the same colors can also be found by selecting swatches in the default color palette.

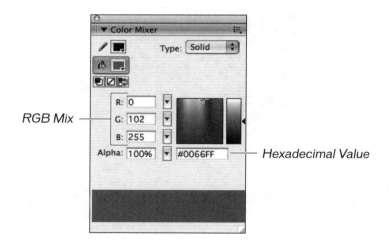

RGB Mix

Hexadecimal Value

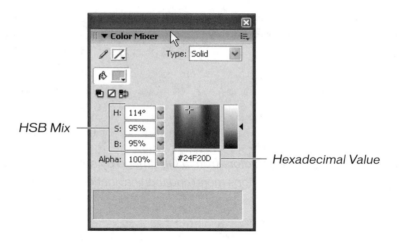

HSB Mix

Hexadecimal Value

You can select a stroke or fill color using the color controls in the Tools panel or in the Property inspector (the color controls are the two color swatches you see in the color area of the Tools panel). When you click a fill or stroke color control, the color pop-up window appears, and the Eyedropper tool replaces the cursor. You can click the Eyedropper tool on a color in the palette, on the Stage, or on the desktop to select a color to use. The Eyedropper tool in the Tools panel is used the same way. You can use the Eyedropper tool to match colors with one another quickly or to pick up a color from a layout you designed in a program such as Fireworks.

Creating Graphics with Drawing Tools

The first graphics you will create for the Tech Bookstore application use the basic drawing tools that create shapes on the Stage. Basic tools allow you to create nice and simple layouts. Combined with Flash 8's built-in components, you can create attractive interfaces without ever having to leave Flash.

Note *If you want to create more complex graphics, you should consider using a tool like Macromedia Fireworks or Macromedia FreeHand. These applications offer more filters than Flash as well as editing controls to produce graphic effects not available in Flash. But you'll probably be surprised at just how much Flash drawing tools can actually do.*

You will learn how to use some of the basic drawing tools in Flash to produce a shape and discover how to select colors for the shape's stroke and fill. You will also learn how to select your shape and modify it using the Property inspector.

1. Open bookstore3.fla from the TechBookstore folder on your hard drive or from the lesson02/start directory on the CD. Open the Publish Settings dialog box and deselect the HTML check box in the Formats tab. Save the file as **bookstore4.fla**.

You are versioning up again because you are about to make some big changes. Make sure to save the new version of the file in your TechBookstore directory on your hard drive.

Open the Publish Settings dialog box, either by selecting File > Publish Settings or by clicking the Publish Settings button on the Property inspector. Make sure that you are in the Formats tab, and uncheck the HTML box. You don't want to produce a whole new HTML file for every new version of the bookstore you produce. You will create an HTML document in Lesson 11.

2. Select the Rectangle tool in the Tools panel, and set the fill color to #CCCCCC and the stroke color to #666666 using the color controls. Draw a rectangle using the Object Drawing model.

When you select the Rectangle tool, you have three places to change stroke and fill color: in the colors area of the Tools panel, in the Property inspector, or in the Color Mixer (which you'll learn to use later).

In either the Property inspector or the colors area of the Tools panel, click the color control for the fill color. A color pop-up window appears. You can search for the right color in the pop-up window or you can enter the color manually by typing it into the white box in the upper left of the pop-up window. Click into the white box and type **#CCCCCC** to specify the fill color; then press Enter. Next, click the stroke color control, click into the white box, and type **#666666**, pressing Enter to set the color.

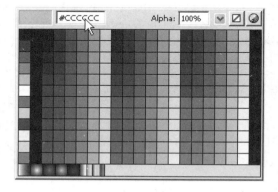

Tip | *You can also set alpha in the color pop-up window. Alpha controls the opacity of the shape, from 100% opaque to 0% opaque.*

After you finish setting the stroke and fill, with the Rectangle tool still selected, press the Object Drawing button in the options area of the Tools panel; then click and drag on the stage to produce a rectangle of any shape or size. You will change its dimensions with the Property inspector.

Tip *You can easily change stroke and fill settings after you have drawn the graphic by selecting the shape and changing the color controls to the color you want. Also, you can change stroke style and size, and fill type, which you will learn to do later.*

Note *If you double-click an object drawn in the Object Drawing model, you will "enter" the object, and your edit bar will show Drawing Object next to "Scene 1." When you draw something in the Object Drawing model, it's more or less grouped, which is not unlike putting something in a box. Double-clicking the object lets you go into the box to change the contents. It can be useful in limited circumstances, but most of the changes you want to make can be done without using this special editing mode, which is called edit-in-place mode. To get out of this model quickly, you can either double-click on the background or click Scene 1 in the edit bar.*

3. Change the dimensions of the rectangle to **779** pixels wide by **15** pixels high in the Property inspector.

When an object on the Stage is selected, the Property inspector shows its width and height in the W and H fields in the inspector's lower-left corner. These are editable properties, and you can type into the fields to change the values. If you want to constrain the proportions of the graphic (keep its width-to-height ratio), you can click the padlock icon on the left of the W and H fields. You can also change the *x* and *y* location of the object on the Stage. By default, *x* and *y* position is based on the graphic's upper-left corner, which really does make it easier to position.

Make sure that the Constrain Proportions icon is unlocked, and click into the W field. Type **779** in the field and press Enter. Move to the H field and type **15**, pressing Enter when done. Notice that both the width and the height of the rectangle have now changed.

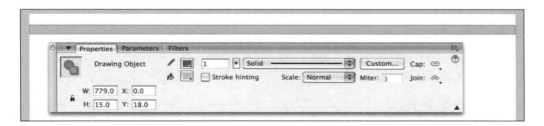

4. Create a circle with the Oval tool that will be used for a glow animation. Give it a fill color of #999999.

Ultimately, the logo will be animated and made of several different graphics. You lay down the foundation for part of the animation now by creating a graphic that will be used in an animation later on.

Select the Oval tool and set the fill color to #999999 using the Fill Color control. Shut off the stroke by selecting the Stroke Color control and pressing the No Color button (it is a small white box with a red line through it, located just under the Fill Color control). It is dimmed unless one of the shape drawing tools is selected.

Create a small circle somewhere on the Stage by holding Shift down while clicking and dragging with the Oval tool. Holding down Shift produces perfect circles rather than ovals and ellipses. Later on in the lesson, you will change the stroke color to something other than grey.

Select the circle you just drew with the Selection tool. In the Property inspector, change the width to **130** and the height to **100** to create an oval that will fit just behind the logo image you will use later.

> **Note** *If you have a drawing tablet connected to your computer, Flash has a special feature that allows you to take advantage of pressure sensitivity and angle of the tablet pen. Pressure and tilt options for the Brush tool can be set in the options area of the Tools panel, or you can take advantage of your tablet because tablets are really the best things ever.*

5. Save the document.

Using Guides, Grids, Coordinates, and Snapping

In Flash, almost everything has to do with a coordinate. Each document has its own x and y coordinates, the point of origin being the upper-left corner of the document, which is used to do everything from precisely positioning graphics to animating things using ActionScript. *x* refers to the horizontal axis of the document, and *y* is the vertical axis. When you create symbols in Flash and are in symbol-editing mode, a cross hair at the center indicates the origin of that symbol's own independent coordinate system. You will learn more about symbols and symbol-editing-mode in Lesson 4, although you will produce a symbol in this lesson just how to see how it's done.

Note *Flash does not have a z index property; it has a depth, which serves the same purpose.*

To help you navigate through all the coordinates are guides, grids, and snapping. Guides and grids are used to assist in layout and drawing. Snapping takes an object you are creating and snaps it to guidelines or gridlines. This is useful in some circumstances and maddening in others, which is why they can all be shut off.

Guides and the grid are visible only when you are in an editable Flash file and are not visible in the final SWF. Also, rulers have to be visible to use guides. To turn on rulers, select View > Rulers. When rulers are on, guides are visible by default (although you don't see them until you make them) and can be toggled on or off by going to View > Guides > Show Guides. To turn on the grid, select View > Grid > Show Grid.

You can change the settings for your guides by selecting Edit > Guides > Edit Guides.

 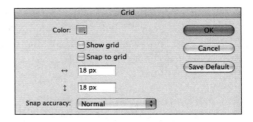

In the Guides dialog box, you can change the color of the guide lines, set whether they are visible, have objects snap to them with different levels of accuracy, and lock the guides down so they cannot be moved by mistake. In the Grid dialog box, you can change the gridline colors, size, and snapping options, as well as set whether or not the grid is visible.

Tip *You can also change snap settings in the View › Snapping fly-over menu.*

Guides are dragged out of rulers by clicking the ruler, dragging down or over (depending on which ruler you're using) and then dropping anywhere on the Stage. When you mouse over a guide on the Stage, a special cursor appears to indicate that you can drag it into a new position. To get rid of guides, shut them off or drag them back into their respective rulers.

In this book, we want objects to snap to our guides.

Creating a New Graphic Symbol

In this exercise, you will create the background graphic for drop-down lists in the Tech Bookstore. You'll then convert that into a *graphic symbol*, which will make it reusable without adding file size. Because there are three menus in the site, it makes sense to use this methodology because it gives you a way to control file size for your project. Don't sweat the details of symbols just now because you will learn all about them in Lesson 4.

You'll use the Rectangle tool again, but this time you round out the corners using the Corner Radius button. You'll also work more with fill colors, tools, rulers, and guides.

Note | *Graphic symbols can contain their own Timeline and layer structure. You can take advantage of this to make a more complex graphic without altering the main document Timeline.*

1. Open bookstore4.fla if it is not already open and save it as bookstore5.fla. Make sure that object snapping is turned on.

To make sure that object snapping is turned on, you can do one of two things. First, in the Tools panel, select the Selection tool, and in the options area, make sure that the Snap to Objects icon is highlighted (it looks like a magnet). You can also select View > Snapping > Snap to Objects.

2. Create a new graphic symbol by selecting Insert › New Symbol and then create three new layers inside of it by clicking the Insert New Layer button in the Layers pane.

When you create a new symbol this way, you are leaving the main document Timeline behind and entering the Timeline of the symbol. All symbols in Flash, with the exception of the Font symbol, have their own Timeline panel, with their own layers. How those Timelines behave is based on what kind of symbol you choose to create.

Select Insert > New Symbol to create a new symbol. The Create New Symbol dialog box appears; it has two modes: Basic and Advanced. Basic is the default. If you press the Advanced button, it sends you to Advanced mode. You want Basic.

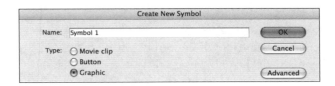

The Name field labels the symbol in your document Library panel, which you haven't learned about yet. The name is not important to Flash because it is a human organizational tool. The symbol type *is* important to Flash however because it tells Flash how the symbol should behave. Name the symbol **grMenuGraphic**, and select Graphic from the Behavior radio button group. Then click OK.

Tip *The "gr" prefixing the name is just a convention you can use to determine quickly what kind of symbol you have, and is not necessary. But a good naming convention can mean the difference between a smooth project development and a bewildering project development. Pick a naming convention and stick with it.*

You are now in symbol-editing mode. If you look at the edit bar, you'll see a small icon and the name of your symbol next to Scene 1, indicating that you are editing the master symbol itself. In the Layers pane of the Timeline panel, you'll see that the symbol's Timeline now appears, with the default Layer 1. Create three more layers, then name them **gradient**, **inner**, **middle**, and **outer** from top to bottom. Remember that to rename a layer, double-click on its name.

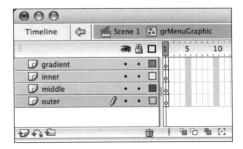

3. Zoom to 800% using the drop-down list in the edit bar and set up the outer guides for the menu graphic you are about to produce.

You need to set up a series of guides for the menu background, which will have several colors for an outline, to create a border effect. You will use a series of rounded rectangles layers on top of one another with differing colors to create the effect and you will use guides to help you layer the rectangles in the symbol.

Turn on rulers by selecting View > Rulers if they are not already on. The rulers appear at the top left of the workspace. Remember that you can't use guides unless the rulers are on. From the Zoom menu at the far right of the edit bar, select 800%. This will make it easer to work because the menu will be only 110 pixels wide by 15 pixels tall.

Click the vertical ruler and drag to produce a guide. Drag the guide to **0** on the horizontal ruler, which should line up with the vertical line of the cross hair on the Stage, which is the symbol's absolute center and the point of origin for its coordinate system.

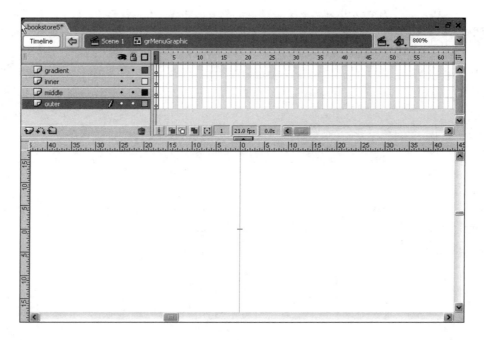

Repeat this step, dropping the guide at **110** pixels. Now, drag out upper and lower guides. The lower guide will be set to **0** in the vertical ruler, and the upper guide at **17** above the lower.

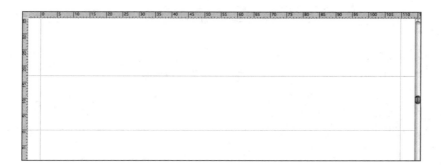

4. Create three guides at one-pixel intervals from the sides and bottom of the menu.

To accurately line up each layer, you need to create guides for each shape to snap to when you create it. Create three more guides on the left of the Stage, but to the *right* of the guide set at 0, spaced one pixel apart. Drag three more guides at the right of the Stage, but to the *left* of the guide set at 110. Finally, drag three more guides set above the horizontal guide at 0. All the guides should be only one pixel apart.

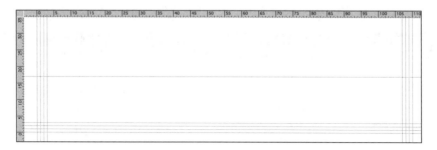

5. Create the menu background on the outer layer using the Rectangle tool with a corner radius set to 2. Set the stroke color to None and the fill color to #666666. Create the rectangle within the outermost guides.

First, select the Rectangle tool and shut off Object Drawing by deselecting it. You need to edit a bunch of graphics at once in this exercise, and Object Drawing makes the process a little more difficult in this circumstance. Switching to Merge Drawing will make the edits easier.

You need to create the outer edge of the menu background using a rectangle with rounded corners. Select the Rectangle tool and then press the Set Corner Radius button to open the Rectangle Settings dialog box. The Set Corner Radius button is found in the options area of the Tools panel. Enter **2** into the Corner Radius field and click OK. You will use the Rectangle tool with this corner radius for each layer.

Use the Fill Color controls and Stroke Color controls in the Tools panel to set your fill color to #666666 and your stroke color to No Color. Select the outer layer to create the first rectangle. The first rectangle snaps to each of the outside vertical guides placed at 0 and 100, and the horizontal guides at 0 and 17.

Tip *You might want to lock your guides first by selecting View › Guide › Lock Guides, so that you don't inadvertently move them.*

Click the cursor very close to the upper-left corner of the guides and then drag the cursor diagonally to the lower-right corner of these guides. When the cursor is clicked or released close to one of the guides, it snaps right to the line.

6. Create another rectangle in the middle layer, with a fill of #FFFFFF and no stroke. Create the rectangle one pixel in from the left, bottom, and right sides of the outer rectangle.

Now click the middle layer to make the next rectangle. Use the Tools panel to set your fill color to #FFFFFF and make sure that the stroke color is still set to No Color. Now you need to create a rectangle shape that is inside the rectangle on the outer layer by one pixel on the bottom left and right sides.

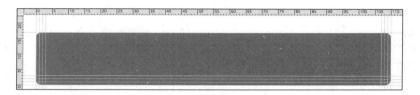

Tip *Use Ctrl+Z or Cmd+Z if you need to undo and redraw the shape.*

The third and fourth rectangles are created exactly the same way, except for moving in another pixel on each side and the bottom. For the rectangle on the inner layer, set the fill color to #999999 and the stroke color should still be off. For the gradient layer, for now, set the fill color to #CCCCCC. Later in this lesson, you will do an exercise on gradients, in which you will apply a linear gradient to this graphic.

7. Trim the top of the menu and then lock the layers in place.

If you have locked any of your layers to prevent from drawing everything in the same layer, unlock them now. Drag a new guide line to **15** pixels on the vertical ruler. Next, with the Selection tool, click and drag from the upper-left corner, down to the 15 pixel guide, all the way to just past the 110 pixel vertical guide, and then let go. You'll see a crosshatch pattern, indicating that area has been selected. This selects the upper portion of all of the graphics only. Press Delete or Backspace to delete that portion of the menu graphic because you won't need it.

Click the Lock Layer icon at the top of the Layers pane to lock all your layers at once.

8. Return to the Main Stage.

Return to the main Stage by clicking the Scene 1 icon at the far left of the edit bar. Remember that you are in symbol-editing mode. When you go back to the main Stage, you will not see your graphic. It is being stored in the library, waiting to be used.

Zoom back out to 100 percent by using the Zoom options menu at the far right of the edit bar.

Tip *You can also double-click on the Zoom tool in the Zoom panel to do the same thing.*

9. Save your work.

Creating and Using Masks

A mask allows you to hide and reveal parts of the Stage based on some shape that you draw. It's a lot like a mat in a picture frame, giving you a glimpse of the image beneath it—but only the interesting part, while everything else is hidden. Using a mask can be very powerful because masks can create some amazing and complex effects. Masks can remain stationary on the Stage, or you can animate them so they move around. The mask effect is really a layer property, and is achieved by setting one layer to be a masking layer, and setting another layer to be masked by it. Flash will do this first step for you.

In this exercise, you will create a basic shape to mask an area of the Stage. The menus will be animated to drop down below the three buttons that are used to control them when you construct that part of the interface. The mask that you will create will ensure that menus are visible only in an area below where the buttons will be. You should still be using bookstore5.fla for this exercise.

1. Add guides to the main Stage by dragging guide lines from the horizontal and vertical rulers.

As this point, you should have a long rectangle on the Stage, but it is not properly put in place. For now, simply drag the graphic off the Stage to the workspace. Repeat this procedure for the other graphics you have on the Stage, such as the oval you created earlier in the lesson for the glow animation. You need to create some new guide lines in the same way you created them in the previous exercise. First, make sure that your guides are not locked. Remember, you can lock and unlock guides in View > Guide > Lock Guides. Next, drag a vertical guide to **115** pixels and a second vertical guide to **405** pixels. Drag a horizontal guide down to **125** pixels and a second horizontal guide down to **140** pixels.

2. **Create a rectangle on a new layer and then change the layer to a mask.**

Select the background layer and then insert two new layers. Name the lower layer **menu** and the layer above it **mask**. On the mask layer, create a rectangle within the guide lines. The edges snap to the guides.

When you finish creating the rectangle, select the mask layer in the Timeline. Right- or Control-click the layer name, and select Mask from the contextual menu. The menu layer is automatically indented in the Layers pane, which means it is now being masked.

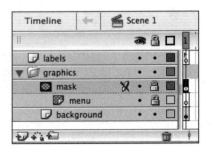

3. **Ensure that the mask layer is locked and remove the guides.**

By default, when you produce a mask in Flash, the mask layer and the layer being masked automatically lock. This causes the mask to work properly in the editing environment. When you unlock either layer, the mask graphic will become visible again, so either the content of the masked layer can be repositioned or the content of the masking layer itself can be reshaped. Even with those layers locked, however, if you test the movie (Control > Test Movie, Ctrl+Enter or Cmd+Enter on OS X), the mask will still behave as expected. It is unnecessary to test the movie at this point because you have no content yet on the layer being masked.

Ensure that the mask layer is locked. In addition, set the mask layer to be hidden by clicking the dot underneath the Show/Hide All Layers icon for the layer. Finally, because you won't need the guides for now, select View > Guides > Clear Guides to quickly put them back in the ruler.

Adding Strokes

Strokes are the outlines around objects or lines all by themselves. Flash 8 has several built-in options for stroke styles, with a limited way of customizing a style, and has some options to control joins and capping. Strokes can be added to a shape with the Ink Bottle tool or drawn with any of the line drawing tools.

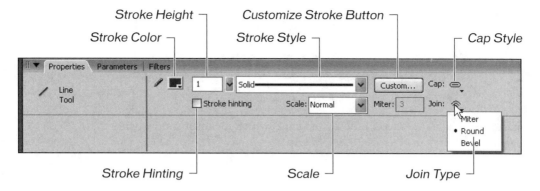

Stroke Height — Customize Stroke Button —
Stroke Color — Stroke Style — Cap Style
Stroke Hinting — Scale — Join Type —

Stroke height controls the thickness of the line on the Stage. Set it by clicking the triangle next to the Stroke Height field and using the slider bar to adjust, or enter a value from 0.1 to 200. Stroke height is measured in points.

The Stroke Style menu holds the generic styles that come with Flash 8. Click the menu to see the styles you can apply. One of the options is *hairline*, which always stays the same size, no matter how much you zoom into the Stage. A *regular* stroke appears larger when you zoom into the Stage, and is what you have been using so far. You can customize the styles further by pressing the Custom button, which presents limited options to altering the stroke style.

Tip *Limit your use of custom stroke styles in your FLA file. The custom styles add more file size to your SWF file. Likewise, the styles other than hairline or normal can increase file size.*

The Cap button is used to determine the appearance of the end of the stroke, and can be *none*, *round*, or *square*. *None* is flush with the path's end, whereas *square* extends beyond the end of the stroke by half of the stroke's width. Finally, *round* just rounds out the stroke's end.

The Join option controls how two strokes meet, and can be *miter*, *round*, or *bevel*. Join types can be changed after strokes are drawn together by selecting the stroke segments and changing the values.

Stroke hinting is used to adjust line and curve anchors on full pixels automatically, which prevents horizontal or vertical lines from being blurry when drawn. This works, of course, only if the option is selected.

Finally, when you have the Pencil tool selected and it is set to draw in Smooth mode in the options area of the Tools panel, a Smoothing slider will appear to control how smooth the resulting stroke is.

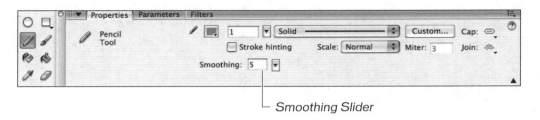

Smoothing Slider

1. Insert a new layer and create another rectangle.

Select the background layer and insert a new layer. Rename the layer **outline** and make sure that the background layer is locked.

Select the Rectangle tool in the Tools panel. Set the stroke color to #000000 (black), set the fill color to No Color, and make sure that the stroke height is set to the default value of 1. In the Cap box, ensure that the cap is set to None. Finally, in the options area of the Tools panel, press the Rounded Corners button and make sure that the value is set to 0. Draw a small rectangle anywhere on the Stage.

> **Tip** If you don't see the changeable options on the Property inspector when you select the Rectangle tool, switch to the Selection tool, click once on the background, and go back to the Rectangle tool.

2. Resize and position the rectangle.

With the rectangle selected, enter the following values into the Property inspector: W of **770**, H of **519**. These values ensure that the rectangle is visible all around the edge of the Stage. If you create it the same size as the Stage, some of the rectangle will be cut off after you publish the SWF file. Next, set *x* and *y* to **0**, **0** respectively. That place matches the graphic's upper-left corner with the upper-left corner of the Stage.

> **Note** Although the right side and bottom of the SWF file might appear to have a double line and be a little rough, the line appears uniform around the edge of the SWF file when you publish the file and view it in a browser. If you set the rectangle to full size, you do not see your outline at the bottom or right of the Stage.

3. Change the rectangle into a symbol and lock the layer.

The rectangle should still be select on the Stage. Select Modify > Convert to Symbol and name the graphic **grOutline**. Select the Graphic radio button to make it a graphic symbol. Click OK, and when you are finished, lock the outline layer.

Using the Library

The library stores the symbols, components, sounds, bitmap images, and digital video items that you use in your Flash FLA file. Any time you create a new symbol or import sound, video, and bitmaps, those items are automatically added to the library. In the library, you can view, organize into folders, rename, or adjust properties of nearly every asset you can use in Flash. You can also add new items to the Stage from the library by dragging items out and dropping them where you like (as long as it is in a keyframe and an unlocked layer).

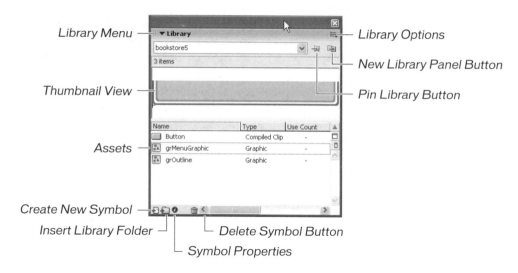

In Flash, every document has its own library. What's more, document libraries can be opened separately from an FLA file, so that you can share or copy assets from one library to the next. When more than one Flash document is open, the Library drop-down list will allow you to switch back and forth to different document libraries quickly. The selection in the drop-down list always shows the active document library unless you click the Pin

Library icon to keep the selection locked in place. The New Library Panel button launches the currently selected library in its own panel.

Buttons for creating new symbols, deleting selected assets, showing asset properties, and organizing assets into folders are all at the lower-left corner of the Library panel.

In this exercise, you will learn your way around the library and create some folders to organize the elements you will import into the document. You should still be working with bookstore5.fla for this exercise.

1. Select Window > Library to open the library if it is not already open.

The library is like any other panel in Flash; it can be minimized, maximized, docked, and undocked. In your library, there will be several named items already showing; the Button component, and the grMenuGraphic and grOutline. The grMenuGraphic and grOutline symbols were automatically added to the library when you converted those graphics into your graphic symbols. Likewise, when you dragged and dropped a Button component to the Stage in the previous lesson, it was added to the library. Why? So these items can be reused. Even when you delete an *instance* of an asset from the Stage, it is still kept in the library.

Note *The graphics that you produced on the Stage with the drawing tools are not symbols, so they aren't added to the library. They're referred to in Flash as raw or primitive graphics. Nothing that is directly drawn on the main Stage is a symbol until you make it one.*

2. Delete the Button component from the library.

To delete an asset from the library, select it and then click the trash can icon in the lower portion of the panel. You can also Right- or Control-click the asset and select Delete from the context menu.

Note *If you have elements in the library that are not used in the application, they are not exported in the SWF file when you publish—with the sole exception of Flash's built-in components. Always delete unused components from your document library to save file size.*

3. Create a new library folder by clicking the **New Folder** button. Name the folder **graphics** and put both graphic symbols in it.

Library folders are very useful in Flash because often you will have many, many assets. Organizing them into well-named folders can make finding things much easier.

Press the New Folder button at the bottom of the Library panel. When the folder is created, you can name it straight away. Name it **graphics**. You can rename the folder by double-clicking the folder name and entering a new value. Click and drag both graphic symbols into the new library folder.

Tip *By default, the library folder is collapsed. To expand it, double-click the folder icon. If you double-click the name, Flash thinks you're trying to rename the folder.*

4. Create four more library folders named **components**, **buttons**, **media**, and **movie clips**.

We will add assets to each of these folders in later exercises.

5. Open the grMenuGraphic symbol from the library.

When you double-click a symbol in the library, you enter into symbol-editing mode. Here, you are changing the master properties of the symbol, which will affect all instances of that symbol used in your document.

If your graphics folder is collapsed, double-click the folder icon to expand it. Then double-click the grMenuGraphic symbol icon to enter symbol-editing mode. Don't make any changes; this step just shows you how to go into symbol-editing mode from the Library panel. Click Scene 1 on the edit bar to exit symbol-editing mode.

6. Save your work.

Importing and Optimizing Bitmaps

You have several graphics on or around the Stage at this point, which are all vector art. Sometimes, however, you need bitmaps for various reasons—for example, to make your interface more visually compelling. Bitmaps are also very useful in animation because animating a bitmap is simply moving pixels around on a screen, whereas vector art has to be completely redrawn from frame to frame.

The problem with bitmaps is that they don't scale well. Scaling up, and sometimes even scaling down, can cause bitmaps to lose resolution on the Stage, so as a best practice, bitmaps should be imported at their intended size, and scaling up or down should be avoided.

Images and graphics can be created using any image editing software, such as Macromedia Fireworks or Adobe Photoshop. What's more, Flash has round trip editing features that work in Fireworks and Photoshop both, so you can Right- or Control-click a bitmap in the graphic, select Edit or Edit With, update the image in Fireworks or Photoshop, and the updates will automatically happen in Flash. No need to reimport.

In this exercise, you will import bitmap artwork that was already created for you. This artwork will be for buttons, the logo, and the title area, and it will be in PNG format. Flash, however, supports very nearly every bitmap format there is.

1. Select File > Import > Import to Library to import six PNG files for the buttons. Then place the items in the buttons folder in the library.

When you select the Import to Library menu option, any assets that import will be placed directly in the library, not on the Stage. You also have the option to import items directly to the Stage, although this does place a copy of those assets in the library as well.

From the File menu, select Import > Import to Library. From the lesson02/assets subdirectory, import company_up, company down, contact up, contact down, products up, and products down. You can select all of them at once by pressing Control or Command (depending on your platform) while clicking. Then press the Import to Library button to make the import.

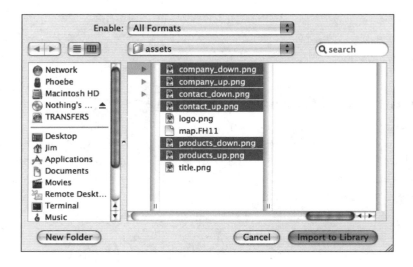

After the graphics are in, drag them and drop them to the library folder labeled buttons. Again, you can select more than one item to drag by Control-clicking or Command-clicking.

2. Check the optimization settings for the imported bitmap images.

Flash allows you to have a bit of control over the optimization of the bitmap images that you import. By default, all images are optimized in JPG format at 50% quality when you publish your SWF file. To change that, select the image in the library and press the Properties button at the bottom (it's the white *i* in the blue circle).

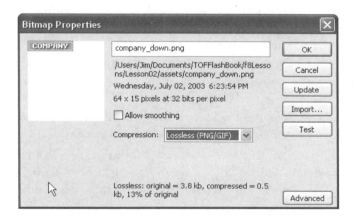

The dialog box has a Compression drop-down list that allows you to switch compression types from Lossless (PNG/GIF) to Photo (JPEG). Lossless is the best option to select for the button graphics you just imported because they have few and simple colors. Photo is the best option to select for graphics that have lots of color and tonality, and gradients. Photo is Flash's default compression type.

> **Tip** | *For optimal control over compression and image quality, optimize your images before you import them into Flash.*

The Allow Smoothing check box lets anti-aliasing smooth the edges of the bitmap. In most cases, anti-aliasing enhances the appearance of the image.

3. Import title.png from lesson02/assets and change its compression properties.

Select File > Import > Import to Library again to bring in title.png. Drag the image into the media folder in the library; then select it, Right- or Control-click the bitmap, and select Properties from the context menu. This is another way to get to the Bitmap Properties dialog box.

Change the compression for the title.png bitmap to Photo compression, uncheck the Use Document Default Quality check box that appears, and change the value from 50% to 80%. Click OK.

4. Place the image on the Stage in the background layer, and use the Property inspector to position it at **0,0**. Lock the background layer when you are finished.

First, make sure that the background layer is unlocked. If it is unlocked, click it to make it active and then drag an instance of title.png from the library out onto the Stage. Notice the braid around the image, indicating that it is a *raw* image, not a symbol.

Use the Property inspector to enter in an *x* of **0** and a *y* of **0** to position the graphic. When you finish setting the new location for this graphic, lock the background layer so you won't accidentally move the graphic away from this position. The graphic was made to fit the width of the Stage precisely, so it wouldn't do to shift it.

5. Import the **logo** graphic into the library and change its compression properties to Photo. Place it on the Stage in a new layer named **logo**.

Import the logo.png graphic from lesson02/assets. When the image is imported, drag it into the media folder in the library. Right- or Control-click and select Properties from the context menu. Set the compression to Photo because this image has gradients, and set the quality to 80%.

Make a new layer above the background layer with the Insert Layer button and rename the new layer **logo**. Drag and drop an instance of logo.png to the Stage and position it in the upper-left corner.

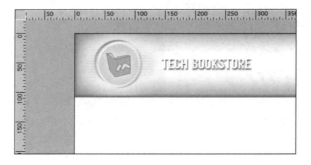

Roughly position the graphic as seen in this image. You can use your own judgment about where the logo looks best in this corner. Just make sure that it doesn't overlap and obscure much of the title text in the image underneath it. When you finish positioning the image, lock the logo layer.

6. Save your work.

Importing Vector Drawings

You can import complex vector drawings into Flash, such as those from FreeHand (.FH7 to .FH11 files) and Adobe Illustrator (.AI files). You can maintain the layers in each kind of document, although you have more control when you import documents made with FreeHand. An advantage of using vector drawings is that when they are scaled, you do not lose quality as you do when scaling bitmap images: Vector drawings are made by math instead of pixels on a grid, so distortion doesn't occur when the image resizes.

In this exercise, you import a file that was created using FreeHand MX. You select how and where the assets in this file are placed and then properly place them in the Flash document.

1. Create a new Flash document and change the document properties.

The map area of the website is dynamically loaded into the main web pages SWF file at runtime. When a user visits the map of the site, the SWF file loads into the main Tech Bookstore SWF file. This means that you need to add the map to a new FLA file so you can export the SWF file that will be used to load into the main bookstore SWF file later.

Select File > New and then click Flash Document from the Type list. Click OK and a new FLA file opens in Flash with its own Document Tab, which makes it easy to switch between open documents when you need to do so.

Maximize the Property inspector. Change the dimensions of the Stage by pressing the button next to Size and entering new values into the W and H text fields in the Document Properties dialog box. Enter a width of **500** and a height of **355**. Then change the frame rate to **21** fps, matching the frame rate you entered for the main bookstore SWF file in Lesson 1.

2. Import a vector file that was made in FreeHand into a new Flash file.

One area of the website includes a vector drawing of a map. Inside the lesson02/assets folder on the CD-ROM is this file, which was created using FreeHand MX. FreeHand files can retain symbols, pages, layers, and text, so you can edit the file contents further using Flash.

Select Layer 1 and rename the layer to **map**. Make sure that it is selected before you import the FreeHand document. Select File > Import > Import to Stage and import map.FH11 from lesson02/assets. The FreeHand Import dialog box opens.

Select either Scenes or Keyframes for the Pages setting. This document does not contain multiple pages, so it doesn't matter which you select. If a document has multiple pages, each page is placed in a separate scene or ascending keyframes on the main Timeline.

Select Flatten for the Layers selection. You don't need to change the placement for the different sections of the map, except for one symbol that you will paste on a new layer.

3. Align the symbols on the Stage.

When you import the file, it doesn't necessarily line up properly with the Stage. Select Edit > Select All to select all the symbols on the Stage, and enter **0, 0** for the x and y coordinates in the Property inspector to line things up properly.

Tip *In the library, a FreeHand Objects folder has been added, which contains the assets that were imported with the FreeHand document. You can work with these symbols the same way as you work with those created in Flash.*

4. Cut and paste a symbol onto a new layer.

With the map layer selected, click the Insert New Layer button. Rename the layer to **map star**.

Select the yellow star symbol on the map layer and select Edit > Cut. This process cuts the symbol to the Clipboard. It looks like as if it has been deleted, but it is being held in memory so you can paste it to a new location.

Select the map star layer and select Edit > Paste In Place, which pastes the graphic in the exact same x and y location it was cut from. You are moving the star to a new layer because in an upcoming lesson you will be manipulating it.

5. Save the file as **map.fla** and publish it.

Select File > Save and save the file to the TechBookstore folder on your hard drive. Type **map.fla** into the File Name field and click OK. You need to publish an SWF file so you can load it into the main bookstore SWF file later. Select File > Publish Settings, and in the Formats section, deselect HTML because you don't need to produce an HTML file. Click the Publish button to create the SWF file.

You will import other media, such as sound and video, into FLA files for other lessons. For now, you should have a good grasp of the process of importing media. Importing is pretty much the same process, no matter what asset you are importing. There are small variations, such as when you are importing video for instance, but for the most part, nothing is radically different.

Using Fills and Gradients

You have already used several fills in this lesson. The menu background graphic you created used fills without any strokes. You used hexadecimal values to select fill colors, although you could have used the color swatches as well. Color Mixer gives you more control over fills than the Tools panel does, and it should already be open in the TechBookstore panel set. If not, open Color Mixer by selecting Window > Color Mixer. You can create gradient and bitmap fills using the controls in this panel.

With bitmap fills, you fill an area using a bitmap graphic that was imported into Flash. You should already have several bitmaps in bookstore5.fla, and you have an Import button to import a new image for the fill. Select Bitmap from the drop-down list in Color Mixer.

The bitmaps currently in the library are then shown in Color Mixer. If you select one of these bitmaps, it is selected as the current fill.

Note *Bitmap fills are tiled when filling in an area. To resize the bitmap fill, use the Fill Transform tool, which can scale, rotate, and skew bitmap fills. You will use the Fill Transform tool with gradients later in this exercise.*

You can fill a shape with a gradient, which is a gradual transition from one color to another. There are two kinds of gradients that can be created with Flash: *linear* and *radial*. A radial gradient makes the transition in a circular fashion, whereas a linear gradient makes the transition along a straight line. You can apply up to 16 colors to either gradient type to make more complex graphics and use the Fill Transform tool to precisely control the gradient focal point.

In this exercise, you create gradients for several of the assets in the main SWF file. You should have a rectangle and a circle that you created in the first exercise of this lesson moved off the Stage. The fill for both of these elements will be modified.

1. Save a new version of bookstore5.fla as bookstore6.fla in the TechBookstore folder on your hard drive.

You should version up whenever you plan to make significant changes.

2. Unlock the background layer. Move the rectangle that you created in the first exercise back onto the Stage and create a gradient using Color Mixer.

In the first exercise, you created a rectangle that was 779 pixels by 15 pixels. Select that rectangle and move it back onto the Stage. Expand or open Color Mixer, and select Linear in the Fill Type drop-down list. A color palette will show below the drop-down list, and your rectangle will have a linear gradient applied to it straight away.

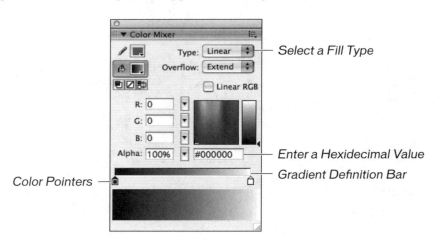

Click the color pointer on the left side of the gradient definition bar. Then enter **#CCCCCC** into the hexadecimal text field just above and press Enter. Alternately, you can press on the color pointer and select a color from the swatches menu that appears. The color pointer on the right side of the gradient definition bar should still be set to white. If it is not, click the color pointer on the right side of the gradient definition bar and change the color to white (#FFFFFF).

Tip *You can change the color using the RGB text fields on the right.*

Tip *To add a color to the gradient, click over the gradient definition area somewhere. A new color pointer appears so that you can add a color. Remember, you can add up to 16 colors. You can remove the color by dragging a color pointer away from the bar.*

3. Modify the gradient with the Fill Transform tool.

If, for some reason, the gradient you added was not applied to your rectangle, select the Paint Bucket tool from the Tools panel and click your rectangle now. That process applies the gradient. The gradient still needs to be scaled and rotated, though, and you will use the Fill Transform tool for that purpose.

Select the Fill Transform tool from the Tools panel and click the gradient fill in your rectangle. A series of control handles appear.

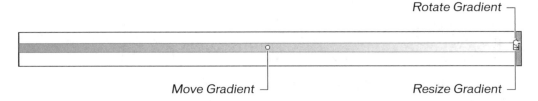

Rotate Gradient

Move Gradient

Resize Gradient

Mouse over the rotation handle at the upper-right corner of the rectangle and click and drag it downward to rotate the gradient 90 degrees clockwise. Thus, the gradient transition will be vertical instead of horizontal. However, now the transition is barely visible because of the narrow rectangle. To make the gradient visible, you need to resize the gradient. Click the square control handle on the Fill Transform tool, which is now below the shape, and drag it upward. Let the bounding box snap to the side of the rectangle, so the gradient is the same height.

4. Convert the rectangle to a graphic symbol and move it onto the Stage directly under title.png.

Using the Selection tool, make sure that the entire rectangle is selected. Because you drew this graphic in the Object Drawing model, you need to click it only once (double-clicking it puts you into edit-in-place mode. Use the keyboard shortcut F8 to convert the rectangle into a graphic symbol or select Modify > Convert to Symbol from the main menus. Name the new symbol **grBar**.

In the Property inspector, place the symbol instance at **0** for x and **109** for y, which puts it just below the title.png image. In the library, drag the symbol grBar into the graphics folder, just to stay neat and organized.

> **Note** Any time you select a symbol, an object drawn In the Object Drawing model, or a grouped item, you see a blue outline, indicating that the item is selected. This is referred to as a bounding box.

5. Open the grMenuGraphic symbol from the graphics folder in the library. Fill the shape on the gradient layer with a linear gradient.

Double-click the graphics library folder icon and then double-click the icon for grMenuGraphic to enter symbol-editing mode. You need to zoom in on the graphic, either with the Zoom tool or with the Zoom options in the edit bar. Right- or Control-click on the gradient layer in the Layers pane and select Lock Others from the context menu. This ensures that you are only editing the graphic on the gradient layer.

You use the same gradient that was used for the rectangle. Because you have not changed the fill type since the last exercise, you can select the Paint Bucket tool and click once on the shape in the gradient layer to apply the fill.

Using the Fill Transform tool, rotate the gradient 90 degrees clockwise to make the gradient vertical. Then resize the gradient to the same width of the shape.

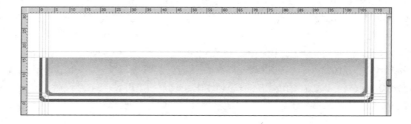

When you finish, click Scene 1 in the edit bar to return to the main Stage.

6. Move the circle that you created onto an empty part of the Stage and fill it with a radial gradient. Convert it to a symbol and then move it to its own layer.

You made a circle in the first exercise, and it is used to create a glow behind the imported logo. Return to the Color Mixer; this time, select Radial from the drop-down list. Click the left color pointer for the gradient and type **#00cc00** into the hexadecimal field just above the gradient definition bar. This selects a bright green color. Although it might not appear too appealing at this point, the glow is mostly hidden and quite transparent. When you finish creating the site, it matches part of the default component set used in the Tech Bookstore.

Select the color pointer on the right side of the gradient definition bar. This time, you set this end of the gradient to fully transparent by clicking the arrow button next to the Alpha field and sliding it to **0** or by typing **0** into the Alpha field directly and pressing Enter.

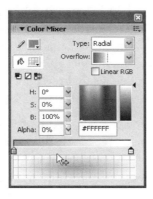

Make sure that the circle is filled with the gradient and then convert it to a symbol using the keyboard shortcut F8. Name the symbol **grGlow**, make it a graphic symbol, and move it to the graphics folder in the library.

On the Stage, select the background layer and insert a new layer above it. Name this layer **glow animation**. Cut the grGlow instance from the Stage in the background layer and paste it into the new layer.

Tip   *You should use gradients sparingly because they can increase file size significantly.*

7. Save your changes.

Manipulating Graphics

You have created, imported, and filled graphics for the Tech Bookstore. But there are more ways to manipulate them: You can also rotate, scale, tint, and change the alpha of graphics. This exercise shows you how to make some more changes to the graphics you just created using tools and the Property inspector.

1. Create a new layer, name it bars, and then move the grBar symbol onto this layer.

Add the new layer just above the background layer. Now click the instance of the graphic symbol grBar that is in the background layer, cut it, and activate the new layer, bars. Select Edit > Paste In Place to paste it into the same *x* and *y* coordinates from which it was cut.

2. Drag the grBar graphic symbol from the library onto the Stage and rotate it.

When you drag another symbol from the library and drop it onto the Stage, you are creating a new *instance*, or usage of that symbol. Instances are separate from other instances on the Stage. You can change one without changing the others. However, if you double-click the symbol instance on the Stage, you will go into symbol-editing mode—in edit-in-place mode at that. Any changes you make to the graphics in the symbol will affect all symbol instances based on it. The moral of this story: Don't get click-happy.

Drag your instance of grBar into the bars layer. With it selected, select the Free Transform tool; you can rotate the symbol so that the gradient is facing in the opposite direction.

3. Use the Align panel to place the second instance of grBar at the bottom of the Stage.

If you don't see the Align panel, open it now using Window > Align. Press the To Stage button at the right side of the panel so that it is highlighted. This allows you to line up objects relative to the Stage; without it selected, multiple selected objects will line up relative to each other.

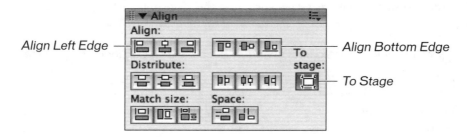

Press the Align Left Edge button under Align so the left side of the symbol aligns with the left edge of the Stage. Click the Align Bottom Edge button under Align so the bottom of the symbol aligns with the bottom of the Stage. Lock the bars layer after you have finished.

4. Change the alpha and scale of the grGlow graphic symbol.

Earlier in this lesson, you imported a logo for the Tech Bookstore onto the logo layer and then placed it on the Stage. Make sure that the logo layer is locked for this step.

The glow animation is placed beneath the logo and is revealed around the edges of the image because transparency was used in the PNG. Move the grGlow symbol beneath the logo and check to see whether the glow is visible around the edges of the logo. If it isn't visible enough, you might need to scale the grGlow symbol up with the Free Transform tool. With the Free Transform tool selected, switch to the Scale option in the options area, click the graphic symbol, and scale up or down with the corner control handles until the gradient is just visible around the edges of the logo.

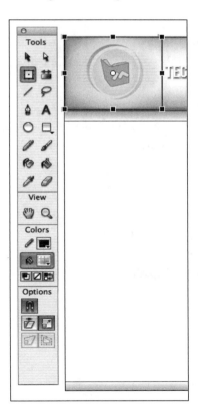

If you feel the color is too bright, you can reduce the alpha for the symbol. In the Property inspector (with the symbol selected), you should see a Color drop-down list. From the Color drop-down list, select Alpha, and either use the slider that appears to change the opacity of the grGlow symbol, or enter a value into the field and press Enter on the keyboard.

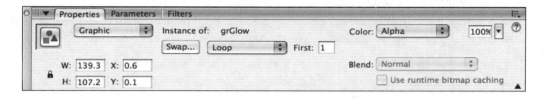

5. Lock all your layers and save your work.

What You Have Learned

In this lesson, you have:

- Navigated the tools (pages 33–34)
- Learned about the Merge Drawing and Object Drawing models (pages 34–36)
- Used vector and bitmap images (pages 36–39)
- Used tools to draw graphics (pages 39–42)
- Learned how to use guides and snap graphics to them (pages 42–44)
- Made a graphic symbol (pages 44–49)
- Created a mask layer (pages 49–50)
- Created and modified strokes (pages 50–53)
- Used the library to organize assets (pages 53–55)
- Imported bitmaps and vector artwork (pages 55–61)
- Used gradients (pages 61–65)
- Modified existing graphics (pages 66–68)

3 Using Text

Text is an important part of most websites, particularly informational or commercial sites. Flash allows you to have a lot of control over the kind of text you can add to a document and of editing the property settings of the text. Text can be loaded from a server or placed directly on the Stage. Kerning, character spacing, justification, color, and anti-aliasing of text can all be controlled by setting properties in the workspace. Text is regularly used in Flash for creative, beautiful, and traditional purposes. In fact, Flash allows you to create many textual effects that are not possible when using HTML or CSS style sheets (Cascading Style Sheets).

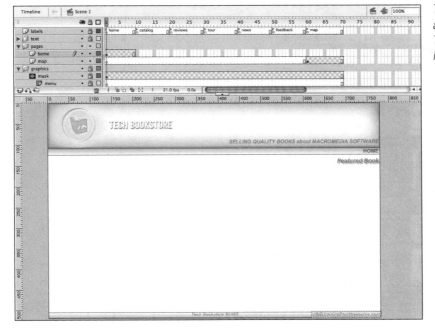

Text fields are added to the Tech Bookstore in this lesson

In this lesson, you will add and format the properties of many text fields in Flash. You will learn how to add a Filter effect to a static text field. You will also spell check the entire document before you finish the lesson. This lesson gives you a foundation in the way text and fonts work and a good basis for using increasingly complex methods of working with text and components in upcoming lessons.

What You Will Learn

In this lesson, you will:

- Learn how to use the Text tool to add text fields
- Learn about static text and device fonts
- Learn to change text properties for legibility
- Align text fields on the Stage
- Learn about embedding fonts and charters in a SWF file
- Use a Filter with text
- Check spelling in a document

Approximate Time

This lesson takes approximately 45 minutes to complete.

Lesson Files

Media Files:
None

Starting Files:
lesson03/start/bookstore6.fla

Completed Files:
lesson03/complete/bookstore7.fla

Using the Text Tool

There are several different kinds of text that you can use in Flash 8. The three text field types available are static, dynamic, and input text, and they are each used for different purposes. Static text is similar to an image or graphic: It displays any kind of text on the Stage and does not change unless you manually edit the text field. Dynamic text can be used with ActionScript to change what displays in the field—for example, it might change based on some user action (such as a failed login) or if you load text into the field from a file on a server. Input text allows a user to type in text when the SWF file is running in Flash Player. You might use this rather often if you are building a form in which you need to gather a person's name and address. ActionScript is used to capture input text that a visitor types into the form and then send it to a server.

Tip *Flash 8 Basic and Flash 8 Professional both ship with built-in components that can also be used to handle text. These components come in handy when you need to build a form quickly or need to display long lines of scrolling text.*

There are many text properties that can be edited using the Property inspector. Flash allows you to have control over the font face (a set of characters in a given design), color, size, kerning (adjusting the space between characters for aesthetic purposes), character spacing and position, justification (alignment), and orientation of text fields. You can also control typefaces, meaning that you can set the characters to be regular, bold, and/or italic. What's more, Flash 8 introduces tools that control font anti-aliasing for different situations, such as animation or plain old display, to make the text as legible as possible. Select the Text tool in the Tools panel and maximize the Property inspector. If you don't see properties similar to the following figure, click the Stage once.

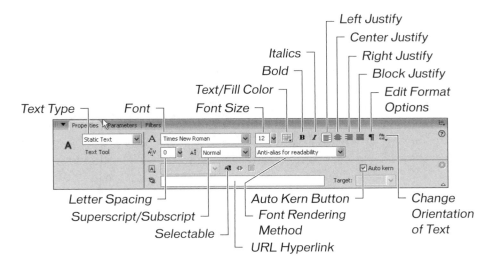

If you send a FLA file to someone to edit, that person needs the fonts you used to be installed on the computer to see the file. A missing font doesn't stop a person from opening and editing the file because any missing font can be mapped to any font currently installed on the system. An alert appears when the file is opened or published, indicating any missing fonts, and allows an available font to be chosen as a replacement. The original correct font is used again if the file is passed on to someone who has it installed.

Understanding Static Text and Device Fonts

When you use static text in a FLA file, Flash creates outlines of each character and uses them to display the text. It doesn't matter what font you select; the characters are visible, no matter who views the file. You can also be sure the fonts display the same way you see them on the Stage. A pitfall of this feature, and therefore of using static text, is that using it does increase the SWF file. Fortunately, there is a way around this: You can choose to use *device fonts*, which use the font installed in the end user's computer, rather than using an outline created by Flash.

Device fonts can be used for horizontal static text fields and are the default for input and dynamic text fields. If the end user doesn't have the font you selected installed on the computer, the SWF file uses the browser default: the sans font. There are also three default device fonts in Flash: _sans, _serif, and _typewriter. The _sans font is similar to Arial or Helvetica, _serif appears like Times New Roman, and _typewriter is similar to Courier.

Flash 8 Basic includes tools to assist with font legibility at any font size. One of the features in Flash that can make font choices problematic is anti-aliasing. Static text in Flash is anti-aliased by default, which can make smaller font sizes look blurry and difficult to read. In the past, the only way to defeat anti-aliasing was to either shut it off altogether, use a device font, or use a dynamic text field to display text. Now you can select several different rendering types in the Font Rendering Method drop-down list: Bitmap text, which is not anti-aliased; Anti-alias for animation; Anti-alias for readability; and Custom anti-alias, which controls the smoothing of the font. Custom anti-alias is available only in Flash 8 Professional.

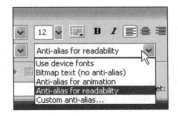 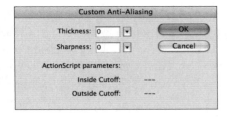

Adding Static Text to a Document

The first step of learning how to effectively use text in a Flash document is to add some basic static text to the Stage. In this exercise, you will add static text to the FLA file. The character outlines are embedded in the file, so you can use any font on your computer system, and it is visible to the site's visitors.

1. Open bookstore6.fla from the TechBookstore folder, and save it as **bookstore7.fla**.

Alternatively, you can open bookstore6.fla from lesson02/start and save it as **bookstore7.fla**.

2. Add a new layer for static text and rename it **page names**. Insert a layer folder and name it **text**.

Select the graphics layer folder and insert a new layer above it. Rename the layer to **page names**. With the new layer selected, click Insert Layer Folder at the bottom of the Layers pane, and name the new folder **text**. Drag the page names layer into the text folder.

3. Extend the main document Timeline to 70 frames.

The various "pages" for the Tech Bookstore will be organized along the main document Timeline. Each of these pages will include a static text field, including the name of the page.

Note   *Although this procedure is not necessarily considered a best practice, it's quite okay for a learning application. In the real world, your different "pages" will be different SWF files loaded into the interface with a user interaction. You will learn how to do that in a later lesson, but for now, the goal is to get used to text, and practice using the Timeline at the same time.*

Click on Frame 70 of the labels layer (only that frame should be highlighted). Now hold down Shift and select Frame position 70 of the background layer. By pressing down Shift, you are highlighting Frame 70 across all the layers, so you can extend each layer to that point in time at once. Press F5 on your keyboard or select Insert > Timeline > Insert Frame to extend all your layers to 70 frames.

4. Organize the layers to form the website's pages.

First, you need to add some keyframes to the labels layer that will represent each of the different parts of the Tech Bookstore website. Select Frame 10 of the labels layer and press F6 to insert a keyframe. Continue to insert keyframes at Frames 20, 30, 40, 50, and 60. Each of these keyframes is labeled with the title of the section.

You already have a frame label in Frame 1 of the labels layer. To add the others, start by selecting Frame 10 on the labels layer, type **catalog** into the <Frame Label> text field in the Property inspector, and press Enter. Leave the Label type at Name. Repeat this process for the next five keyframes on the label layer, entering **reviews**, **tour**, **news**, **feedback**, and **map**.

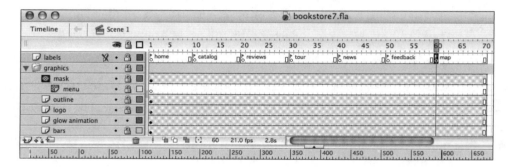

5. Select the Text tool and change the font properties in the Property inspector.

Select the Text tool from the Tools panel and maximize the Property inspector.

Select Static from the Text Type drop-down list. Then select Arial from the Font drop-down list and select 12 for font size. Click the Text (fill) color box and enter **#666666** into the Hexadecimal field above the palette. Click the Bold button so the text appears boldface. Click the Align Right button on the Property inspector to right-justify the text field. All the other settings can remain at the default settings. In the Font Rendering Method drop-down list, select Anti-alias for readability. Your Property inspector should match the settings in the following figure.

6. Add the page name text to each area of the bookstore site using static text.

Now you need to create the text field on the Stage. The page names are placed on the far right of the bar graphic that sits beneath the title area.

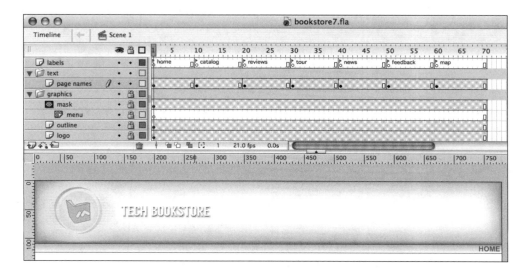

Select Frame 1 on the page names layer. Remember that the text is right-aligned in the text field. Therefore, click the Stage where you want the text to end. Type **HOME** into the text field and select the Selection tool from the Tools panel after you finish. Select the text field you just created and move it to where you want all the page names on other pages to appear.

Tip | *You can create text fields in two different ways. If you want your text field to expand as you type into it, simply click the Stage and start typing. A white circle at the upper-right corner of the field depicts an expanding text field. If you want to set your text field to a fixed width, click the Stage and drag the Text tool to your desired width. A white square at the upper-right corner of the field depicts a fixed-width text field. Both of these handles also can be used to resize the field.*

The frames in the page names layer should extend right up to Frame 70 because you added the layer after you extended the Timeline. Select Frame 10, which is labeled catalog, and insert a keyframe by pressing F6. Continue by inserting keyframes at each labeled frame: 20, 30, 40, 50, and 60.

Now you need to add the actual page names to each page because every one of them says HOME! Go to Frame 10 and double-click the page name. The text returns to an editable state, so you can change the text from HOME to **CATALOG**. Make sure that you do not move this text field on the Stage or any text properties, so it remains consistent and aligned with all of the other text fields.

Repeat this step for all the other pages, giving them the same name (in all caps) as the frame labels you created in Step 4. All you need to do is double-click the text field and edit HOME to the name of the current label.

Lock the page names layer when you finish. The Timeline should look like the previous figure.

7. Add the bookstore's slogan using static text on top of the title area.

You need to add another text field above the page names. However, you need to create a new layer because the slogan stays the same throughout the website, whereas the page names change on every page.

Select the page names layer and then insert a new layer. Rename that layer **propaganda**. An empty keyframe and frames should extend right to Frame 70 already. Select the Text tool and maximize the Property inspector. All the current settings will be used for this text field, except you should click the Italic button and change the Text (fill) color to #999999.

In the propaganda layer, click on top of the title area of the layout and type **SELLING QUALITY BOOKS about MACROMEDIA SOFTWARE**. When you finish, select the Selection tool and move the text field to a desired location in the general lower-right area of the title area. If you want to align the slogan with the page names, use a vertical guide. Drag the guide from the vertical ruler and align it with the right side of the page name. Then select the slogan and snap the right side of the text field to the guide.

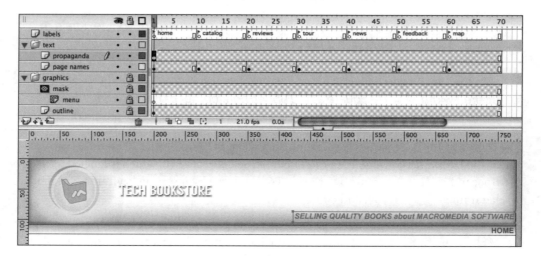

8. Add aliased small text to the bottom of the Stage.

Small fonts can sometimes be very hard to read in Flash because Flash has to create outlines for the fonts, which can cause them to be blurry. Choosing Bitmap Text (no anti-alias) from the Font Rendering Method drop-down list can prevent the blur. Aliased text is not smoothed out.

Note *Small fonts are small fonts. It's not always such a good idea to produce text less than 8 points in size, simply because the text is hard to read at those sizes. If you must use fonts smaller than 8 points, always use the Bitmap Text option.*

The next step is to add some more text on the propaganda layer. At the bottom of the web page is copyright and contact information for visitors to use. You should use a very small text size because you probably don't want to make it too distracting.

Select the Text tool and maximize the Property inspector. Then leave the text type as static, and select Arial as the font. However, change the font size to 10, change the Text (fill) color back to #666666, make sure that Bold and Italics are not selected, and select the Align Left button to left-justify the text.

Next, from the Font Rendering Method drop-down list, select Bitmap Text (no anti-aliasing) so the text you create renders clearly on the Stage. Using the Text tool, click in approximately the center of the bar on the bottom of the Stage and type **Tech Bookstore © 2005**.

Tip *On OS X, the keyboard shortcut to insert the © symbol is Option+G. On Windows, select from the Start menu All Programs › Accessories › System Tools › Character Map, and copy and paste the copyright symbol from there.*

Create a second text field within the bottom bar area. Because this text field has exactly the same properties, you don't need to use the Property inspector before you create the field. Click the Stage and enter the following e-mail address: **info@trainingfromthesource.com**.

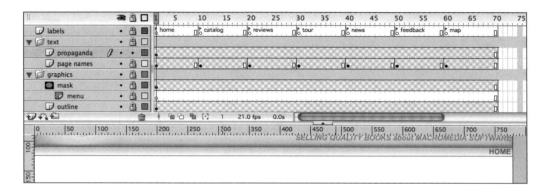

9. Align the small text on the Stage using the Align panel.

When you finish creating both text fields, click the Selection tool and maximize the Align panel. Make sure the To Stage button is selected. Click the first text field you created and then click the Align Horizontal Center button, which centers the text in the middle of the Stage. Use the Up and Down arrow keys on your keyboard to fine-tune the text placement vertically approximately in the center of the lower bar graphic, but depending on where it looks best against the gradient.

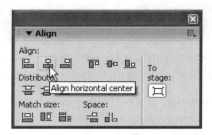

Note *Moving things around with the arrow keys is called nudging. Just so you know.*

Select the second text field that contains the e-mail address and click the Align Right Edge button in the Align panel. This procedure aligns the bounding box around the text field with the right edge of the Stage. If you think it is too close to the edge, select the text field and use the Left Arrow key to move it a few pixels to the left.

These two text fields are probably already lined up horizontally, but let's make sure that they are aligned perfectly. Select both text fields by holding down Shift while clicking them with the Selection tool. In the Align panel, click the To Stage button again so it is not selected. Now click the Align Vertical Center button so both fields are vertically aligned. When you finish, the text should look similar to the previous figure.

10. Add a link to the bookstore's e-mail address using URL link in the Property inspector.

Sometimes you need a quick and sturdy way to add a URL type link to a line of text. One way is to create an invisible button, which serves as a hot spot, over the text, and then use a button action to specify the URL or e-mail to link to. Or, you can select the text block, and apply a URL link in the URL Link field.

Note *Unlike HTML text, this doesn't turn your text blue and add an underline to it. It's up to you to make sure that your users clearly understand that the block of text is clickable.*

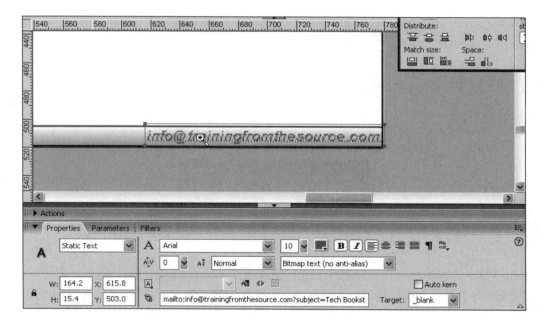

Select the text field with the e-mail address and maximize the Property inspector. At the URL Link field at the bottom, enter **mailto:info@trainingfromthesource.com?subject= TechBookstore** into the text field. When you finish, the text field has a dotted underline to signify that there is a URL link applied to it.

Tip *Adding a question mark at the end of the e-mail link and typing "subject=Tech Bookstore" automatically fills out the subject line. The end user can, however, still change it. Bummer, right?*

Tip *Remember that not all of your users have a default e-mail client on their machines. Some visitors to the site might be using a shared computer, might not have an e-mail client installed, or might not use the e-mail software that is currently the default. Thus, the Tech Bookstore site uses a built-in contact form, so all users can send feedback or questions from the site.*

If a visitor clicks the link, a new e-mail message will open in the user's default e-mail client addressed to *info@trainingfromthesource.com*, with *Tech Bookstore* entered into the subject field. When you finish, lock the propaganda layer so you do not accidentally add something else to this layer.

11. Save the changes you made to the bookstore7.fla file.

The changes you made in this exercise are saved to the file.

Using Embedded Fonts

In contrast to static text, dynamic and input text fields use device fonts by default, which you learned about near the beginning of this lesson. You might want to use the option of embedding your fonts if you want more control over the exact size and look of your dynamic or input text. Dynamic and input text both rely on system fonts, so whatever font you use for the text field must also reside on the computer that the SWF file is running on by default. The SWF file contains only the name of the font and then looks for a similar name on the end user's computer. If a matching font isn't found on the computer, the user cannot see the correct font in that field. The closest matching font is used instead. Embedding a font gets around that troublesome issue.

When you embed a font in a dynamic or input text field, the font outlines are stored in the SWF file when it is published and ensures proper rendering when the SWF file plays on a visitor's computer. The main issue with embedding fonts is that it increases your file size, depending on how much information (how many characters, or *glyphs*) you choose to store in the SWF file.

In this exercise, you will create a dynamic text field and embed a font in it.

1. Create a dynamic text field.

Select Frame 1 of the propaganda layer on the Timeline. Unlock the layer, select the Text tool, and maximize the Property inspector. Select Dynamic from the Text type drop-down list. Click anywhere on the Stage and type **my cat eats chicken** into the text field.

2. Open the Character Options dialog box.

Select the dynamic text field you just created and click the Embed button in the Property inspector. The Character Embedding dialog box opens, in which you can specify a range of characters (or individual characters) to embed. Or if you clicked the Embed button by mistake, you can click the Don't Embed button as well as a Cancel button to get out of the dialog box.

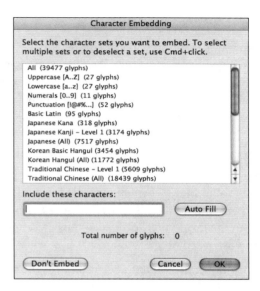

3. Control-click on Windows to select the characters you want to embed. On OS X, Command-click to select them.

To help reduce the amount of information Flash stores for the font, you can specify for only a particular range of character outlines to be embedded in the SWF file. Select the first two options in the list by simply clicking both listings. Press the Ctrl or Command keys while making your selections.

Tip *Specifying a range is particularly useful if you want to limit what characters are used, such as numbers only.*

Note *If you want to display only certain characters—say only the letters A through M for example—don't select any character ranges, but instead type the characters you want to include in the Include These Characters Field.*

4. Click Cancel and delete the text field.

Obviously, visitors to the Tech Bookstore don't need to know that your cat eats chicken. Click Cancel at the bottom of the Character Embedding dialog box to close it. Then delete the dynamic text field from the Stage and lock the propaganda layer again.

Looking at Font Properties

In Flash, and in other programs in which you can edit text, there is a wealth of options available for formatting text to change its appearance. So far, we have used only the most basic and common of them. In this exercise, you will use some new properties that you didn't use in earlier exercises and learn how they are used and what they do in Flash. You should still be using bookstore7.fla for this example.

1. Add Static text to the map page and set the properties for the text in the Property inspector.

The map page will contain some store information and a title, and load a map into a placeholder. Loading content into a SWF file is dealt with in Lesson 6, but the address and title are created here. Open the Property inspector so you can set properties for the store information that needs to be placed on the Stage.

Change the Text Type drop-down list to Static. Select Arial as the font and then set the font size to 12 and the color to black. Click the Align Center button to set the alignment (justification), which centers the characters you will enter in the text field. Also, choose to anti-alias the text for readability.

Kerning refers to the spacing between characters; however, it is not uniform like the Character Spacing setting. Kerning is built into the font and determines how two particular letters are spaced. For example, some letters might be spaced closer together based on the way they are shaped. The character W is usually placed closer to an A character than O is. Kerning helps the spacing look uniform based on the shape of each character by spacing two characters in varied amounts. Check the Auto Kern check box in the Property inspector to use the built-in kerning information for the font.

2. Enter the store information and place it on the Stage.

Select the graphics folder, insert a new layer, and rename it **map**. Click Frame 60, also labeled map on the labels layer, and insert a keyframe (F6). Select the Text tool and click and drag on the Stage to produce a fixed-width text box. Enter the text in the following figure into the text field, using the Enter key to create new lines.

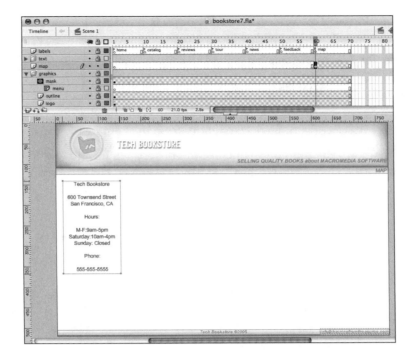

3. Format parts of the address text in the Property inspector.

If you need to resize your text field, click and drag the drag handles around the text box. To edit the field, double-click on it with the Selection tool or click once on it with the Text tool. Highlight the first line. With the line highlighted and the Property inspector maximized, click the Bold button and then select a dark grey swatch from the color control palette for Text (fill). Repeat this step for all headings in the text field.

It is also a good idea to make the address *selectable*. For example, some of the website visitors might want to copy and paste this information into an e-mail, send it to a portable device, or save the text. Select the text field with the Selection tool, and then click the Selectable button in the Property inspector so visitors can highlight and copy all the text in the text box at runtime.

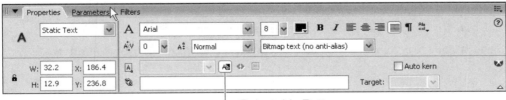

Selectable Button

4. Select the Bitmap Text option in the Property inspector.

An aliased image has a hard and definitive edge, and curves tend to appear jagged. Anti-aliasing creates the illusion that lines are smoothed or curved by using blending and shading to smooth the image or lines. Anti-aliasing reduces the jaggedness of aliased text or graphics. Although anti-aliasing is often a good choice for web graphics, it does not work well with very small text because blending and smoothing usually make small text appear fuzzy and unclear. When you select the Bitmap Text options from the Font Rendering Method drop-down list, anti-aliasing is shut off.

Select the text field you just created in Step 3. Expand the Property inspector and then switch to Bitmap Text in the Font Rendering menu. Notice the change in appearance for your text. Return the text field to Anti-alias for readability.

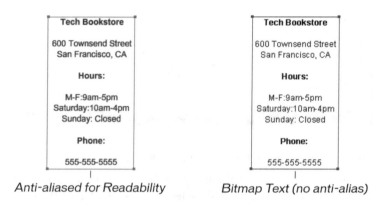

Anti-aliased for Readability   Bitmap Text (no anti-alias)

5. Change the properties for the map title using the Property inspector.

Maximize the Property inspector to change the font properties again. You will use some large text this time.

You will still use a black Arial font, so don't change those properties. However, change the font size to 26 by typing into the field or using the numerical slider next to it. Make sure that the Bold and Italic buttons are selected. You can leave Auto Kern checked, or deselect the check box. Because you are increasing the Character Spacing in the next step, it doesn't particularly matter.

6. Enter the text for the map title and position it on the Stage.

Create a static text field on the Stage, and enter the following text: **How to find us**.

You might need to edit the exact placement later on when you add the map to this page. For now, change the values of the *x, y* coordinates in the Property inspector to **70** (*x*) and **470** (*y*).

7. Change the Character Spacing value to **2**.

When you change the character spacing for a text field, a uniform amount of space is set between each character. You can enter a positive value to space the characters further from one another, or enter negative values so they are closer. Select the text field you just created and enter **2** into the Character Spacing field. Take note of the way the characters change in the text field and adjust the amount as desired.

| Tip | You might want to take this opportunity to play around with some of the other settings in the Property inspector. Because the size of this text is so large, it is easy to see how the text is changed. Double-click the text field and select half of the characters in the text field. Try applying changes only to those characters. Remember to remove the changes you make before going on to the next step.

8. Save your work.

Timeline Effects are used to add certain effects to assets in Flash. Flash installs with several Timeline Effects made by Macromedia, but you can also find many more on the web for download to install into Flash, in places like Macromedia Exchange.

Adding a Timeline Effect to a Text Field

Timeline Effects are used to add certain effects to assets in Flash. Flash installs with several Timeline Effects made by Macromedia, but you can also find many more on the web for download to install into Flash, in places like Macromedia Exchange.

Timeline Effects are applied from Insert > Timeline Effects. To add a Timeline Effect to something, select it first; then select Insert > Timeline Effects > Effect and choose the particular effect you want, such as Drop Shadow. When you add an effect, you will see a preview window that will show you what the effect will look like when done, and provide you with options to modify how the effect is applied.

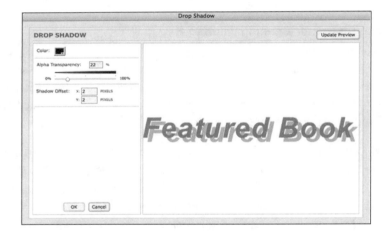

1. Create a new layer and layer folder for the home page on Frame 1.

Move the playhead back to Frame 1 on the Timeline, labeled home. Select the map layer, insert a new layer, and give this layer the name home. With it selected, insert a new layer folder and name it pages. Drag the home layer (and the map layer you created in the earlier exercise as well) into this folder. The pages folder will eventually hold all the layers created for each page in the website.

Select the home layer again. Click just to the right of the final frame on the layer, and drag the cursor back to Frame 10 and release the mouse to select the row of frames. Right-click or Control-click and select Remove Frames from the contextual menu. Because the contents of the home page will display only in the first 10 frames of the Timeline, it isn't necessary to have this layer extend all the way out to Frame 70.

2. Create a static text field with the words Featured Book.

Open the Property inspector, so you can change some of the text properties. Leave the text as a static text type and Arial. Change the font color to #CCCCCC and the font size to 14. Make sure that the typeface is set to Bold and Italic, and that Anti-alias for readability is selected. You probably need to change Character Spacing back to 0 and make sure that Auto Kern is selected.

With the home layer selected, click the Stage to create a new static text field and type **FEATURED BOOK** into the field. Place the text field on the upper-right side of the Stage under the Home text, similar to the following figure.

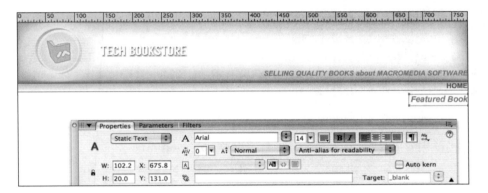

3. Add a Timeline Effect to the text field.

Select the text field you just created. Select Insert > Timeline Effects > Effects > Drop Shadow to add the drop shadow effect.

In the Drop Shadow dialog box, experiment with the settings until you find something you like. After you have entered values into any of the fields, press Update to see your text field update in the preview window. Press OK to exit the Drop Shadow dialog. This creates a graphic symbol in your library called Drop Shadow 1. You will learn more about symbols in the next lesson. For now, simply be aware of the addition.

Tip *If you hate the Timeline Effect altogether, you can remove it by selecting Modify › Timeline Effects › Remove Effect.*

Note *Many designers also use an image editor to apply various filters or effects to the text and then save the image and import it into Flash. This way, you can have complex text in your SWF file with effects you couldn't create using the tools in Flash.*

4. Lock the home layer and save your work.

Spell Check Your Document

The spell checker tool in Flash allows you to check your spelling in all text in a FLA file. Cleaning up the spelling in a FLA file before you publish it for the world to see is a great habit to adopt. The spell check feature in Flash allows you to have a lot of control over how the FLA file is checked. You can check the spelling of all text fields and even layer names or ActionScript. Now that you have added a lot of text to the FLA file, you should spell check the text you added.

1. Use the Spelling Setup dialog box to select your settings.

If you haven't used the spell check feature yet, select Text > Spelling Setup. You need to open this dialog box before you can use the spell check for the first time. Even if the Spelling Setup has already been run, open the dialog box and explore the settings available. Notice that you can control what text is spell checked in the FLA file under the Document heading. The options under Checking Options allow you to decide what kinds of words and changes are included or omitted in the spell check. In the Spelling Setup dialog box, check off the selections seen in the following figure before getting started.

Make any additional selections if desired. All the options are quite self-explanatory, and tooltips explain what each option does, as shown in the previous figure. Remember that you can change these settings at any time.

2. Check the document's spelling using the Check Spelling dialog box.

Select Text > Check Spelling to open the Check Spelling dialog box and start the spell checker. Currently, it is set to check the spelling of all text fields in the FLA file. If a word is correct but is not recognized by the spell check dictionary, you can click Ignore to ignore the word or you can add it to your personal dictionary by clicking the Add to Personal button.

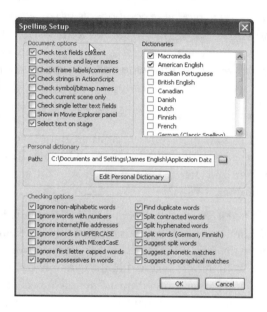

An alert pops up when the spell check is complete. Click OK to exit the Check Spelling feature.

3. Save your work as **bookstore7.fla**.

Save the new version in the TechBookstore folder on your hard drive. If you want to look at the completed file for this lesson, open bookstore7.fla, which can be found in the lesson03/complete folder on the CD-ROM.

Using Text-Based Components

One of the ways you will add text to the Tech Bookstore application in upcoming lessons is by using text components. Text components include the TextArea and TextInput components. TextArea is used when you need to display larger blocks of text that can be scrolled. TextInput is when you need to have users enter data into a text field that can be collected and used. In some ways, these two components are replacements for the dynamic and input text fields discussed earlier. A drawback of using TextArea and TextInput instead of dynamic or input text fields is a greater file size, and sometimes you have to write or use more ActionScript to get them to work the way you need them to. The advantage of using these components is the wealth of things you can do using them, and the scroll bars that are automatically attached to the field.

> **Note** Code to load content into these components will be added later on in Lessons 9 and 10. For now, you know where the components will go on the pages you just added. Later on in the book, you will add TextInput fields to a feedback form that will be created. Users will enter information that will be stored in an XML file.

Understanding Dynamic Text Fields

Dynamic and input text fields are quite different from the static text fields you have worked with earlier. These different kinds of text fields can each handle changing text. This means you can load text into them and change the text based on some kind of event that happens while the SWF file is running.

Dynamic and input text fields can also understand HTML formatted text. This means you can use HTML tags within the text you enter or load into the field, and Flash will display the font type according to the tags within the text. For example, you could enter <b> tags to boldface text, and Flash will render text within the dynamic text field as bold. You can also place URLs, images, and paragraphs within a dynamic text field using HTML tags. You will explore these techniques in Lesson 9, except you will use a TextArea component, which works in almost the same way.

What You Have Learned

In this lesson, you have:

- Learned about the Text tool (pages 71–72)
- Learned more about static text and device fonts (pages 72–80)
- Tried embedding characters in a SWF file (pages 80–81)
- Changed text properties using the Property inspector (pages 82–85)
- Added a Filter to a static text field (pages 86–88)
- Learned how to check spelling in your document (pages 88–89)
- Learned more about text-based components and dynamic text fields (pages 89–90)

4 Creating and Editing Symbols

If you're going to do anything useful in Flash, you need to use symbols. Symbols provide structure to a Flash document, can help to reduce file size, are vital to motion animations, and what's more, are necessary to add interactivity to your Flash application. In short, a Flash file without symbols is like trying to cook without using pots and pans and casserole dishes. Sure, you can manage to make bread on a hot flat rock. But why would you want to?

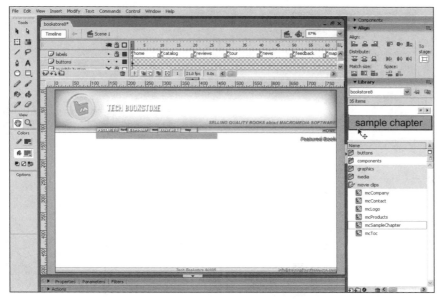

MovieClip, Graphic, and Button Symbols added to the Tech Bookstore

In this exercise, you're going to start whipping out the cookware. You'll learn about the different symbol types in Flash 8 and what each one of them is used for. What's more, you'll see how your symbols have a unique structure that can be reused in many places and updated once. You'll learn how to nest symbols inside of each other to make complex effects, and finally you'll learn how to use symbols to produce interactivity. Sorry, but you won't end up with a chocolate cake at the end of this lesson, but the Tech Bookstore will be richer just the same.

What You Will Learn

In this lesson, you will:

- Learn about symbols and how they're used in Flash 8
- Learn more about the graphic symbol
- Create a visible and invisible button symbol
- Define a button symbol hit area
- Nest symbols inside of one another
- Create a movie clip that acts as a button

Approximate Time

This lesson takes approximately two hours to complete.

Lesson Files

Media Files:

None

Starting Files:

lesson04/start/bookstore7.fla

Completed Files:

lesson04/complete/bookstore8.fla

Symbols Explained

You worked with a symbol in Lesson 2 when you created some of the graphics for the background of the website. The specific symbol that you used was a graphic symbol, which is great for displaying multiple instances of the same graphic. You also took items from the library and placed them onto the Stage, and found out that the library is used to store assets you use in FLA files. The second point here is important because the library *stores* symbols (graphic, movie clip, button, and the often-forgotten font symbol), not to mention video clips, bitmap images, sound files, and components. In fact, if it can be seen or heard, it's usually stored in the library; with the notable exception of the graphics you draw yourself on the Stage. Well, unless you convert them *into* symbols. But I digress.

Flash has three primary kinds of symbols that you can build within the authoring environment: movie clips, buttons, and graphics. You created graphic symbols in Lesson 2 and found out that symbols can contain images such as the vector graphics you created using the drawing tools. New to you is the button symbol. Buttons are symbols that contain four *states* that determine how the button looks and works in relation to the mouse. You use buttons to create interactive elements in the SWF file, such as navigation menus, rollover effects such as tooltips, and hot spots.

Also at your fingertips is the movie clip symbol. This symbol is *the* symbol to get to know. Even your Stage is a movie clip symbol. Movie clips are essentially little Flash applications with their own independent Timelines that do whatever you want them to do. They are scriptable Objects, too, which make them ideal for interactivity, nested animations, and a whole host of radically cool things (if you're a proud geek, that is).

You can also create font symbols in Flash, which are stored in the library and never dragged onto the Stage. You would use a font symbol for asset sharing, which can keep file size down and allow team members to use a font outline from within Flash if for some reason they don't have the font itself. Everybody forgets about the font symbol, which is sad because it's very useful in a pinch.

Tip *You can find out more about using font symbols and embedding fonts on the book's website at www.TrainingFromTheSource.com/bonus.*

Symbols always reside in a library. When you drag a symbol from the library onto the Stage, it's referred to as an *instance*. An instance is really just a reference to the symbol in the library (meaning that you can have many instances on the Stage derived from a single symbol). Instances have some small measure of independence and can be scaled, tinted, made transparent, rotated, skewed, and made darker or brighter without affecting its brother and sister instances. Movie clip and button instances can be named using the Property inspector, so you can boss them around using ActionScript or one of the canned behaviors that comes with Flash 8. If you modify the properties of instances using ActionScript or the Property inspector, it does not affect the symbol in the library. If you edit the symbol from the library in symbol-editing mode, all the symbol's instances you have on the Stage are affected, which is good because it means than any updates to the graphics contained in the symbol are automatically pushed out to the symbol instances on the Stage. Of course, if you didn't mean to edit a symbol's master properties, it's not such a good thing, but that's why the thoughtful engineers of Flash included the lovely Undo function.

All the hullabaloo of symbols really comes down to this: Symbols are reusable. If you need to have 18 squares that might differ only in tint or scale, it doesn't make sense to make whole new square graphics. Make a symbol, draw a square in it, drag 18 instances of it out on the Stage, and change their respective tint and scale. Because those instances are really just references, your file size stays nice and small. Drawing 18 more squares adds weight.

Note *Remember that when you import assets such as video clips, bitmaps, fonts, and sounds, they are added to the library as well. So when the assets are added to the Stage, they are essentially copies (or instances) of the item stored in the library.*

Creating and Editing Symbols on the Stage

There are two ways to create a new symbol: You can create a symbol from an item already on the Stage (such as a raw graphic or another symbol), or you can make a symbol from scratch and drop graphics into it while in symbol-editing mode. If you already have a graphic and want to convert it, select it on the Stage and press F8 on the keyboard. This actually places the graphic inside of the symbol itself.

Tip *You can also convert items to symbols in the following ways: by selecting Modify › Convert to Symbol; Right-click or Control-click the graphic and select Convert To Symbol from the context menu; or drag the item into your open document library.*

For example, if you have drawn a square on the Stage, select it and select Modify > Convert to Symbol. The square is then placed inside of the symbol you create, so you are essentially wrapping a symbol around the shape you selected. You could just as easily do the same thing that you did to the square to a bitmap, or even another symbol, such as a movie clip.

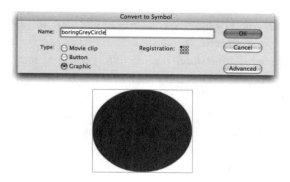

The second way to create a symbol is to start from scratch and add new content into the symbol using symbol-editing mode. As you might remember from Lesson 2, symbol-editing mode takes you to a separate editing area independent from the Stage. You can enter symbol-editing mode by double-clicking a symbol in the library. While you are in symbol-editing mode, the edit bar (directly above or below the Timeline on Windows and the Mac) reminds you that you are editing the symbol by the links you see on the bar.

You can also edit symbols "in place," which allows you to edit a symbol and still see the placement and size of the symbol in relation to the other elements on the Stage. To edit a symbol in place, double-click the symbol on the Stage. Everything else on the Stage is dimmed and not selectable while you edit the symbol. The edit bar indicates that you are editing the symbol in place.

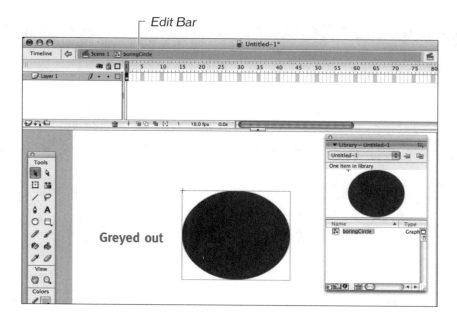

Tip *It's considered a best practice to change any vector drawings that you make directly on the Stage (which is raw data) into symbols before publishing the FLA file. Vectors that are raw data have a crosshatch pattern over them when they are selected. Raw data placed on the Stage has to be rendered out (drawn on the Stage using calculations when the SWF file plays) every time the playhead reaches that frame on the Timeline because the information is not stored in the library, and this can slow performance down. By changing the raw data into a symbol, you can reduce the SWF file size so the information has to be referenced only once in the library instead of perhaps many times individually on the Timeline. It also makes the graphic easier to select on the Stage if you drew it in Merge Drawing mode.*

Looking at Symbols in the Library

You can view the symbols within your FLA file in the library, which is opened using Ctrl+L (or Command+L on the Mac). An icon and name represent each symbol, and you can tell what kind of asset the symbol is by referring to the *Kind* column. The *Use Count* column lets you know how many instances of a symbol are used throughout the document. *Linkage* lets you know whether the item is exported, associated with a shared library, or even linked to something in the FLA file (such as a component). You will learn more about linkage later in the book.

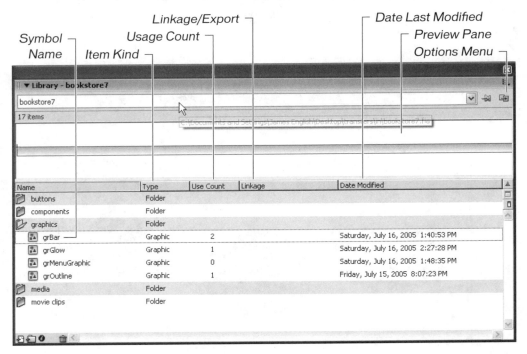

Tip *To make sure that your use counts update automatically, from the Library Options menu, select Keep Use Counts Updated.*

Button and movie clip symbol instances can be named in the Property inspector. You give them a unique name in the Property inspector's <Instance Name> field so you can *target* the symbol using ActionScript. An *instance name* is different from the name you give a symbol when you initially create it. The name in the library really is just for people to use for organization, and although an instance on the Stage can be named the same as the master symbol in the library, each instance name you create after that for the same master symbol must be unique, or else things stop working. You will learn more about naming instances in Lesson 6.

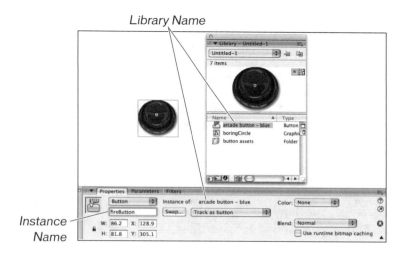

Library Name

Instance Name

Nesting Symbols and Timelines

Every symbol except the font symbol has a Timeline of its own that can hold text, video, graphics, and other symbols. How each Timeline works really depends on the type of symbol you're producing. Buttons, for example, can only display four frames per layer: Up, Over, Down, and Hit. Graphic symbols can have as many frames as you like, which means you can create animations in them, but a graphic symbol's Timeline is completely dependant upon its parent Timeline and therefore won't move unless its parent is also moving. Lastly, movie clip symbols have their own independent Timelines that can do anything that the main document Timeline can do. You can place movie clips inside of buttons, buttons inside of movie clips, or graphic symbols inside of movie clips and buttons, all to make more complex animations and interactions. You cannot, however, place a button symbol in a button Timeline or place a button instance inside of a graphic symbol because graphic symbols cannot be controlled with or contain ActionScript.

In Lesson 2, you learned about the edit bar. As you work more with symbols in this lesson, you'll find out how important it is to use the edit bar to navigate through documents that contain nested symbols because it tells you what Timeline you happen to be editing at any given moment.

Revisiting Graphic Symbols

You already created some graphic symbols when you worked with the drawing tools in Lesson 2. Graphic symbols are useful when you have static graphics or bitmaps in the library and want to use them throughout your Flash document (and particularly when you want to reuse the images). Static graphics refers to graphics that are just going to sit around dressing the Timeline up a bit without having any kind of "nested" animations of their own. Graphic symbols can't be controlled with ActionScript, so they can't take instance names.

You *can* create animations inside of graphic symbols, but here's something to be aware of: The animation *inside* the graphic symbol will play only if the Timeline the graphic symbol is *in* is playing. Think of graphic symbols like kids holding hands with their parents. If the parent stops, so does the child, even though the child is its own self-contained identity. When the parent moves, the child moves with the parent. This can be useful in very limited circumstances, so by convention, *nested* animations (animations inside of symbols and not on the main document Timeline) tend to be reserved for movie clips because they are totally independent of their parents (like teenagers!).

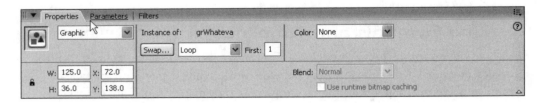

Note *You cannot apply filters to graphic symbols.*

When you have a graphic symbol instance on the Stage selected, you can change its Properties in the Property inspector. The Instance Behavior drop-down list allows you to change that one instance of the symbol so that it can behave like a button or a movie clip. The Swap button lets you switch it out with any other symbol in your library. Options for Graphics is used to control (to some degree) any animation that the graphic symbol might contain in its own Timeline. You can tell it to *Loop* continuously while the parent Timeline is animating, *Play Once* only, or display only a *Single Frame*. The Color menu is used for *instance effects* and it contains options for altering *brightness, tint, alpha* (opacity), or a combination of those things in the *advanced* option. You will look more at the properties of graphic symbols in Lesson 5 on animation.

Creating Buttons

Buttons are used to make your Flash application interactive. As you'll learn in Lessons 6 and 9, buttons can be used to submit forms or execute ActionScript code that controls your Flash document. Buttons also have events that are *broadcast* when something happens in the SWF file. An example of an event is a user clicking a button. Using ActionScript, you can write a small script that then responds to that event. That response is generally termed an *event handler*, but that's too complex for now. You'll learn more about that in Lesson 9.

The first buttons you need to create for the bookstore are three basic buttons that go under the title area. Each button will reveal a menu below it and will be built using the six PNG bitmap images that you imported into the FLA file during Lesson 2.

Every button symbol has four *states* that determine how the button will look when someone interacts with it in the published SWF file.

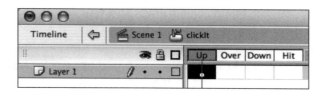

The graphic that you put in the button for the Up state displays when the button is not being interacted with; it's just hanging out, being a button. The Over state displays when the mouse cursor hovers over the button's hit area. The Down state displays when the mouse is clicked within the hit area. Any image or drawing that's placed in the Hit state determines the hit, or clickable, area of the button. The Hit state more or less *is* the button because the Up, Over, and Down states are strictly aesthetic and don't need to be used. The graphics in the Hit state are also not visible, which gives you a way to create an invisible hot spot to use.

> **Note** In most SWF files, the cursor will change to a hand in this clickable region, notifying the user that the graphic can be clicked and something will happen. The cursor can be changed using ActionScript.

1. Open bookstore7.fla from your TechBookstore folder, and save a new version of the document as **bookstore8.fla**. You can also open bookstore7.fla from the lesson04/start folder on the CD-ROM.

Use the Save As command under the File menu and click OK to save a new version of the file to start the lesson with.

2. Select Insert › New Symbol to create a new button symbol called **btnProducts**.

The Create New Symbol dialog box opens. Type **btnProducts** into the Name field and select the Button radio button. This procedure names the button symbol in the library. You will put it on the Stage later on and also give it an instance name (which is different from the library name, remember). Click OK, and symbol-editing mode opens. The symbol can also be found in the library.

> **Tip** *You are prefixing the symbol name with "btn" simply to make it easier to organize your library. You can use any naming convention that you want in everyday life, as long as you stick with it!*

3. Open the library and find the bitmaps that you put into in the media folder.

Double-click the media folder's icon to open it up so you can find the bitmap files. The bitmaps should still be called products_up.png, products_down.png, company_up.png, company_down.png, contact_up.png, and contact_down.png. These bitmaps will be used for different button states in the bookstore.

4. Select the Up state and add the products_up.png bitmap to the button. Set the *x* and *y* position of the graphic to **0** and **0**.

After you open the button symbol, notice in the Timeline that there are four states that you can give the button. These four frames represent the Up, Over, Down, and Hit states discussed at the beginning of this exercise. Select the Up frame on the Timeline and drag products_up.png from the media folder in the library into the button symbol.

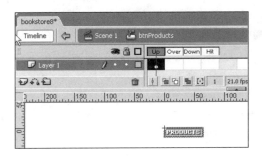

Select the graphic on the Stage, and in the Property inspector, set the *x* and *y* position both to **0** and **0**.

5. Add the products_down.png bitmap to the button symbol's Over state.

Just like anything else, all assets inside of a button Timeline have to live in keyframes. Select the frame Over frame in Layer 1 and insert a blank keyframe using Insert > Timeline > Blank Keyframe. You want a blank keyframe so that the bitmap in the Up frame isn't copied to the new keyframe. You'll place a different bitmap in the Over frame.

Drag the products_down.png bitmap from the media folder into the button for the Over state. This is the image seen by visitors when they hover the mouse over the button. So when they move the mouse over the button, the button changes its appearance. Using the Property inspector, place the bitmap at *x* and *y* of **0**, so that it matches the graphic in the Up frame.

> **Tip** | *A crosshair shows you where the registration point of the symbol is located. Sometimes you want to change the registration point of a button or movie clip, particularly if you are using ActionScript. When you want to change the position of the symbol, you assign the x and y coordinates. The registration point is placed at those assigned coordinates.*

6. Select the Hit frame and press F5 to add frames to the Down and Hit frames.

Pressing F5 applies the products_down.png bitmap to both the Down and Hit states, while making sure the bitmap position is the same for each of the frames. The Hit state defines the area where you click the button. Because it is the same image at the same location (which you already set), you know that the clickable area will exactly match the other areas of the button.

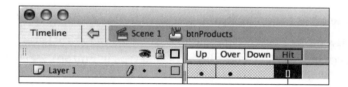

> **Note** | *Remember, the hit area is not visible on the Stage. You could substitute a bright lime green rectangle in place of the bitmap image, and it wouldn't be visible to your visitors when they see the SWF file. In this case though, it's easiest to just use the existing graphic already on the Timeline, which is sized and positioned correctly, to serve as the hit area for the button.*

Tip *Text is not suitable for defining a hit area. The reason for this is that the graphic portion of text is the letters themselves. Spaces between letters, the center of an "o" are all background and therefore not clickable. If you have text in a button Timeline, you should place a graphic like a rectangle in the Hit frame and size it so that it covers the whole text box. If you don't, you'll get lots of hate mail about your button not working correctly.*

7. **You need to create two more buttons and add the symbols to the button folder in the library in order to organize the new buttons you created.**

You need to create two more buttons for the area beneath the main title area for company and contact buttons. Repeat Steps 2 through 7 to create the btnCompany and btnContact. When you finish, open the library and move the three button symbols into the buttons folder. Just leave the buttons in the library for now; you will add the buttons to the Stage in the next exercise.

8. **Save your file before moving on to the next exercise.**

Select Ctrl+S or Command+S to save the file. You do not need to create a new version of the file.

Placing the Buttons On the Stage

You now have three buttons in the library that should be placed on the Stage before you can progress with adding other elements on the Stage. The three buttons need to be placed on top of the grBar graphic instance on their own layer. At the end of this lesson, you will create an *invisible* button that will surround these three buttons and also align menus with these buttons.

1. **Create a new layer called buttons.**

Select the text layer folder in the Timeline and click the Insert New Layer button. When the new layer is created, double-click the name and type in **buttons** to rename the layer.

2. **Drag the three buttons that you created from the library onto the Stage.**

btnProducts, btnCompany and btnContact should all be within the buttons folder in the library. When you drag the buttons onto the Stage, you should notice how the three buttons were created to be about the same height as the grBar.

3. Move the three buttons into order, and place each button at the correct *x* coordinate using the Property inspector.

Place the three buttons slightly apart from each other similar to the following graphic in the following order from left to right: btnProducts, btnCompany, and btnContact. Now that they're in the correct order, you need to move the three buttons into a correct vertical position. Select the btnProducts instance and change the *x* coordinate to **115** using the Property inspector. Then select btnCompany and set its *x* coordinate to **200** in the Property inspector. Finally select btnContact and set its *x* coordinate to **285**.

4. Align the three buttons horizontally with each other using the Align panel.

Maximize the Align panel and make sure that the To Stage button is not selected. Select the three buttons by holding Shift while clicking each symbol. Then click the Align vertical center button so the buttons align with each other.

5. Group and align the three buttons with grBar using the Align panel. Ungroup the three buttons and lock the buttons layer when you are finished.

You can group symbols so they can be edited together as one object. Sometimes you have a couple of symbols on the Stage that you want to resize, rotate, or move together as one symbol, and you can achieve this by grouping the symbols together.

Select the three buttons by holding down Shift as you click each symbol. Then select Modify > Group from the main menu. The three buttons can now be aligned as one object. Select the group of buttons and move the group below the grBar on the Stage. Unlock the bars layer and press Shift to select grBar. Now the grBar symbol and the group of buttons should be selected.

In the Align panel, click the Align top edge button to align the grouped buttons to the top of grBar. Ungroup the three buttons by choosing Modify > Ungroup and then lock the buttons layer and the bars layer.

6. Save your work.

Now you have three buttons on the Stage that are aligned with the bar behind them. The three buttons should align to the top edge of the grBar and be evenly distributed. The buttons are placed so that when you have the menus attached to each button, they line up fine with the mask you created earlier in the book.

Creating Text Buttons

Sometimes you need to create a button that is made out of only text with no background. You will use text buttons like this for part of the menu. You will create text buttons in this exercise and then insert them into the menu later on in the lesson.

One of the more important parts of creating text buttons is properly defining hit areas for them. The hit area refers to the area in which a user can click the button. It is particularly difficult to click a text button if you leave text on the Stage without a hit area defined. A person who is trying to click the button would have to click within the small lines defining each character, which isn't easy to do!

Note *It is not really a best practice to make text buttons because they aren't really reusable. It makes more sense to create a button with no text in it, but merely a graphic of some sort, and use many instances of it underneath a text layer. Remember, each button you make in the library increases file size.*

In this exercise, you will create text buttons that will be placed in the menu and define a hit area for each button. Creating a proper hit area for a text button is easy. All you need to do is follow these steps.

1. Select the Text tool and click the Stage to create a text field. In the Property inspector, select Static text from the drop-down list, set the font to Arial, text color to black (#000000), font size to 8. Click the Bold button. Set the text rendering to Anti-alias for readability.

After you click on the Stage with the Text tool, maximize the Property inspector and enter the new settings for the font, color, and size. Ensure that you have the correct text type (Static) and that the Bold button is selected. Make sure that the text is set to Anti-alias for Readability.

Select the buttons layer on the Timeline (make sure it is unlocked) and then click the Text tool on the Stage and type **CATALOG** (all capitals) into the new text field.

Note *It doesn't matter which layer you create the text field on because you will temporarily delete the buttons from the Stage when you finish the exercise.*

2. Select the text field and then press F8 to place it inside a button symbol.

Select the Selection tool from the Tools panel and then select the text field. Use F8 on your keyboard or select Modify > Convert to Symbol to convert the text field into a button symbol. Type **btnCatalog** into the Name field and click OK when you're finished.

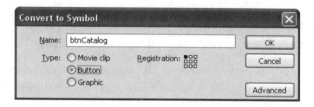

3. Open **btnCatalog** in symbol-editing mode and center the text field in the symbol.

Double-click the button to open it in symbol-editing mode. Select the text field and then use the Align panel to center the text field. Make sure that the To Stage button is selected in the Align panel, and then click the Align Horizontal Center and Align Vertical Center buttons in the panel.

4. Add Over, Down, and Hit states for the button.

Select the Down frame and press F5 to insert a frame. The same text is displayed for the Up, Over, and Down frames of the button because you don't need a different visual appearance for each state of these text buttons.

> **Tip** *If you want rollover or click colors for the text, you need to insert a keyframe in the Over frame and/or Down frame, then select the text field and change the text fill color using the Property inspector. The text color changes when a visitor rolls the mouse over the text in these buttons.*

5. Create a hit area for the button in the Hit frame with the Rectangle tool.

Select the Hit frame and press F6 to enter a new keyframe. You can see that the text from the Down frame is entered into the Hit frame. You can use the text field as a reference for where the hit area needs to be created. Select the Rectangle tool and select any color for a fill color and No Color for the stroke. Then draw a rectangle that completely covers the text that's in the frame. You want to make the rectangle slightly larger than the text area so the button is easy to click.

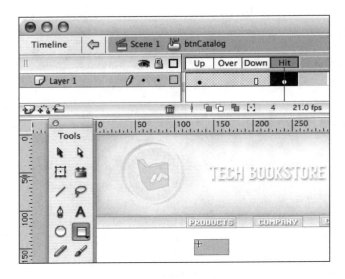

6. Create five more buttons for the menu: **REVIEWS, TOUR, NEWS, FEEDBACK,** and **MAP.** Then delete them from the Stage and lock the buttons layer.

Repeat Steps 1 to 5, except add different text (**REVIEWS, TOUR, NEWS, FEEDBACK,** and **MAP,** all in capital letters) for each button. You should have six new buttons in the library when you finish: btnCatalog, btnReviews, btnTour, btnNews, btnFeedback, and btnMap. After you have checked you have the correct number of buttons in the library, delete the text buttons from the Stage. In the library, move the symbols into the buttons folder. You will add these buttons that are stored in the library to three menus you create later on in the lesson.

Lock the buttons layer when you finish.

7. Save your file.

Remember to save the changes to the file before moving on.

Creating an Invisible Button

You found out that what is entered into the Hit state of a button is not visible when you view a SWF file. You will take advantage of that now and create an *invisible* button that contains only a hit area and does not have any graphics. An invisible button is very much like a "hot spot" in HTML. When you roll over or click a hot spot, something happens, even if it does not look like a button is there. Invisible buttons do the same thing in a SWF file. You will use an invisible button as a trigger to close the three menus that serve as the main navigation for the Tech Bookstore.

When you roll over one of the three buttons in the bookstore, the menus open by animating downward. Then when you roll over the invisible button, the menus will animate upward so they appear to be closing. Whenever the mouse rolls outside of the menu area, you want the menus to close. The invisible button uses a button symbol's hit area to enable it to serve as a trigger to close the menus.

1. Create a new layer called invisible button below the buttons layer.

Select the text layer folder and click Insert New Layer. Double-click the new layer and type in **invisible button**. This layer is layered beneath the three buttons you created on the buttons layer that will be used to open menus. You are layering the invisible button underneath the three buttons so the invisible button does not interfere with opening and closing the menus. If you layer buttons, whatever button's on top is the one that takes precedence in the SWF file. If the invisible button were layered on top of the three buttons, the menus would not open because the invisible button on top of the three buttons would trigger them to close. Thus, the importance of layer order!

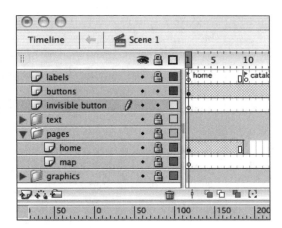

2. Add three horizontal guides to the Stage at **120,140**, and **160** pixels. Create a fourth guide that is vertical at **450** pixels.

If rulers are not visible, select View > Rulers from the main menu. Click and drag a new guide from the horizontal ruler above the Stage and drag it downward until you reach **140** pixels on the vertical ruler. Create a second one that sits at approximately **120** pixels on the horizontal ruler. Then click and drag a guide from the vertical ruler and drop it at the **450**-pixel mark.

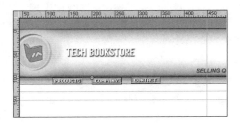

3. Select the Rectangle tool, and select any color for the fill in the Tools panel. Switch to Merge Drawing mode and draw a rectangle from the document's upper-left corner to the intersection of the guides at **450** and **120**. Draw a rectangle that covers the area between the guides at **140** and **160**, from the document's left edge to the vertical guide at **450**.

The buttons that trigger the menus are within the grBar graphic, and the menus extend below it to where the guide is placed. You want to cover all the areas around where the menus will be, but not the area the menus are in. You also don't need to cover the rest of the Stage. The button should cover some of the Stage below the menus, which is the area below the guide. You are switching to Merge Drawing mode so that you can create a slightly more complex shape. You'll be drawing several rectangles so that they all overlap, merging into one larger graphic, making your invisible button custom built to the menu system you are creating.

Create a rectangle that covers from the upper-left corner of the Stage—about 450 pixels wide. The rectangle should stop just about the bottom of the buttons, at the **12**-pixel point on the vertical ruler (where you set the guide to in Step 2).

Tip *If you want to be able to see what's on the Stage while creating the hit area for this button, maximize the Color Mixer panel, click the fill color icon, and reduce the Alpha percentage to about 20%. This makes the fill color for the rectangles transparent so you can see through to the Stage, which helps you define the hot spot. If you have already created some of the rectangles, select the shape on the Stage before reducing the Alpha percentage.*

The second rectangle you create below the guide should be the same width of the Stage and just below where the menus open. Draw a rectangle beneath the guide set at 140 (created in Step 2). This rectangle should be approximately 20 pixels tall.

4. Add two more rectangles on either side of the buttons, making sure that the graphics overlap with your two previous rectangles.

In case a user moves the mouse off the left or right side of the menu, you also need to have two more rectangles spanning either side of where the menus will be. When you are finished, your rectangles should be merged together and appear as in the following figure.

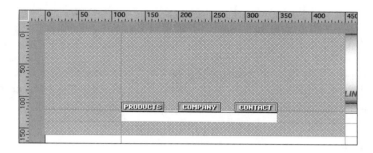

Note *After you actually build and animate the interactive menus, you might need to slightly modify the invisible button, depending on where you precisely place the buttons and menus in your FLA file.*

The height of the rectangles you just created does not matter, as long as they overlap the rectangles above and below them so there are no gaps in-between. The empty space between the rectangles is where the drop-down lists will appear.

5. Click the keyframe in the invisible button layer to select the rectangle you just drew. Select Modify > Convert to Symbol and select the Button radio button. Name the button **btnInvisible** and then click OK. Double-click the symbol on the Stage to get into symbol-editing mode.

After creating the btnInvisible symbol, the content on the Stage should now have a bounding box around the edge of it. Double-click the symbol to open symbol-editing mode. The rectangles you just drew should all be in the first (Up) frame in the button. However, you need content only in the Hit frame because you are using only the clickable part of the button.

6. Drag the rectangles to the Hit frame.

Click the keyframe in the Up frame and then drag it over to the Hit frame.

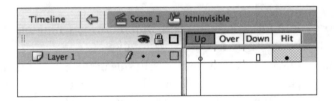

You can just leave all of the other states empty, so the button does not have any states with graphics. Nothing placed in this frame is visible after you publish the SWF file: The button is completely invisible.

Tip *To quickly convert a selection into a symbol, press F8 or drag the selection into the library. You have to drag it into the area below the Preview pane (under the Name list) and then the Convert to Symbol dialog box opens.*

7. Click on Scene 1 to return to the main Stage, and hide and lock the invisible button layer.

The Stage should now have a large turquoise and slightly transparent area covering a portion of it. The turquoise area is where the invisible button's hit area is. You will use this area as the trigger to close the menus. Even if this transparent turquoise area is not visible in the SWF file that you publish, it might interfere with your work in the Flash authoring environment.

Go to the Timeline and click the Hide layer dot (the dot under the large eye icon) in the invisible button layer. Click under the Lock icon to lock the layer. This means that the layer cannot be seen, be selected, or have content accidentally added to it.

8. In the document library, drag the btnInvisible symbol into the buttons library folder.

You created a new library folder in Lesson 2 called buttons. Move all the button symbols you created in the previous three exercises into the buttons folder. In Lesson 9, you will add some ActionScript for the invisible button that makes it target the menus so they close when the mouse rolls over the area.

9. Save your work.

Creating and Using Movie Clips

Movie clips are arguably the most common type of symbol used by Flash designers and developers. In essence, movie clips are miniature applications themselves. Each movie clip has its own Timeline that operates independently from the Flash document's main Timeline. This means that you can create looping animations while minimizing file size because you can use the Timeline in the same way as the Timeline you find on the main Stage.

You don't have to create long repeating animations: Simply create one loop and then place the movie clip on the Stage. It repeats over and over, independently of the main Timeline. Movie clips don't have to loop, either. You can create a clip and have it animate after a particular event happens. Or a movie clip can play and then stop at the end.

Movie clips do a heck of a lot more than just hold animations though. For instance, you can use blends with movie clip symbols. Blends determine how the colors of a movie clip interact with the colors of objects on a lower stacking order; we don't cover blends in this book, but there's tons of stuff about it in your documentation. You can also create mini applications with them, drag and drop applications, and all kinds of other useful stuff. The movie clip is your friend, and you should know it and love it. Because you'll be working with the movie clip throughout the book, don't fret all the details now. At this point, simply get to know your new friend.

In the next exercise, you will create several movie clips for the Tech Bookstore. The movie clips in this lesson will be used to contain animations for user interface elements. Later on in the book, you will use movie clips as containers for miniature applications and even to hold content loaded from a server.

You create movie clips in the same way you create graphic and button symbols. However, movie clips enable you to add more functionality to a symbol than button or graphic symbols do. You can also create and manipulate movie clips using ActionScript, which can be a powerful tool in your applications. You assign an instance name to a movie clip instance, which is used in your ActionScript to target and manipulate that instance. You will learn more about ActionScript in Lesson 6 and Lesson 9.

Note *Movie clips add a bit more file size to your SWF file than equivalent button or graphic symbols. If you can create the same effect using either a graphic or button, it is wise to do so. Often you will need the additional capabilities that movie clips offer, however.*

1. Select the logo symbol and press F8 to insert the symbol inside a new movie clip.

Type **mcLogo** into the Name field, select the Movie clip radio button, and click OK to create the new movie clip. The mcLogo will contain a couple of independent animations within it, so you need to insert the logo.png bitmap inside of a movie clip so you can nest other movie clips on layers inside one main clip.

Tip *If you cannot select the logo on the Stage, make sure that the logo layer is not locked.*

2. Double-click `mcLogo`, rename Layer 1, and then add a new layer to the movie clip.

You will see the logo.png bitmap on Layer 1 inside the movie clip. Rename Layer 1 to **logo**. Click Insert New Layer so a new layer is added above the logo.png image. Rename the new layer **pageTurn**.

3. Use the Line tool to create a line on the pageTurn layer.

Make sure that the pageTurn layer is selected before you create a line. Select the Line tool and return to Object Drawing. Click the stroke color control in the Tools panel and change the stroke color to #999999 in the color pop-up window. Select the Line tool from the Tools panel.

As shown in the following figure, click and drag from one end of the left side of the book cover from the outer to the inner edge of the cover. Position the line so it is the same angle and length as the left book cover edge.

Tip *With the line unselected, mouse over the ends of the lines until you see a cursor containing an "L" shape. If you click and drag the line with this cursor, you can change the position and length of the line. This can help you properly position the line in relation to the logo and fine-tune a little bit. If you select the entire line, the cursor changes to a four-way arrow when you mouse over it. Clicking and dragging the line moves the entire line instead.*

4. Place the drawing you made into a new movie clip by pressing F8.

Select the entire line you just created, without moving it. Press F8 to convert the line into a movie clip symbol. Type **mcPageTurn** into the Name field, select the Movie clip radio button, and click OK. A new movie clip is created *inside* mcLogo, so mcPageTurn is nested within mcLogo. Look at the edit bar, which shows you a visual representation of where you currently are nested within movie clips.

Tip *If you double-click mcLogo and then mcPageTurn, you are taken inside of the mcPageTurn movie clip, in which you can edit the line you created. The line is left as a raw graphic, so you can shape tween the line. You will learn how to create shape tweens in Lesson 5.*

You need to create a movie clip that will eventually be animated within the mcLogo movie clip. The animation will loop independently from the main Timeline, which means that it should be placed within a movie clip.

5. Insert a new layer in mcLogo and move it to the bottom of the layer stack.

The glow needs to animate beneath the logo itself, so it appears behind that area. Therefore, it needs to be placed beneath the logo itself. Click Insert New Layer to create a new layer and rename it **glow**. Make sure this new layer is on the bottom of the stack in the Timeline.

Return to the main Timeline by clicking on Scene 1 in the edit bar.

6. Lock the logo layer. Select the glow animation layer on the Timeline, cut its contents, and place the glow symbol inside the mcLogo movie clip.

Expand the graphics layer folder. The grGlow symbol should still be on the Stage from when you created it in Lesson 2. Return to the Stage by clicking Scene 1 in the edit bar. Select the grGlow symbol and select Edit > Cut.

Double-click mcLogo in the library to open it in symbol-editing mode and select the glow layer. Then select Edit > Paste in Place so the grGlow symbol and the logo graphic line up correctly.

7. Return to the main Stage and delete the glow animation layer. Save the changes you made to the file before moving on.

Click Scene 1 on the edit bar to return to the main Stage. Notice that the glow animation layer is now empty because you cut and pasted the content from the layer into the movie clip that is on the logo layer. Right-click or Control-click the glow animation layer and select Delete Layer from the contextual menu. The layer is permanently removed from the Timeline. Don't forget to save the FLA file before you proceed to the next step.

Now that you have put together the pieces for the logo's animation, you need to create the main menu that controls the Tech Bookstore. In the next exercise, you will create a movie clip to hold both graphic and button symbols.

Creating the Menu

You already created the background graphic for the menu in Lesson 2, so you have a good start on creating the menus for the Tech Bookstore. The next steps include nesting grMenuGraphic into a movie clip symbol, adding a few more graphics, and nesting the text buttons.

1. Drag the grMenuGraphic instance onto the menu layer and insert it into a new movie clip symbol; then drag two more instances of grMenuGraphic onto the Stage and also insert them into two new movie clips.

The menu background graphic should be in the graphics folder in the library, named grMenuGraphic. Drag three instances of the graphic symbol onto the masked layer called menu in the Timeline.

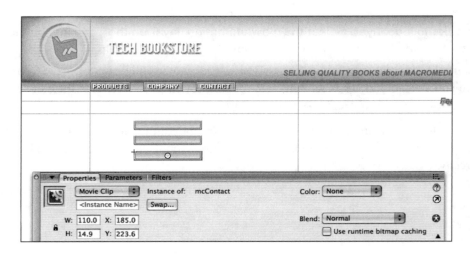

Select the first instance and press F8 to insert the graphic instance into a new symbol. Type **mcProducts** into the Name field, select the Movie clip radio button, and click OK. Convert the second instance into a movie clip named mcCompany and convert the third instance into a movie clip named mcContact. You should now have three movie clips created for each menu, sharing a graphic symbol for the background image.

2. Open the mcProducts movie clip by double-clicking the instance on the Stage and rename Layer 1 to bg. Insert a new layer and create a vertical line that is 11 pixels high and colored #666666.

The menus need a division down the middle of the background to divide the text buttons on either side. After you rename Layer 1 to **bg**, insert a new layer inside the mcProducts movie clip and name it **divider**. Select the Line tool in the Tools panel and change the stroke color to #666666. Create a straight vertical line on the Stage. With the line selected, open the Property inspector and change the height to **11**.

3. Create a second vertical line on the Stage that is white (#FFFFFF) and also 11 pixels tall.

Change the color in the stroke color control and then create a second line of the same length on the Stage to the right of the one you just created. Select the line and use the Property inspector to change the height to **11**.

4. Move the two lines together to be next to each other and select both lines. Convert the lines to a new graphic symbol called grDivider and move the symbol to the center of the grMenuGraphic.

Move the lines on the Stage so they are directly next to each other; then select both lines by pressing Shift while clicking each line. Press F8 to convert the lines into a symbol. Type **grDivider** into the Name field, click the Graphic radio button, and click OK to create the symbol.

Select grDivider using the Selection tool and move it to the middle of the menu. The symbol should be placed at about **55** pixels to the right of 0 on the ruler.

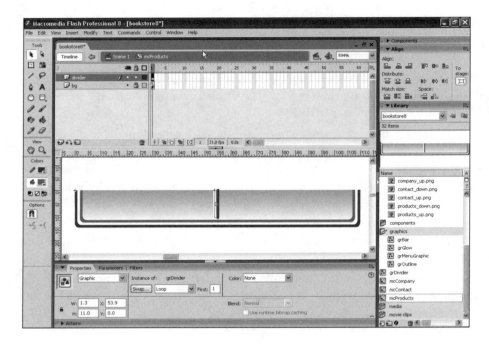

5. Add grDivider to the mcCompany and mcContact movie clips. Align grDivider so it is in the middle of each movie clip.

Click Scene 1 to return to the main Stage and open the library. Double-click mcCompany to open it up and rename Layer 1 to **bg**, as you did earlier. Then add a new layer called **divider**. Drag an instance of grDivider from the library onto the divider layer and align it in the center of the menu.

Do the same for mcContact.

In the next part of this exercise, you will insert the text buttons that you created earlier in the lesson into the menu.

6. Open the library and add the text buttons to each menu.

Find the text buttons you created for the menus in the library within a folder called buttons. Open mcProducts, insert a new layer above the divider layer on the Timeline, and rename it **buttons**. Drag btnCatalog to the left of grDivider and then drag btnReviews to the right of grDivider. Center btnCatalog between the left edge of mcProduct and grDivider. Similarly, center btnReviews between grDivider and the right edge of mcProduct.

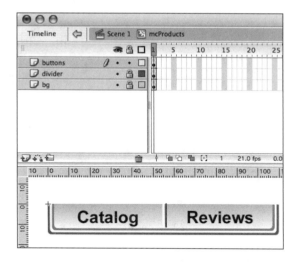

Repeat this step with the other two movie clip menus. Add a new layer to mcCompany and rename it **buttons**. Drag btnTour and btnNews to the left and right of the grDivider. Finally, repeat these steps with mcContact. Drag btnFeedback and btnMap to the left and right of grDivider and align them on either side of grDivider, as you did with the other menus.

Return to the main Stage. You should now have three menus on the menu layer, each containing two text buttons.

7. Clean up the library and save the FLA file.

You should now have several movie clips in the library. Drag the movie clips into the folder called movie clips you created in Lesson 2. Move the grDivider into the graphics folder. Save the changes you made to the FLA file by choosing File > Save from the main menu.

In Lesson 5, you will animate the menu so it appears to be opening and closing, and in Lesson 9 you add ActionScript to make it work when you play the SWF file.

Creating Movie Clip Buttons

There is another way to make buttons in Flash: by using movie clips. Movie clip buttons allow you to create buttons that are more complex than the standard button symbols you made earlier in this lesson. This doesn't mean you should change all your button symbols into movie clips, though! Remember that movie clips are slightly larger in file size than button symbols, and movie clip buttons usually take more time to create than regular buttons. It is beneficial to use movie clip buttons when you want to add extra states to the button, such as a visited state (after an area has been visited by the user, similar to HTML pages), or animate them in a unique way.

For this next exercise, you will create a couple of movie clip buttons that will be used in the catalog section of the site. You will create a button used to download sample chapters of a book from the bookstore and a button that links to a site where you can purchase the book.

The first parts of the movie clip button you need to create are the graphics and text for the button itself.

1. Select the buttons layer on the Timeline and then select the Rectangle tool in the Tools panel. Set the fill color to #CCCCCC and the stroke color to black.

Click the Round Rectangle Radius button after selecting the Rectangle tool. Make sure that the corner radius is set to 0 before creating the rectangle. Then set the fill color to #CCCCCC and the stroke color to black (#000000).

2. Create a rectangle and then convert it into a movie clip.

Create the rectangle after you have entered the settings in the Property inspector. Double-click the rectangle's fill to select both the rectangle's fill and stroke. Then change the width of the rectangle to **85** and the height of the rectangle to **15**.

With the rectangle still selected, select Modify > Convert to Symbol to convert the rectangle into a movie clip. Name the movie clip **mcSampleChapter**, select the Movie clip radio button, and click OK when you finish.

3. Open the movie clip, select the stroke, and place it on a new layer called fill.

Double-click mcSampleChapter to open the movie clip in symbol-editing mode. Once in symbol-editing mode, select Insert New Layer to add a new layer to the Timeline. Name this layer **stroke**, double-click Layer 1, and rename it to **fill**.

On the fill layer, select the rectangle's stroke outline by double-clicking the stroke itself. After it is selected, select Edit > Cut. Select Frame 1 of the stroke layer and select Edit > Paste in Place.

4. Modify the stroke by selecting two of its segments and changing the color to #999999; then lock the stroke layer.

On the stroke layer, press Shift and click the top and left stroke segments. Change the stroke color to #999999 using the stroke color control in the Tools panel. Changing these two stroke segments creates the effect of depth around the button. When you finish modifying the stroke outline, lock the stroke layer.

5. Add the text **sample chapter** to the button on a new layer called **text**, and then lock the text layer.

So far, the button is not overly descriptive, so you need to add a label to the button using static text. Select the stroke layer, insert a new layer on the button's Timeline, and rename it **text**. Select the Text tool in the Tools panel and click on the Stage. Change the text properties to Static, Arial, 10 text size, black for the text fill color, and Anti-alias for readability. Type **sample chapter** into the text field on the Stage.

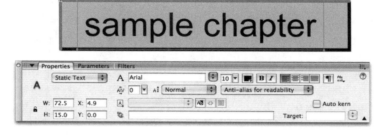

When you finish, lock the text layer.

6. Select the fill layer, select the shape's fill and convert it into a graphic symbol called **grFill**. Then lock this new layer.

This procedure nests a new graphic symbol within the movie clip button. The grFill symbol will be animated, which is why it was separated onto its own layer and converted into a graphic symbol (because the stroke doesn't need to be animated).

Tip *Whenever possible, you should always turn a raw graphic into a symbol before animating it and put each animation on its own layer.*

Lock the fill layer when you're finished.

7. Add a **labels** and **actions** layer to the Timeline.

Add two new layers to the Timeline and name them **labels** and **actions**. These two layers will hold frame labels and frame actions, respectively. It is good practice to keep actions and labels on their own layers so they do not interfere with other aspects of the SWF file.

8. Click Frame 25 of each layer and press F5 to insert new frames. Then insert keyframes on the labels layer at Frames 5 and 15.

The movie clip button needs several states, which span across the Timeline. Flash understands the Up, Over, and Down states of a typical button by entering specific frame labels in a movie clip button, which will be added in the following step. Each of these states is treated the same way as in a button symbol's Up, Over, and Down frames. You can then add drawings, graphics, or text at each of these frame labels, just as you did in the button symbols created earlier.

Note *The hit area is the movie clip itself, unless you define a different hit area manually. If you do, you use a separate movie clip symbol and then set it up as the hit area by using ActionScript. These buttons are solid, so it works just fine for the clickable area to be the visual area of the button. Because of this, you don't need to define a separate movie clip to be the hit area.*

Insert keyframes on the labels layer at Frames 5 and 15. Frame labels will be added to each of these keyframes in the next step.

9. Add frame labels at each keyframe on the labels layer. Make sure that each layer is locked and the file is saved before moving on.

If you add frame labels at each keyframe, Flash recognizes each area as a button state. Maximize the Property inspector and select Frame 1 on the labels layer. Type **_up** into the <Frame Label> text field. Select Frame 5 and type **_over** into the <Frame Label> text field. Finally, select Frame 15 and type **_down** into the field.

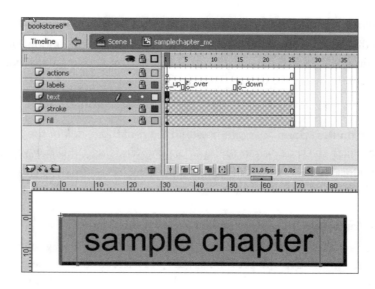

You will add the animation for these buttons in Lesson 5, in which you learn how to animate using *motion tweens*. You will use motion tweens to animate the button to create an interesting effect.

The button won't work yet if you try to test the SWF file in Flash because Flash needs ActionScript or a behavior to recognize the movie clip as a button. You will add the ActionScript in Lesson 6.

Duplicating Symbols and Adding Symbols to the Stage

Instead of re-creating a button, it is possible to duplicate the symbol to avoid having to follow all the steps you just went through all over again. It isn't lazy, just economical! Okay, so it's a *little* lazy, but by duplicating the button, you can add to or modify the symbol (such as the text contained within it) without having to rebuild the symbol from scratch.

1. Open the library and find the mcSampleChapter you created. Duplicate the symbol by Right-clicking or Control-clicking the symbol and choosing Duplicate from the contextual menu.

After you select Duplicate from the contextual menu, the Duplicate Symbol dialog box opens. Name the new symbol **mcToc** and click OK. The new movie clip is added to the library.

2. Double-click `mcToc` in the library and change the movie clip's text.

After you double-click the movie clip, it opens in symbol-editing mode. Unlock the text layer and double-click the static text field. The same font and text size remain. Enter **table of contents** into the text field.

Select the Selection tool and center the text over the background.

Note *If the text does not quite fit within the rectangle, select the text and change the font size to 9 pt or change the Character Spacing to -0.5. If you do this, remember to open* mcSampleChapter *and make the same modifications to the text so both buttons look the same.*

3. Delete the `mcSampleChapter` movie clip from the Stage.

Because you edited `mcToc` from the library, it was not added to the Stage as `mcSampleChapter` was. Select the movie clip and press Backspace or Delete to remove the `mcSampleChapter` instance from the Stage. You will add it to a different FLA file in a lesson later on, but for now you can leave both of these clips in the library until you need them.

You have many new symbols on the Stage and in the library. You should take a moment to lay them out on the Stage before moving on to the next lesson. The `btnProducts`, `btnCompany`, and `btnContact` buttons were already placed on the Stage earlier. You still need to place the menus that are associated with those buttons on the Stage.

4. Align the three menus with their associated buttons.

The three menus should still be on the Stage, but they won't necessarily be lined up with their respective buttons. Select the menu with catalog and reviews, and match up the lower-left corner of the menu with the lower-left corner of the `btnProducts`. You might need to unlock the menu layer before you can change the location of the three menus. Lock the buttons layer if necessary while you move the menus because the menu should be directly behind the button. When you move the menu close to the button, by default, you should see a dotted line that helps you align the menu with the button.

Note *If you do not see dotted lines to help you align objects on the Stage, select View › Snapping › Edit Snap Align. You should set the Snap Tolerance for around the default amount of 10 pixels. This means that the objects being moved will snap to other objects that are 10 or fewer pixels away and help align them either horizontally or vertically. This means that you will see a dotted line, and objects will snap when they are aligned along their edges. If you want to also align the vertical or horizontal centers of objects (as you did with the three buttons earlier in this exercise), check both check boxes under Center Alignment.*

Repeat this for the other two menus. The menu containing tour and news should be aligned with btnCompany. And the final menu with feedback and map aligns with btnContact. When you finish, lock the buttons layer if it isn't already locked. Then lock the menu layer.

Note | *The mcSampleChapter and mcToc buttons will not actually be used in the main Tech Bookstore website. Instead, you will copy these buttons from this file to a new FLA file that is created later on in the book.*

5. Clean up the library and save a new version of your file as bookstore8.fla in the TechBookstore folder.

In the library, move all the movie clips you just created into the movie clip folder and move the grFill graphic into the graphics folder. Save your work.

What You Have Learned

In this lesson, you have:

- Learned what symbols are (pages 93–94)
- Created, edited, and viewed symbols on the Stage and in the library (pages 94–97)
- Nested symbols within other symbols (pages 97–98)
- Learned more about graphic symbols (pages 98–99)
- Created buttons and hit areas (pages 99–102)
- Placed buttons on the Stage (102–104)
- Changed the hit area on a text button (pages 104–106)
- Built an invisible button (pages 106–110)
- Created movie clip symbols (pages 111–117)
- Made a movie clip button (pages 117–121)
- Duplicated symbols (pages 121–123)

5 Creating Animations

You've been waiting to get to it, and now you're here...creating animations, everyone's favorite thing to do in Macromedia Flash. Animations spice up an application and can make for some very interesting web experiences. At its heart, Flash is an animation tool, and most of the animations produced in Flash are deployed over the web. However, Flash animations are springing up on CD-ROMs, Computer Based Training (CBT) systems, mobile devices, and even broadcast production. Why? Because Flash produces such lightweight files that it is ideal for delivering on all kinds of platforms.

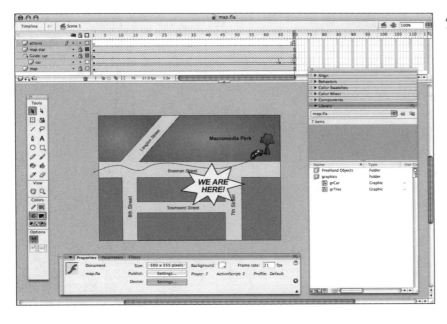

Animation in the Tech Bookstore

It's not terribly difficult to produce animations in Flash 8, although it does take just a little getting used to and good organizational skills. Flash does most of the work for you, in fact, and Macromedia has included some prebuilt effects that can help speed the process along. In this lesson, you'll look at some different ways to create animations using the Timeline—motion and shape tweening in particular. You'll also have a better idea of what purposes you can put animation to because it isn't just for making cartoons any more.

What You Will Learn

In this lesson, you will:

- Learn about the different types of animation
- Create a motion tween
- Use easing to speed up and slow down motion tweens
- Change brightness and alpha over time
- Add a shape tween
- Create a simple frame-by-frame animation
- Use a motion guide to animate a symbol along a vector path

Approximate Time

This lesson takes approximately two hours to complete.

Lesson Files

Media Files:

None

Starting Files:

lesson05/start/bookstore8.fla
lesson05/start/mapStarter.fla

Completed Files:

lesson05/complete/bookstore9.fla
lesson05/complete/map.fla

Animating Explained

An *animation* is a sequence of images that create the illusion of movement when viewed in rapid succession. In Flash, these images are formed by content that's placed in frames on the Timeline. You might use drawings, photos, or even ActionScript-generated graphics to create an animation in your FLA files.

There are several different ways to create animations using Macromedia Flash 8. Additionally, there are several different *types* of animations that you can make use of. You can create *motion tweens, shape tweens,* or *frame-by-frame animations.* The term *tween* may be new to you. It's actually a carryover from traditional animation, in which a master animator draws all the animation cells where some change takes place, big or small. Assistant animators then draw all the "in-between" steps from cell to cell. Because human beings *hate* having to pronounce extra words and syllables, the process was referred to simply as *tweening.* Scout's honor. In Flash, the concept behind the process holds true. You define the areas in which an animation changes, and Flash draws the in-between steps, or tweens, for you. Isn't that lovely?

You define the beginning points (points where changes are going to occur) and end points in *keyframes.* When you apply a motion tween betwixt keyframes, Flash fills in the *frames* between the starting keyframe and the next keyframe it encounters on the Timeline. Likewise with shape tweens, although the goal of a shape tween is not motion, but the physical changing of an object's shape. You will create both motion and shape tweens in this lesson.

A frame-by-frame animation is a more traditional way of creating animation. Instead of having Flash create a tween for you, you draw each frame of the animation yourself in many, many keyframes, thereby allowing you to create more-complicated effects. Automatically produced tweens just can't do *everything,* after all. Frame-by-frame animations are usually more time-intensive to create, though, and they generally add more file size to the final SWF file.

> **Note** *You can also create animation using ActionScript and (typically) movie clips. Although it goes beyond the scope of this book, it is definitely worth looking into, if and when you choose to learn more about ActionScript.*

Setting Up for a Motion Tween

Motion tweens are used to change the position of an object over a fixed period of time. What's more, you can change properties such as scale, alpha, tint, or rotation using a motion tween. An optional *motion guide* lets you make more-complicated animations by animating an item along a vector path, which you will do later in this lesson. Here's the catch: You can only motion tween symbols, so you should *always* change an object into a symbol before motion tweening the instance. Because motion animation is an illusion affected by producing many copies of the same graphic in slightly different positions, using a symbol makes sense. It helps keep your file size much lower when exporting the SWF file. The file size is kept low because Flash can reuse assets from the library instead of re-creating a whole new copy of them each time one is encountered on the Timeline.

Note *Shape tweening is the reverse: You can shape tween raw data, but you cannot shape tween symbol instances, grouped items, or bitmaps. They have to be broken apart into raw data first by choosing Modify > Break Apart. You will learn how to apply a shape tween to raw data (vector drawings) later on in this lesson.*

There are a few different ways to add motion tweens to a FLA document, which you will learn to do in the following exercises. In this particular exercise, you will be adding a motion tween to the bookstore menus you built in earlier lessons. Ultimately, the menus will open and close when a user presses a button or rolls off a menu after it's been displayed. You will also add a *stop action* to stop the animation from repeatedly looping when the SWF file plays.

1. Open bookstore8.fla from your TechBookstore folder or from the lesson05/ start directory, and save a new version of the file as bookstore9.fla in your TechBookstore folder on your hard drive.

In Lesson 4, you created most of the symbols you will animate in this lesson. You want to version the file up because you will be making some significant changes, and if you break something, you'll have a stable file to go back to.

2. Find the instance of mcProducts on the Stage, press F8 to place it inside another movie clip, and name the movie clip mcProductsMenu.

You're probably wondering why you put a movie clip inside of another movie clip. In Flash, for various reasons you often need to have animations, but don't want to make those animations on the main document Timeline. The solution is to create your animations inside of movie clip symbols and then place an instance of that movie clip on the Stage. In this circumstance, you will be creating a motion animation inside of the mcProductsMenu movie clip. Don't forget that you can create motion tweens only with symbols, which is why mcProducts has to be nested inside of mcProductsMenu.

Tip *The buttons layer is on top of your menu layer, which may make the menu movie clips difficult to select. Lock the buttons layer and hide it to make it easier to select the menu movie clips.*

3. Double-click `mcProductsMenu` to edit it on the Stage. Zoom in on the menu if necessary.

After you double-click `mcProductsMenu`, the rest of the Stage is dimmed, so you can concentrate on the symbol you're editing. You're actually editing the symbol's master properties, which would affect all instances of that symbol in your document. Because there is only one instance of this movie clip on the Stage, edit-in-place mode won't have any unintended ill effect. You're specifically editing in this mode because your animation has to start and stop at specific places on the Stage, and this mode lets you see the Stage and entire graphics while you work.

4. Select Layer 1 and rename it **menu tween**; then insert a new layer and rename it **actions**. Add keyframes to the actions layer on Frames 11 and 20.

Select the menu tween layer, click the Insert New Layer button, and rename it **actions**. Create new keyframes on Frames 11 and 20 of the actions layer by selecting each frame and pressing the F6 key. You will change the position of the movie clip in each keyframe. Changing the movie clip position creates the animation after you add the tweens in-between each keyframe. You will add the tweens in the following exercise.

One of the important things to remember about movie clips is that they have their own independent Timelines. They're like teenagers: They won't do anything unless you tell them to—or worse, won't stop doing something unless otherwise instructed. (No offense to you teenagers reading this book, of course.) What that means for you is that when you make an animation in a movie clip, it will loop over and over unless you tell it to stop, and not only to stop, but when it should.

You want your animation to work like most drop-down lists: A user clicks on one of the buttons (Products), the menu animates down until it's fully displayed, and then stops to display all of the options. When an option is chosen, or the user rolls off of the menu, you want it to animate back up until it's gone. So you will ultimately want to tell the movie clip to stop animating in two different places: Frame 11 and Frame 20.

5. Add stop actions on the Timeline to control the animation.

Stop actions are added from the Actions panel. Although you haven't learned about ActionScript yet, you can still make use of ActionScript with a simple point-and-click operation.

Open the Actions panel by selecting Window > Actions from the main menu. The Actions panel opens, docked below the Stage on Windows or as a floating panel on OS X. The Actions panel is separated into three different panes: the Script pane, the Script navigator, and the Actions toolbox. The Script pane is the large text field located to the right of the

Script navigator and Actions toolbox. The following figure shows you the different parts of the Actions panel.

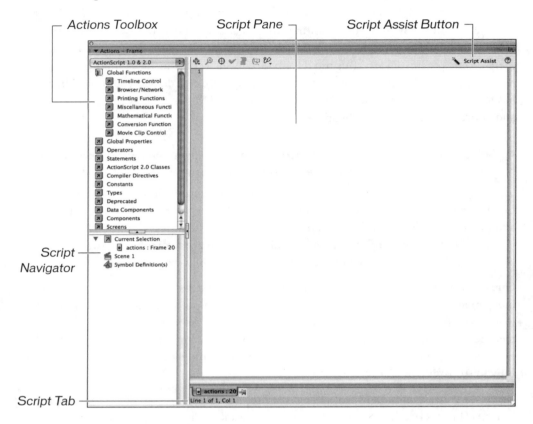

You'll add stop actions to keyframes 11 and 20 of the actions layer using Script Assist. The Script Assist feature is very useful if you're new to ActionScript because you select an action that you want to add, and Script Assist helps you fill it in correctly with a series of menu options and buttons.

Select keyframe 11 of your actions layer and make sure that your Actions panel shows Actions-Frame in its title bar. The Actions panel title bar will let you know if you have a frame or an object selected. So will the Script navigator—look at the Current Selection option in the Script navigator, and it should show Frame 11 of the actions layer. So does the script tag at the bottom of the Script pane, for that matter.

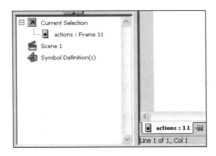

Press the Script Assist button in the upper-right corner of the Script pane. In the Actions toolbox on the left, click once on the Global Functions category, and select Timeline Control. From the Timeline Control category, double-click on the stop action to add it to the Timeline. Script Assist will indicate at the top of the Actions pane that the stop action takes no parameters. Repeat these steps to add a stop action to keyframe 20 of the actions layer.

Tip Script Assist will describe the action you have selected in the Actions toolbar in the upper-left corner of the Script pane. Underneath the description are instructions on how to add the action to your script.

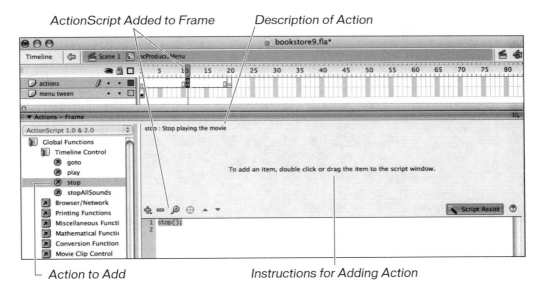

ActionScript Added to Frame   Description of Action

Action to Add   Instructions for Adding Action

When you finish adding the ActionScript, lock the actions layer by clicking the dot underneath the Lock Layer icon, which prevents anything being added to the Stage on the actions layer. It is a good practice to never place any raw data, symbols/instances, components, or assets onto a layer that has ActionScript. If you place code on the same layer as objects, such as components or movie clips that contain ActionScript, and then sometimes code conflicts can arise in the SWF file. Your FLA file might also be more difficult to debug.

Note *Actions, like any other element on a Timeline, must be placed on keyframes if you are adding frame actions. You cannot add ActionScript to a normal frame.*

6. Insert a new layer and rename it **labels**. Then add new keyframes and frame labels to Frames 2 and 12, and lock the layer when you finish.

Select the menu layer and press the Insert Layer button. Rename this layer **labels**. Create new keyframes on Frame 2 and Frame 12 by selecting each frame and pressing F6. You will use ActionScript to tell the playhead to move directly to these keyframes and play when someone presses on the Products button or rolls away from the menu after it has animated. The easiest way to use ActionScript for this task is to label those keyframes. Here's why:

You may decide that you don't like how long it takes for your menu to animate down or up, so you may adjust the amount of frames in which those animations occur. When you do that, where your animations begin and end might move to different frames. If you've told ActionScript to go to a frame *number* then you have to go into your Actions panel and change the script to reflect the new numbers. If you choose to send the playhead to a labeled frame, however, when the start and stop frames move, the label goes with it, and you won't have to adjust your Script.

Select Frame 2 on the labels layer and enter a frame label named **slidedown** into the <Frame Label> text field in the Property inspector. Then select Frame 12 on the labels layer and enter **slideup** into the <Frame Label> text field. When you finish, lock the layer as you did in the previous step to prevent accidentally adding any content to it later on.

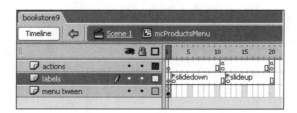

7. Insert new keyframes on Frame 12 and Frame 20 of the menu tween layer.

These frames determine how the menu animates. Frame 12 is the end of the animation for the menu opening and the beginning of the animation for the menu closing.

8. Change the position of the `mcProducts` movie clip at Frame 12.

Select `mcProducts` on the Stage at Frame 12. Move the movie clip straight downward by holding the Shift key and pressing the Down arrow key until the clip is directly underneath the `grBar`, as shown in the following figure.

Tip *When you hold down the Shift key while pressing the Down arrow key on the keyboard, your selected graphics move in 10 pixel increments. Pressing the Down arrow by itself moves items in 1-pixel increments, and is often referred to as "nudging."*

9. Return to the main Stage and repeat each of these steps for the other two menus.

Click Scene 1 in the edit bar to return to the main Stage. Repeat Steps 2 through 8 for `mcCompany` and `mcContact`. Name their wrapper movie clips **mcCompanyMenu** and **mcContactMenu** respectively. Then, all three menus can be animated tweening.

10. After you finish, remember to save the changes you have made to the FLA.

You have now set up each of your movie clips for motion tweening.

Note *In motion tweening, you can only animate one symbol instance to another instance of the same symbol in the same layer. Those symbol instances are the only things allowed to be in those keyframes, because Flash can only tween one thing at a time in a keyframe. If you put other items in the same keyframe as the symbol that's going to animate, Flash isn't capable of understanding which item you want to animate; It has too many decisions to make. Like a very hungry person in a grocery market. If you need to animate more than one thing at a time, separate those animations into their own layers.*

Tip *Flash 8 comes with a feature called Distribute to Layers, which is useful when you need to animate individual characters of a text block (that has been broken apart) or if you are importing a group of items onto the Stage while you are creating your FLA. When you select multiple objects on the Stage, and then select Modify > Timeline > Distribute to Layers, Flash places each selected object on a new layer and renames each layer for you, although you'll probably want to go through and make sure they've been named the way you want them to. While you don't use it here, this feature is a useful way to keep your FLA organized not to mention the fact that it certainly speeds up development.*

Adding the Motion Tweens

As you learned earlier, you can use motion tweens to change the position, brightness, alpha, or tint of a symbol instance on the Stage. In the Property inspector's Properties tab is a drop-down menu called Color, which is used to change the brightness, alpha, or tint of an instance as well as an advanced option, which allows you to change both color and alpha values. If you have an instance you are motion tweening, changing the values using this drop-down menu for one of the keyframes creates a transition to or from the new property you have set.

Now that you have set up the movie clip with keyframes and have the beginning and end positions for the instance, you are ready to add the motion tweens that will actually move the menus. You will also animate the brightness of the menu using the motion tween and changing a value in the Property inspector.

1. In bookstore9.fla, double-click to open mcProductsMenu if it isn't already open. Select the menu tween layer again.

You will be working with the same movie clips and content you set up in the previous exercise.

2. Create a motion tween between Frames 1 and 12 to slide the menu downward.

Right-click or Control-click any frame between Frames 1 and 12 on the menu tween layer, and select Create Motion Tween from the context menu. The first thing you notice is that the background color for the frames spanning the menu tween layer have changed into a purple color, and an arrow spans from the beginning to the end of the span of frames. The change in appearance indicates that you have correctly added a motion tween on that layer. The figure following Step 3 shows you a Timeline containing motion tweens.

> **Note** *Had you incorrectly added a motion tween, you would see dotted lines in your layer instead of a solid line with an arrow. Usually, this happens because there is more than one item in one of the keyframes you are animating between.*

> **Note** *If you attempt to set a motion tween between keyframes that do not contain symbols, Flash will convert the graphics in those keyframes to graphic symbols named Tween1, Tween2, and so on. Always convert your graphic assets to symbols before you even extend your Timeline (when possible) to avoid this.*

3. Add a second motion tween to animate the menu upward, and then review the animation by scrubbing the Timeline.

Repeat Step 2 to add a motion tween between Frames 12 and 20. Select any of the frames between Frames 12 and 20, Right-click (or Control-click), and select Create Motion

Tween from the contextual menu. When you finish, the movie clip animates downward between Frames 1 and 12, and then animates upward between Frames 12 and 20. Click and drag the playhead to view the animation.

Tip *After motion tweens are applied to a series of frames, you can still change the duration of the tween by adding or removing frames in-between the two keyframes. You can add frames by selecting a frame within the tween and pressing F5 (to add more frames), or remove frames by selecting Remove Frames from the contextual menu (to delete frames). Flash automatically modifies the tween for you.*

4. **Add easing to the menu motion tween using the Property inspector.**

The Ease slider is found in the Property inspector when you select the beginning keyframe of a motion tween. You can ease the animation so it appears to be speeding up or slowing down along the duration of the motion tween, which is very useful for gravity-type effects. By default, easing is set to 0 (no ease), but by moving the Ease slider to a positive number (between 1 and 100), you are telling Flash to begin the animation quickly and then slow the animation down at the end of the tween. Setting the amount of easing to a negative number (−1 to −100) starts the animation a bit more slowly, but speeds the movement up toward the end of the tween. Either way, the animation still has to execute in the same amount of time.

Select Frame 1 and expand the Property inspector. Use the Ease slider to set the easing to **100**, which means it is easing out and gradually slowing down as it animates downward. Then select Frame 12 and set the Ease slider value to −**100**, which means that the menu is easing in toward the end of the animation. The menu gradually speeds up as the menu closes.

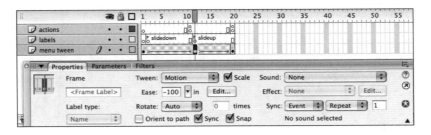

Note *When performing a motion tween, there is also an option to set the direction and amount of rotation for the selected symbol. There are four choices for rotation: None, Auto, CW (Clockwise), and CCW (Counterclockwise). If you chose Auto, the item is rotated in the direction that requires the least amount of movement. Clockwise and Counterclockwise rotate the object a specified number of times in either of those directions.*

5. Add a brightness tween to the menu, and then test the animation by scrubbing the Timeline.

Select the instance of mcProductsMenu on Frame 1 of the menu tween layer. You must select the instance, not the frame, to access the Brightness property. Select Brightness from the Color drop-down list on the Property inspector's Properties tab and change the value to 85%. Select the instance of mcProductsMenu on Frame 12 and make sure that the brightness is still set to 0. Scrub the Timeline by dragging the playhead back and forth. Take a look at how the animation looks so far.

Tip *You should try to use a brightness tween instead of an alpha tween whenever possible because alpha tweens, particularly over detailed bitmaps, are much more processor-intensive than brightness tweens are. Flash needs to perform many more calculations when tweening with transparency than when you tween the brightness of a color.*

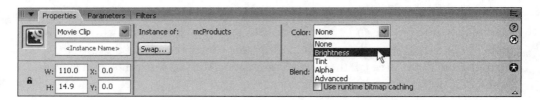

6. Repeat Steps 2 through 5 for the other two menus in the FLA file. Scrub over the animation to make sure that the animations work correctly.

Repeat Steps 2 through 5 for the remaining two menus in the FLA file so that all three menus have animation added to them. When you are finished adding animations for the three menus, click the playhead directly above the frames on the Timeline. Drag it to the right—you can see the animation play as you drag the playhead. You can also play the animation in the Flash authoring environment by pressing Enter, and the animation begins to play right on the Stage and then stops at the end of the animation.

7. Return to the main Stage. Clean up the library and then save the FLA document.

Click Scene 1 in the edit bar to return to the main Stage. Clean the library by moving `mcProductsMenu`, `mcCompanyMenu`, and `mcContactMenu` into the movie clips folder in the library. Save the changes you made to the FLA file.

Animating Alpha Levels and Size

Changing a symbol instance's alpha isn't much different from moving an instance around the Stage and is pretty much the same as changing its brightness level, which you did in the previous exercise. As you read in earlier lessons, alpha refers to the amount of opaqueness (or transparency) that an object has. If an object's alpha is set to 0, it is fully transparent and invisible on the Stage. If an object has a visibility of 100%, it is completely visible. Using the alpha property of a symbol instance with a motion tween produces fade in and fade out effects.

In the following example, you will use motion tweens to fade the glow that is animated behind the logo and then to change the scale of the graphic. You are still working with the bookstore9.fla file where you left off from the previous exercise.

1. Select `grGlow` and convert it to a movie clip symbol named mcBookGlow. Then rename Layer 1 to glow animation.

Make sure that you are on the main Stage by clicking Scene 1 in the edit bar, if necessary.

Find the instance of the `grGlow` inside `mcLogo`. The easiest way to do this is to either double-click `mcLogo` in the library, or double-click it on the Stage. Either will get you into symbol-editing mode, in which you can then select the `grGlow` instance and press F8 to convert it into a movie clip symbol called **mcBookGlow**. You need to change the graphic symbol into a movie clip because the animation you add needs to loop repeatedly. Make sure that the pageTurn and logo layers are locked so you can select the `grGlow` instance. Double-click `mcBookGlow` to open the instance and rename the default layer from Layer 1 to **glow animation**. You are now three Timelines deep (see figure on the next page).

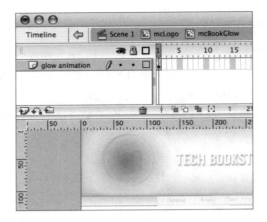

2. Create keyframes on Frame 35 and Frame 70 of the glow animation layer.

Select Frame 35 of the glow animation layer and add a new keyframe. This procedure copies the contents of Frame 1 into the keyframe on Frame 35.

Insert another keyframe on Frame 70 on the glow animation layer. You will next change the alpha and size of grGlow across the sets of frames.

3. Resize grGlow using the Transform tool.

Select Frame 35 on the glow animation layer. Select the Transform tool from the Tools panel and drag one of the corner handles toward the center of grGlow to make the instance smaller. To prevent the symbol from distorting and to maintain the symbol's aspect ratio while you resize it, press and hold Shift while dragging the mouse. Resize the instance so it is mostly hidden behind grLogo, as seen in the figure in Step 4. grLogo is visible below grGlow, just dimmed-out because it is in a different Timeline (if you are in edit-in-place mode, that is).

Tip *You can also select the scale option in the Options section of the Tools panel with the Free Transform tool selected. When the scale option is chosen, an object's proportions are constrained when you drag any of the corner handles.*

4. Change the alpha of grGlow using the Property inspector and motion tween.

You have changed the size of the graphic on Frame 35. Now change the alpha of the instance. Select the instance on Frame 35, again by using the Selection tool. Select Alpha from the Color drop-down list in the Property inspector's Properties tab and move the Alpha slider from 100 to **80** percent.

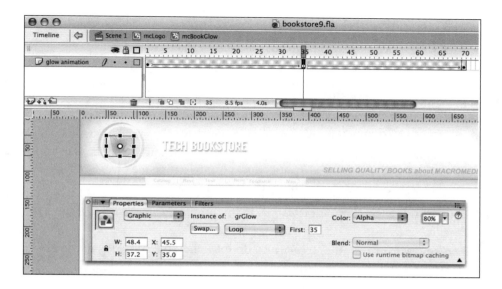

If you find the amount doesn't look quite right on your screen, modify the new alpha value you gave the instance.

Tip *Remember that the changes you are making to the instance on the Stage do not affect the symbol in the library. You can pull another copy of grGlow from the library, and it appears on the Stage as it originally appeared before you made the modifications.*

5. Add motion tweens to scale the graphic and then scrub the Timeline to view the animation.

Click on any frame between Frame 1 and 35 and expand the Property inspector. Change the Tween drop-down list from None to Motion. Follow the same steps for a frame between Frame 35 and 70. The movie clip should now scale the glow larger and fade it out slightly before returning to its original state when you view it on the Timeline. You can also test this individual movie clip (and not the entire SWF file) by moving your playhead to Frame 1 of the mcBookGlow symbol and selecting Control > Play from the main menu.

6. Move mcBookGlow into the Movie Clips folder in the library. Save the FLA file before proceeding to the next exercise.

Animating the Movie Clip Button

In Lesson 4, you created two Movie Clip buttons: one for a table of contents, and the second for a sample chapter. In this exercise, you'll animate the Movie Clip button to create a mouse-over effect. The effect will be produced by a brightness tween inside the movie clip. When the visitor mouses over the button, the button animates, and what's more, it also animates when the cursor moves off the button as well so that the brightness returns to its initial state. The Movie Clip buttons use special frame labels so Flash knows to treat each labeled keyframe like a button state instead of as a normal frame label. These special labels you are going to work with are _over, and _down (representing the Over and Down states of a normal button symbol). Remember, you set these labels already in Lesson 4.

You are still working with bookstore9.fla file in this example.

1. Find `mcSampleChapter` in the library and double-click the movie clip.

After you double-click the symbol, the movie clip opens in symbol-editing mode. Unlock the fill layer and make sure that the other layers are locked before proceeding with the animation, which helps prevent selecting the text or stroke layers.

2. Select the fill layer and insert a keyframe on Frames 5, 14, and the last frame in the movie clip (Frame 25).

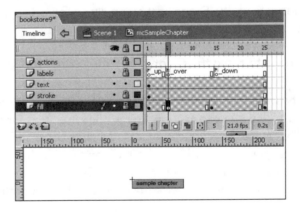

Frame 5 on the Timeline corresponds with the frame labeled _over. This frame will begin an animation when a user rolls the mouse cursor over the Movie Clip button.

Click to select the Frame 5 and press F6 in order to add a keyframe; repeat this process on Frame 14 and 25 on the same layer. There are two animations: one for the _over state, and a second for the _down state. You want to create an animation for the _over state that is reversed for the _down state, so the beginning of the _over animation and the end of the _down animation are exactly the same.

3. Add a brightness tween to `grFill` and then insert a keyframe on Frame 15.

Select Frame 5 in the fill layer and expand the Property inspector. Select Motion from the Tween drop-down list to insert a motion tween. Select `grFill` on Frame 14, select Brightness from the Color drop-down list in the Property inspector, and change the value to **85%**.

When you finish, select Frame 15 and press F6 to insert a keyframe. Change the Tween drop-down list in the Property inspector to Motion. Scrub the Timeline to view both of the motion tweens you have created.

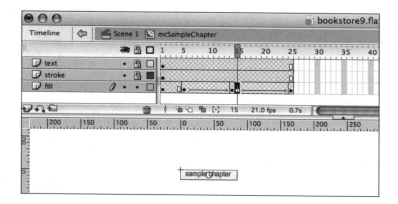

Tip *If you test the button at this point, you cannot see the brightness tweens because Movie Clip buttons in Flash are engineered to go to each special frame label and stop. You need to add a bit of ActionScript code to tell it to actually go and play each animation and then stop at the end of the animation. You will do this in another lesson.*

4. Repeat Steps 1 to 3 with the `mcToc` instance.

The `mcToc` movie clip should also be in the library. Double-click the symbol in the library and it opens in symbol-editing mode. Repeat the same steps as with `mcSampleChapter`, so that each of the buttons animates the same way.

5. Lock the fill layer in the movie clip's Timeline, save the changes, and return to the main Stage.

Creating a Shape Tween

Shape tweens allow you to change the shape of an editable vector graphic over time. You can change the length of lines, bend lines, or alter a vector drawing to create some very interesting effects, including changes of color. Instead of having to manually create each change in the appearance of the shape, Flash does the calculations to create the animation for you: All you have to do is set the beginning, the key points where the shape will change, and the end—just as you did with motion tweening. You can have one or several shapes tween on a single layer, although if you have many shapes in the same keyframes, they might affect one another in unpredictable ways. But be warned: The more complex a shape tween is, the more CPU will be eaten up on the end user's computer, which isn't a very nice thing to put your end users through.

Note *Shape tweens can only be applied to raw vector graphics (they show the crosshatch pattern when they are selected). You cannot shape tween bitmaps unless they have first been converted to vector graphics. Changing the shape of one bitmap image to another bitmap image requires different software.*

Shape tweening can often produce very unexpected results because your control over how the tween executes is somewhat limited. The path that a particular part of a shape takes between the beginning and the end of the tween might go all over the place. To assist you in controlling how the shape changes, Flash 8 has included *shape hints*, which allow you to specify corresponding points across keyframes on tweened shapes (meaning that a particular point on the beginning shape should go directly to a second specified place on the ending shape during the shape tween). Each shape hint has a specific letter. Therefore, wherever shape hint "a" is placed at the beginning of the tween, that point moves to the location of shape hint "a" at the end of the tween.

For example, you might have a cat shape that tweens into a dog shape. If you had a triangle representing the cat's ear with a shape hint "a" at the cat's ear tip, and its corresponding shape hint at the dog's ear tip, the cat's ear should directly tween to the dog's ear instead of taking a more indirect route in the tween between the two locations. The more shape hints you have, however, the worse playback becomes, so they should be used very sparingly. They are added from Modify > Shape > Add Shape Hint when shape tweening has been turned on.

Tip *To make your shape hints behave properly, use at least four, and distribute them clockwise (a,b,c,d) instead of placing each lettered shape hint out of order.*

Leaving behind shape hints, there are two blend options when performing a shape tween: Distributive and Angular. Distributed blending generates a smoother transition that tends to look a bit irregular, whereas Angular blending preserves corners and lines when tweening. Angular is available only when you're working with shapes that have straight lines and sharp corners.

In this exercise, you'll be working on building a subtle page-turning effect in the book's logo in the top-left corner of the bookstore website. You're still working with the bookstore9.fla file.

1. Find mcPageTurn inside the mcLogo movie clip on the Stage. Double-click mcPageTurn to open the movie clip for editing and zoom in to at least **800%**.

You created a movie clip in Lesson 4 that was a single line that was created for a page turn animation. The animation for the page turn is in two parts. The first part of the animation is to create a shape tween, which you will create in this exercise.

2. Rename Layer 1 to **animation**. Add a keyframe at Frame 10 and then modify the contents of the new keyframe.

After you have renamed the layer to **animation** and added a keyframe, you can modify the contents of Frame 10. Remember, Frame 10 contains a simple line drawing. Switch to the Selection tool and then click once on the background to ensure that the line is not selected. Mouse toward the line until you see the cursor change to show a curved line at its lower right, which is shown in the following figure:

Click and drag the line so it bends. Bend the line until it resembles the following figure.

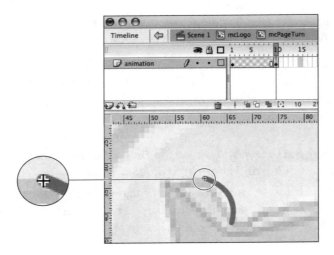

Mouse over the upper end of the line until a cursor appears that has a corner point that's next to the arrow. Click and drag the end of the line slightly to the right until it resembles the following figure.

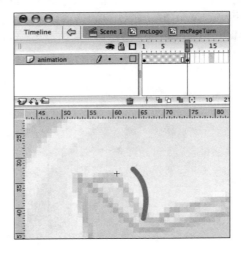

3. Insert a shape tween using the Property inspector, and then check out the animation.

Select Frame 1 and expand the Property inspector. Select Shape from the Tween drop-down list. A green arrow spans across the animation layer, which means that a shape tween has been added to those frames.

Click and drag the playhead across the span of frames and view the animation that has been added to the logo. The lower point of the line should remain in the same place, which is the spine of the book. The page turn animation will be completed in the following exercise.

4. When you finish creating the shape tween, save the changes that you made to the document by choosing File > Save from the main menu.

In the next exercise, you will add a frame-by-frame animation directly following the shape tween to complete the page turn animation.

Creating Frame-by-Frame Animations

When you were a kid bored in school, you may have drawn a little happy face in your notebook corner that turned to a frowning face, little by little. Then you flipped the pages (quietly so you didn't get in trouble, of course) to make it look animated. That little exercise that got you a D in math because you weren't paying attention was your first introduction to frame-by-frame animations (shame on you for getting a D in math, though!).

As you might imagine, frame-by-frame animating means two things. Lots of time will be taken making the animation because you are doing it "manually" in gobs of keyframes, and also the potential to create bigger file sizes goes up. Yet, they can be very useful tools in your Flash 8 toolbox (the one in your brain) because you can create more complicated effects and animations than tweening can. Tween is a joy, but it just can't do everything. Not yet, anyway. So until the day when tweening *can* do everything, well, a little frame-by-frame tradition won't hurt.

Frame-by-frame animation is best-suited to more-complex animation sequences, in which the image must be different for each frame, such as trying to animate facial expressions or create a walk cycle. Because most frames change in a frame-by-frame animation, the penalty is a higher file size because the frames you create have new data that Flash has to store in the exported SWF file.

Tip *If you are hand-drawing your animations, you might want to try using a pen tablet to create your drawings with, such as those made by Wacom. Flash recognizes pressure sensitivity and pen tilt, depending on the features in your tablet.*

In the following example, you'll complete the page turn animation that you started in the previous exercise.

1. In bookstore9.fla, open the mcPageTurn movie clip where you created the shape tween in the previous exercise.

You already have a shape tween on the animation layer spanning between Frame 1 and 10, which begins the first half of the page turn animation. To get the level of detail necessary for the second half of the page turn, you'll use a frame-by-frame animation. Although you could certainly create another shape tween to finish the animation, using frame-by-frame animation allows you to have more control over the motion. Obviously, it also helps you learn how to create frame-by-frame animation, too.

2. Insert a new keyframe at the end of the shape tween, and then turn on onion skinning.

Select the Onion Skin Outlines button to turn on onion skinning, which is a very powerful tool to assist you in creating frame-by-frame animation. Onion skinning allows you to view not only the current frame you are editing but also the contents of the previous and next frames. This feature helps you line up your drawings across your keyframes to ensure that the animation is smooth. The current frame that you are editing appears in full color (similar to working with onion skinning disabled), whereas neighboring frames appear to be slightly faded out or as an outline.

Click the empty frame following the shape tween (Frame 11) and press F6 to insert a new keyframe. The contents of the previous frame are added to the new keyframe, which you will modify in the following step. Click and drag the edges of the onion skin markers above the Timeline to see more frames of the animation.

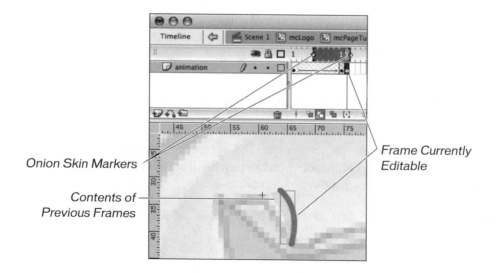

Onion Skin Markers

Contents of Previous Frames

Frame Currently Editable

3. Modify the contents of the new keyframe.

In the previous exercise, you bent the line into a curve to create the appearance of a page turning halfway. In this exercise, you will bend the page a little bit further and modify its length on each new frame that you create. All the while, you will keep the base of the page (at the spine of the book) stationary.

Each keyframe created should contain an incremental change to the line graphic to create the page turn animation. Select the keyframe you created in Step 2 (Frame 11) and then deselect the line on the Stage. Mouse near the upper end of the line, and when the cursor changes, drag the tip of the line the right so the line bends. The frame is now modified from the one to the left.

4. Insert new keyframes and modify the page graphic until the page is on the other side of the book cover.

When you finish the modifications to the contents of Frame 11, select Frame 12 and press F6 to enter another keyframe. The contents of Frame 11 are copied into Frame 12, where you can modify the line again. Make the same kind of modifications that you did for Frame 11 by dragging the upper tip of the page further to the right. Bend the page, if necessary, by mousing near the middle of the line and dragging the page to modify its bend when you see the curved line cursor. However, most of the modifications can be made by moving the upper tip of the line (or "page"). Just make sure that you do not move the bottom tip of the page by the spine. Only bend the middle of the page or move the upper tip of the line.

Because the onion skin feature shows you an outline for each frame around the one you are working on, it should help you figure out how the animation will appear while you are editing. You can also scrub the Timeline by dragging the playhead back and forth.

Tip *Make sure that you do not modify the lower point of the line. If you modify the lower point of the line, it appears as if the page is shifting in the book instead of being bound to the spine!*

Enter as many keyframes as you require until the animation is complete. When you get toward the end of the animation, you probably have to drag the end of the page outward to make it slightly longer in length.

The animation is finished as soon as the page animates all the way to the front book cover. You might have about 9 or 10 keyframes when the animation is complete.

Tip *You can make the animation look a bit better by fading out the page during the frame-by-frame animation. To do this, you can return to each keyframe you created in this exercise and select a different amount of alpha for the line. You can do this using the Alpha slider in the Color Mixer panel. Select the first line in the frame-by-frame animation using the Selection tool, and then drag the Alpha slider downward to about 90%. For each frame, gradually fade out the page more until you reach around 10% for the final page.*

5. Insert frames at the end of the animation in order to add a pause between the page turns.

Select Frame 85 and press F5 to add a frame to the layer, which means that the animation will appear to pause before turning the page again. Remember that because this is a movie clip, it loops on the Stage endlessly, unless otherwise directed with ActionScript. This means that the page will appear to turn over and over again, with a pause in between each one.

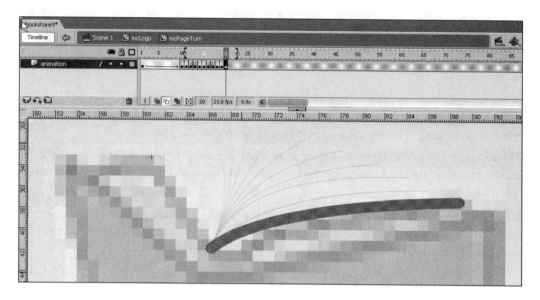

6. Select File > Save As and enter **bookstore9.fla** into the File Name field.

Click Scene 1 in the edit bar to return to the main Stage. Save the file as **bookstore9.fla** and close it. You are done with this file until the next lesson.

Animating Along a Path

When you produced a motion tween earlier in this lesson, your symbol instances animated in a straight line from one point to the next. Although this is fine for most tasks, occasionally you'll want an animation to follow a slightly more complex path, like a wavy line, for instance (think drunken bumble bee). You can accomplish this quickly and almost even painlessly with a motion guide in a motion guide layer. You can make a path in this special layer by drawing a stroke with the Pencil, Pen, or Line tools and then attach a symbol in the layer below the motion guide to either end of the path. This path *must* be placed on a motion guide layer; whatever you draw here will not be visible after you publish the Flash document. Motion guides allow you to animate objects along the outside of a circle, square, straight line, curve, or any sort of shape you can draw—as long as the shape is a stroke. In this final exercise you will make some modifications to the map.fla file you created in Lesson 2. You'll use a motion guide to animate a small symbol over the map.

1. Open mapStarter.fla from the lesson05/start folder on the CD-ROM and save it into the TechBookstore folder on your hard drive.

You'll recognize this file as similar to the one you worked on in Lesson 2. The only difference with this starter file is that there are two graphics in the library that you need to work with. All the layers and positioning are the same. At the end of the exercise, you'll save this file as **map.fla**. That file replaces the map.fla you began in Lesson 2.

2. Select the map layer and insert a new layer called car. Then open the library and locate grCar and grTree in the graphics folder. Drag an instance of grCar onto the car layer and drag an instance of grTree onto the map layer.

There is a symbol in the library called grCar that you can use to animate. The grTree symbol will be a static graphic on the Stage. You will probably have to unlock the map layer before you make changes to it.

Move grCar so it is just beyond the left edge of the Stage on Brannan Street. Move the tree so it is at the right edge of the map at the lower-right edge of Macromedia Park on the map. See the following figure for guidance.

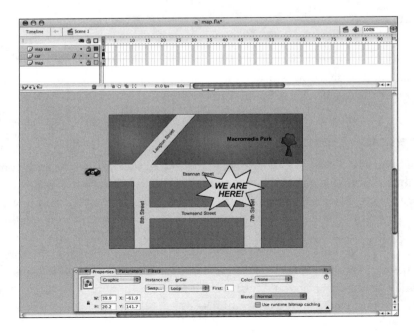

3. Create a new motion guide layer and draw a path on the Stage.

Make sure that the map layer is locked. Select the car layer and click the Add Motion Guide button that's next to the Insert New Layer button. This process automatically indents the car layer, so the motion guide will be applied to it. This is a lot like creating a mask layer, as you did in Lesson 2. The new layer is automatically called Guide: car and is located above the car layer.

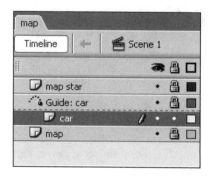

Select the Pencil tool and make sure that you are using the Merge Drawing model. You cannot use the Object Drawing model to draw a motion guide because the graphic is technically grouped, and the path won't be accessible to the symbol that needs to follow it as a result. Also, select the Smooth modifier in the Options section of the Tools panel.

The Smooth modifier helps you draw a path that isn't too ragged, although it still allows you to add a few "bumps" to the path. Now the car doesn't have to follow a ruler-straight path! If you find that the path you create is *too* smooth, select the Ink modifier instead, which does not alter the strokes you create at all (although the path still appears to be aliased, so it does seem to be smoothed to some extent) and redraw the path.

Tip Lock your other layers before drawing the path, so that you do not inadvertently draw the stroke in the wrong layer.

Draw a path on the new Guide: car layer you just created using the Pencil tool. The path should be drawn going down Brannan Street from the left side of the Stage to the right side near the tree. Ultimately, the car will appear to "crash" into the tree, so you want the path to end at the tree's trunk. The path that you create should follow along the road, bending around the "We Are Here" star, and then curve into the tree at the end of the path. Add a few bumps and curves along the path. When the path reaches the tree, curve the line upward, similar to the following figure.

Lock the motion guide layer (Guide: car) when you finish drawing the path.

4. Add a keyframe on the car layer at Frame 70, frames on the `motion guide`, `map star` and `map` layers at Frame 70. Then snap grCar to each end of the path.

Select the car layer and insert a keyframe on Frame 70 by selecting the empty frame and pressing F6. Then select Frame 70 of the map layer and press F5 to insert a frame. Repeat this step for the motion guide and map star layers.

Select the Selection tool in the Tools panel and ensure that the Snap to Objects modifier is selected. On Frame 1 of the car layer, click and drag grCar and snap it to the end of the path near the left side of the Stage. It helps to drag the instance from its center.

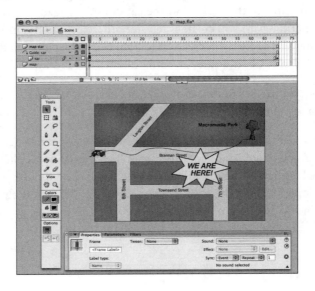

Click Frame 70 on the car layer and then select grCar by its registration point in the center of the graphic and snap it to the end of the path near the tree.

5. Select Frame 1 of the car layer and insert a motion tween from the Property inspector.

Select Frame 1 of the car layer and expand the Property inspector. Select Motion from the Tween drop-down list in the Property inspector. When the frames on the layer are selected, make sure that the Snap check box is selected and Orient to path is not selected. The car layer changes to a purple color with an arrow spanning the length of the animation, meaning that the motion tween expands across those frames.

> **Note** *There are three options on the Property inspector that are related to motion guides and tweening: Orient to path, Sync, and Snap. Orient to path allows you to point objects in the direction they are moving along the path. The object rotates to align with the curve. Sync allows you to sync the animation in the instance to the main Timeline, and Snap allows you to grab an object by its registration point and add it to the motion guide path.*

> **Tip** *If the car has not be snapped to the guide correctly, it will animate from the beginning point to the end point in a straight line. If this happens, make sure the care is properly attached to the guide at both the starting and ending keyframes.*

6. Add easing to the end of the animation, so the car speeds up while it is tweened from one side of the Stage to the other.

Select the first frame in the animation and expand the Property inspector. Enter **–100** into the Ease text field, which means that the car speeds up between the two keyframes when you play the animation in the Flash Player. Select Control > Test Movie to see the animation in the test player. It loops repeatedly at this point in the exercise.

7. Scrub the Timeline to view the animation and then make a modification to the motion tween.

Click and drag the playhead to scrub the Timeline and see the motion tween along the path you drew. If the car doesn't move along the path, make sure that the car is snapped to each end of the pencil line you drew on the motion guide layer.

You probably notice that the motion path doesn't work properly next to the tree that it is supposed to crash into because it doesn't rotate to appear like it is tilting upward or crashed. You need to rotate grCar to correct the effect. Scrub the Timeline again, find a spot around

Frame 65 on the car layer where the car should begin to rotate, and press F6 to insert a new keyframe. This location will be where the new part of the animation will begin.

Select Frame 70 at the very end of the animation and then select the Free Transform tool in the Tools panel. Handles will appear around grCar. Mouse over the upper-right corner of grCar until the rotation cursor appears.

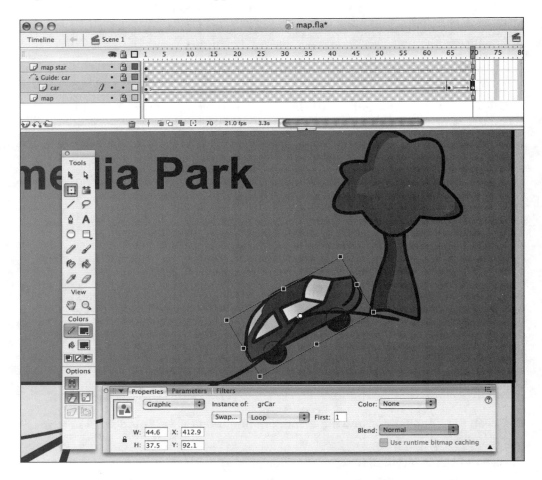

Click and drag the corner to rotate the car until it appears to be leaning against the tree. When you finish, use the playhead to scrub the Timeline again and view the change to your animation.

8. Place a stop action on the last frame on a new layer called **actions**.

If you test the animation as a SWF file before adding a stop action, you will notice that the animation loops repeatedly. To stop the animation at the end, you need to add a stop action on the final frame.

Select the map star layer and then click the Insert New Layer button. Double-click the name of the layer and rename it **actions**. Click Frame 70 (or the final frame in your animation) and press F6 to add a new keyframe. Select the new keyframe and open the Actions panel. Turn off Script Assist if it is still on by pressing the Script Assist button. Type the following ActionScript directly into the Script pane:

```
stop();
```

When you finish, press Ctrl+Enter (or Command+Enter on the Mac) to watch the animation in the testing environment.

9. Save your file as **map.fla**, overwriting your previous version of map.fla produced in Lesson 2.

When you save this file, you will be prompted to over-write the previous version of map.fla you produced in Lesson 2. Over-write the file with the new one that you just finished with, then close map.fla.

What You Have Learned

In this lesson, you have:

- Learned the differences between frame-by-frame animation, motion tweens, and shape tweens (page 127)
- Added a motion tween to a movie clip (pages 127–137)
- Used an instance effect with a motion tween to change alpha (opacity) over time (pages 137–139)
- Used an instance effect with a motion tween to change brightness over time (pages 140–141)
- Added a simple shape tween to animate the turn of a page (pages 142–145)
- Created a frame-by-frame animation (pages 145–149)
- Animated a symbol along a vector path drawn with the Merge Drawing Model (pages 149–155)
- Used a stop() action to prevent an animation from looping (page 155)

6 Adding Basic Interactivity

For the Tech Bookstore, so far you added text, used symbols, made animations, and built your own graphics. You displayed all this in Timelines. These days, all of these things together will earn a big fat whoopdy-do from the millions of users using the web every day. Why? Because they want your web application to *do* something. Displaying graphics and animations and text is all very fine and good, but if end users can't interact with it in some way, it really doesn't merit their sticking around on the site or even coming back. Let's leave the boring old display of information to posters and museum curators and add a little interactivity to your work.

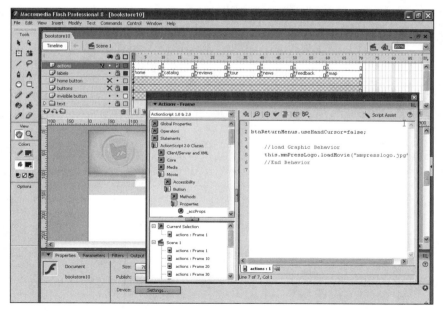

Interactivity is added to the Tech Bookstore Website.

In this lesson, you'll take the big leap and start making things interact with your users. Before you get all sweaty with panic, thinking that you'll have to write ActionScript fresh-outta-your-head, take a deep breath, go to your happy place, and rest assured that in this unit you won't have to think too heavily with your left brain. You'll use *behaviors* that come with Flash to add ActionScript and you will use *Script Assist* to do some tasks that behaviors don't handle. Script Assist will help you ensure that the ActionScript you're adding is well-constructed without forcing you to learn everything there is to know about this very powerful, not-at-all scary scripting language. Feeling better? Good, let's get started then.

What You Will Learn

In this lesson, you will:

- Add behaviors with the Behaviors panel
- Modify behaviors after they have been added to your document
- Load a JPEG image from the server
- Learn about the Actions panel
- Use Script Assist to add ActionScript to an object
- Use Script Assist to add an action to the Timeline
- Use ActionScript to control a movie clip Timeline
- Use the Script navigator

Approximate Time

This lesson takes approximately one hour and 30 minutes to complete.

Lesson Files

Media Files:
lesson06/assets/mmpresslogo.jpg

Starting Files:
lesson06/start/bookstore9.fla

Completed Files:
lesson06/complete/bookstore10.fla

Making Flash Documents Interactive

Interactivity covers a very broad canvas. At its most basic level, making something interactive simply means that a person can click a button, type in text, or in some way respond to events happening in the application that you build. Users do something in your application, and your application responds to whatever it is they do, whether it's dragging an item over top of something or pressing keys on their keyboards. There are, of course, much more complex concepts that relate to interactivity, but for most purposes, instructing your application to react to what a user does while in your application is pretty much enough.

In Macromedia Flash, the most commonly used elements added to produce interactions are buttons, movie clips, and text fields. Buttons in Flash respond to mouse and keyboard events initiated by the user. Movie clips can respond to either user-driven interactions or server-type interactions such as data loading. Text fields can be used to collect information from a user, display information for a user, or both. No matter the purpose, very nearly every Flash 8 application you produce will use all three of these items.

You do not need to write ActionScript to add interactivity, believe it or not, so you don't have to be a whiz kid programmer. Obviously, the more you know, the better equipped you are to make sophisticated applications, but Flash 8 Basic has some built-in features that you can leverage to add interactivity with very little effort (but with lots of forethought). These built-in features come in the form of *behaviors,* which are out-of-the box ActionScripts that you can quickly add to something, and *Script Assist*, a feature of the ActionScript panel used to add more complex actions without necessarily knowing everything about ActionScript.

Introducing Behaviors

Behaviors are a collection of some of the more commonly used applications of ActionScript organized in a panel. The panel's name: the *Behaviors* panel. Strange, but true. In this aptly named panel, you will find behaviors to open web pages, control movie clip Timelines, load JPEG images or SWF files into movie clip instances, and behaviors to control sounds. These behaviors are added directly from the panel, and the panel has a feature that lets you change what event causes the behavior to trigger in all but one circumstance. When you become an ActionScript ace, you can write your own behaviors and add them to the panel, but until then you can download and install additional behaviors that are written by third-party companies and members of the Flash community. One of the best sources for these third-party behaviors is Macromedia Exchange (`www.macromedia.com/go/exchange`).

There are two places in which you can add behaviors: keyframes in a Timeline or directly to movie clip, button, or component instances (ever after referred to collectively as *objects*). When you select an item to add a behavior to, be it an object or a keyframe in a Timeline, the Behaviors panel itself will show what has actually been selected, so you can avoid adding a behavior to the wrong item by mistake. The behaviors you can add will depend on what's been selected.

Tip *Many of the behaviors in the Behaviors panel were written with the idea that the developer or designer would add them directly to object instances. Although this is okay when you're starting out, it's generally considered a better practice to add all your ActionScript to a keyframe in the Timeline because it's easier to find and fix when things start to go wrong. More on this practice in Lesson 9.*

The next couple of exercises cover how to use behaviors to add basic interactivity to your application. First, you'll add a behavior that loads a JPEG image off your hard drive and into your Flash application on the fly. Then, you'll add some behaviors that control movie clip Timelines.

Using a Behavior to Load a JPEG

Dynamic loading of an image is one of the more important features to understand in Flash because images are often used to display catalogs of products or photo galleries of some sort. Because images tend to be big, importing all the images you would need to display for galleries or product catalogs would make your Flash application a little on the large side. Add to that the fact that the images often have to be sorted based on some kind of interaction with the user so that some images display and others are ignored, and you have a recipe for a bloated application that would take roughly two thousand years to download off the web (hyperbole intended). Keeping your images external and retrieving them only when needed really takes care of this problem for you. It also makes your Flash file kind of like a shell that can be easily updated or repurposed to meet changing needs because most of your visual content is externalized. Flash 8 Basic and Professional both have the ability to dynamically load JPEG, PNG, and GIF formatted images at runtime (when the SWF is loaded in the browser and runs, that is to say).

Tip *Flash 8 Basic introduces the ability to load progressive JPEGs as well as standard JPEG images. Progressive JPEGs draw as they are loaded, which is a good visual cue to an end user that something is in fact happening in the application.*

When you load a JPEG, GIF, or PNG image using ActionScript, you have to put it in something for display. You can't really load it into the main document Timeline because it will force all the other content out in favor of the newly loaded image. Even if you did, the image would display at the upper-left corner of the Flash document and wouldn't be able to be repositioned because images are not ActionScript objects and therefore can't be controlled. To gain control of those unruly images, you'll need to load them into individual movie clip instances, which, by the way, have to be named. Movie clips, buttons, components, and nonvisual ActionScript objects (which you will use in Lesson 9) can accept instance names, which are essentially used to boss the aforementioned objects around.

Tip *You can also load JPEG, GIF, or PNG images into Loader components. You will load PNG images into Loader component instances in Lesson 9.*

As you will discover in this exercise, instance names are necessary to *target* the movie clip and button symbols you placed in your Flash document. You have to give the movie clip instances a name so Flash knows what object to manipulate when you add ActionScript to tell something what to do. You can add instance names using the <Instance Name> field in the Property inspector, or you can provide an instance name when you add behaviors. However, it's a better practice to name them in the Property inspector because the option to give something an instance name when you add a behavior is really only there in case you forgot to name it to start with. No getting sloppy now. You will give an instance name to a movie clip so you can load an image file into that movie clip in this exercise.

1. Open bookstore9.fla from your TechBookstore directory or from the lesson06/ start directory on the CD-ROM and save a new version of the file as bookstore10.fla.

Save the new version of the file into the TechBookstore folder on your hard drive.

2. Copy the Macromedia Press logo from the lesson06/assets directory on your CD-ROM and paste it into your TechBookstore folder.

There is a file named mmpresslogo.jpg located within the lesson06/assets folder on your CD-ROM. This is the image that you will use a behavior to load. Placing it in the root directory of your TechBookstore folder will make it easier to do this exercise, but in the real world, you can place it in any folder you want, as long as your directory structure is maintained from your development computer to your web server.

3. Select the home layer in the pages layer folder and create a new rectangle on the Stage. Convert the rectangle into a movie clip and give it an instance name.

Select the home layer that is within the pages layer folder on the Timeline. Make sure that the playhead is at Frame 1. Select the Rectangle tool from the Tools panel and set the stroke color to No Color and the fill color to black (#000000). Draw a rectangle on the Stage and change its dimensions to **128** pixels wide by **96** pixels high in the Property inspector.

Double-click the rectangle that you created and then press F8 to convert it into a symbol. Name the symbol **mcMMPressLogo** and then click the Movie clip radio button. Set the registration point for the symbol to the upper-left corner (click the upper-left black square in the grid) and click OK. On the Property inspector, give the new movie clip the instance name **mmPressLogo**. Move the movie clip near the lower-right corner of the Stage, similar to the following figure.

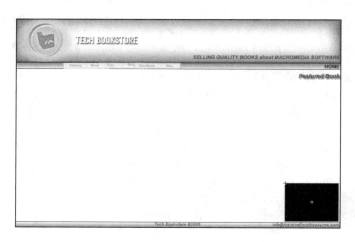

You'll be using this movie clip as a container for the image that you're going to load dynamically when the SWF file runs. The black graphic will be replaced by the mmpresslogo.jpg image, so it's serving as a placeholder for the actual content in this circumstance. That way, you know where to place it.

4. Add a new layer called **actions** to the Timeline and add keyframes for each page.

Select the labels layer and press the Insert New Layer button. Rename the new layer **actions**. It should be the top layer on the stack of layers in the Timeline.

When you finish creating and naming the layer, select the frame above each label and then press F6 to insert a new keyframe, as shown in the following figure. This is where your actions will eventually be placed for each page. For now, you are concerned only with the actions on the home page.

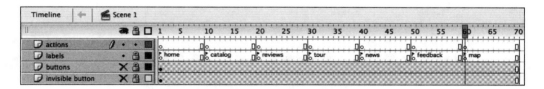

5. Add a behavior by using the Add (+) menu to load `mmpresslogo.jpg` into the SWF file.

There are two different places where you can add a behavior: on a keyframe or on the instance itself. The behaviors that you can add depend on what it is you have selected. For instance, some behaviors can't be added to frames, so they won't be available. Others can only be associated with buttons. You'll see what you can add when you press the Add Behavior (+) button and make choices from the drop down and fly over menus.

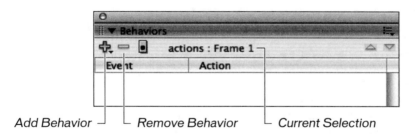

Add Behavior — └ Remove Behavior — └ Current Selection

The behaviors are arranged by category. When you press the Add Behavior button, you'll get a menu of choices that displays these categories. Loading an external graphic image is a special feature of movie clips, so the behavior you want is in the *Movieclip* category.

Select Frame 1 of the actions layer and open the Behaviors panel. If it is not already open, select Window > Behaviors. With Frame 1 selected, click the Add Behavior button in the Behaviors panel and select Movieclip > Load Graphic from the Add Behavior menu.

In the Load Graphic dialog box, type **assets/mmpresslogo.jpg** into the upper text field, and select the mcMMPressLogo movie clip from the tree below both text fields listing the instances available. Click the Relative radio button, which refers to the kind of address used to target the image outside of the SWF file. Ultimately, you're specifying which image should load, and where it should go when you load it in. Apart from that, don't worry about the fine details just yet. You will learn about absolute and relative addressing of instances in Lesson 9. Press OK again to return to the main Stage.

6. Save the changes you made to the document.

At this point, you can't yet effectively test this functionality because you haven't added the ActionScript that stops the Timeline from moving beyond the first frame. You will test the FLA file later on in the lesson as well, and you'll also take a look at the ActionScript that the Behaviors panel just added on your behalf.

Choose File > Save to save your changes before moving on.

Using Behaviors to Open a Web Page

You saw how to use a behavior to load in an external JPEG image in the previous exercise, although you haven't checked to see whether it works yet. In this example, you will learn how to use one of the behaviors in Flash to open a web page in a new browser window. You will be adding the behavior directly to a movie clip instance instead of to a frame in the Timeline this time. This is sometimes referred to as an object action.

You should still be using bookstore10.fla for this exercise.

1. Make sure that you are on the main Stage and then select Frame 1 of the home layer.

Using the Selection tool, click the instance of mcMMPressLogo that you created in the previous exercise. There is an action in Frame 1 of the actions layer that references this instance, but you are going to place an action on the movie clip itself so that if a user happens to click it, it will launch a web page.

2. Add a behavior directly to the mcMMPressLogo movie clip instance using the Behaviors panel.

With mcMMPressLogo selected, click the Add Behavior button in the Behaviors panel and choose Web > Go to Web Page from the menu. The Go to URL dialog box appears and gives you the option to select a target: *_self*, *_parent*, *_blank*, or *_top*. Each of these options is the same as the HTML counterparts; change the value to **_blank**.

3. Set the target URL for the behavior in the Go to URL dialog box.

Setting the target URL to redirect to is as simple as replacing the default value in the URL text field with your desired target. For this exercise, set the target URL to: **http://www. peachpit.com**. After you type in the URL, press OK and return to the Stage.

<table>
<tr><td>Note</td><td>*If you are trying to go to a web page within a different domain, don't forget to prepend your URL in the Go to URL dialog box with* http://. *Modern browsers are making us lazy because we no longer have to type* http:// *into the address window to go to a web page these days. When you're developing or setting a link to another page, however, you absolutely must specify the protocol, which in this circumstance is Hypertext Transfer.*</td></tr>
</table>

4. Change the behavior's triggering event using the Behaviors panel.

Click the mcMMPressLogo instance on the Stage. You can alter when the behavior executes by opening the Behaviors panel and changing some settings. Open the Behaviors panel and look at the Event and Action lists below the Add Behavior and Delete Behavior buttons.

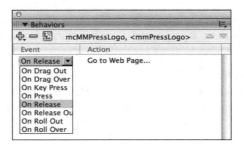

If you click the On Release text to the left of the Go to Web Page action, you will see a drop-down list of events to trigger this behavior on. By default, the event is On Release, which means the user presses and releases the mouse button over the mcMMPressLogo movie clip. You can choose a new value from the drop-down list and trigger when the user moves his or her mouse cursor over the instance, or when the mouse cursor moves off the instance entirely. You can also cause the event to trigger when a certain key is pressed.

Change the event to a Key Press event. Flash prompts you to press a key on the keyboard that will be used to open the Peachpit website in place of a mouse click. Change the event back to On Release because this is the interaction that people are used to.

5. Modify the behavior properties using the Behaviors panel. Then click OK to apply the changes.

From time to time, you might need to change some aspect of the behavior or correct a spelling error in any of the parameters that you had to manually type when you applied the behavior to a frame or object. Lucky for you, you can get back in to the behavior to fix it or change it at any time you like from the Behaviors panel.

If you want to modify the behavior and redirect the user to a different URL, you can modify the behavior by double-clicking it in the Actions column on the Behaviors panel. This will pull the dialog box back up that you used to set the URL. Make any changes that you like and press OK.

Tip *You can also edit the ActionScript that the behavior added directly in the Actions panel. You haven't really used the Actions panel so much yet, and because you haven't learned ActionScript basics at this point, it's not advisable to try. After you've learned a little more, though, it sometimes is the smartest alternative to changing how a behavior operates.*

Loading an External SWF File with a Component

The previous example demonstrated that Flash 8 Basic has the capability to load JPEG (or GIF's and PNG's if you prefer) files into a SWF file on the fly (or dynamically) at runtime. Besides loading JPEG images, Flash can also load other SWF files into movie clips on the fly. In everyday practice, a Flash application is broken out into many SWF files that are loaded when a user requests them, and each SWF file contains a specific category of content. Like externalizing images, breaking your Flash application into smaller content modules that are loaded on demand keeps your application file size manageable and makes it easier to update content. When you have smaller content modules, you only update the SWF file that's being changed, rather than the whole application. Like JPEG images, these smaller content SWF files can be loaded into movie clips. Flash 8 does, however, come with a special prebuilt component that makes the process a little easier, because you can add the component to your document without adding a behavior or ActionScript of your own to tell it to go and retrieve the external SWF file or JPEG image. This component is called the Loader component.

The Loader component allows you to easily embed SWF files or JPEG, PNG, or GIF images into an SWF file without having to write any ActionScript or add a behavior. All you have to do is drag an instance of the Loader component onto the Stage; once the component is on the Stage, you alter a special parameter on the Property inspector called *contentPath*, which tells the component where to get external data to load up. When the component is fully drawn in the SWF file, it will go and get the external content without being told and then display it. Of course, you can control that retrieval of external content with ActionScript if you need to be fussy about when that process occurs.

Note *The Loader component does make it easier to load up external SWF files or JPEG images. It has a dark side, though: It adds extra file size—to the tune of 25K. You can reuse it as often as you like, though, without it adding any further size to your application.*

In this exercise, you will learn how to load the SWF file you created in Lesson 2 into the Loader component. Specifically, you will be using the Loader component to load map.swf, which was initially created in Lesson 2, into the SWF file.

1. Select Frame 60 of the map layer and add a Loader component to the Stage.

On the main Timeline, select Frame 60 on the map layer, which is labeled map. The frame is already a keyframe and has a couple of text fields for the address and map title already positioned on the Stage that you created in earlier exercises.

Open the Components panel, expand the User Interface category and find the Loader component. Drag an instance of the component onto the Stage.

2. Select the Loader component and then look at the component parameters found in the Property inspector.

Select the instance of the Loader component on the Stage and open the Property inspector. In the Property inspector, switch to the Parameters tab; all components have modifiable parameters (things you can change, for those of you not accustomed to geek speak). The Loader component has three:

- **autoLoad:** This parameter controls whether the content should load automatically or whether you have to explicitly trigger the content for it to load (using ActionScript). A value of true means the content automatically loads; false means you need to trigger it before it loads.

- **contentPath:** The text entered into this text field sets the path to the SWF file or JPEG, GIF, or PNG image that you want to load into the component.

- **scaleContent:** This parameter controls whether the content is scaled to match the size of the component (`true`) or if the component is scaled to match the size of the content (`false`).

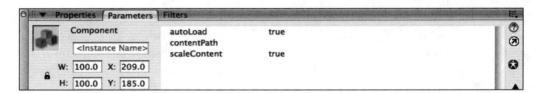

Tip *You can also control and modify components with the Component inspector panel. Open the Component Inspector panel by choosing Window > Development Panels > Component inspector panel. What you can change depends on which component you're using, but all the changeable options are listed in the Parameters tab. The bindings and the Scheme tabs are not covered in this book.*

3. Set the parameters in the Property inspector for the Loader component instance.

Because you'll just be loading map.swf into this component right away, set the `autoLoad` parameter to **true** and then type **map.swf** into the `contentPath` text field.

Note *If you saved map.swf into a folder different from bookstore10.fla, you have to modify the path. You need to use a relative URL such as lesson05/map.swf. This means that you can store certain files in other files in the directory for better organization.*

Set the `scaleContent` parameter to **false** to make the component resize on the Stage to match the size of the external SWF file.

4. Resize the component so it is the same size as map.fla, which can be found in the lesson05/complete folder, and position it on the Stage.

With the component selected, open the Property inspector. Change the width to **500** and the height to **355**.

The map should be aligned to the bottom of the How to find us text field and aligned to the right edge of the bookstore's slogan and the page title, similar to the layout in the following figure.

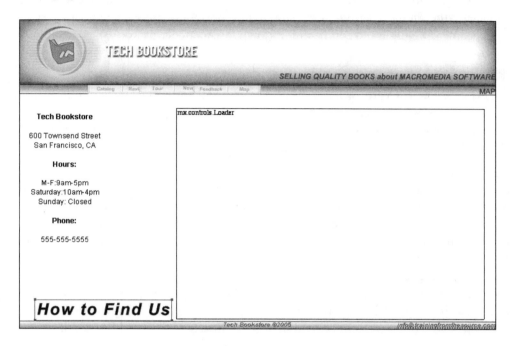

You probably still have guides visible that will help you align the component on the Stage. Just remember to allow enough empty space below the drop-down lists so they do not overlap the map. Make sure that the map either aligns or is (preferably) below the horizontal guide located at 140 on the vertical ruler.

Note *Depending on your own layout, you might need to move the How to find us text field.*

5. Save the changes you made to the file.

In the next section, you will begin to add more ActionScript to the FLA file. You will also use more instances of the Loader component in subsequent lessons. Right now, you won't be able to see the content loading into the map section of the Tech Bookstore website. However, when you test the file in Lesson 9, it should show up. If not, you'll have to check your contentPath parameter to make sure it's set right!

Introducing Script Assist

You are about to leave the safety of behaviors behind for the more sophisticated realm of ActionScript. Don't panic yet, however, because you won't get thrown into the thick of the language. You will meet Script Assist again in these next few exercises, and Script Assist will become your guide and companion through the ActionScript world. At least until you get good enough with ActionScript to go it alone. You can think of Script Assist then as training wheels for the ActionScript scripting language.

In Lesson 9, you will learn all about the general construction and usage of ActionScript and write your own scripts without using Script Assist. Here, you need to understand a few things about the language before moving on, so that you have a better understanding about what's going on in your Actions panel at any given time.

First, you already learned why something needs to have an instance name. Instance names are what you use to tell symbols or ActionScript objects what to do. They serve the same purpose in ActionScript that people names do in real life (although we have to be picker in ActionScript applications because no two instances can technically have the same name). If you're in a room full of kids, and you want to tell one of them to get you some aspirin, you don't shout "Hey kid, get me some aspirin!" because none of the kids will know which kid you're referring to. You have to call them by name: "Hey Cheyenne, go get me some aspirin!" As long as there aren't any other kids named Cheyenne in the room, she will (if she is being good that particular day) go and get you the aspirin you so desperately need when you're in a room full of children. So ultimately, we name symbols and ActionScript objects (such as the Sound object) so we can tell them what to do.

All symbols, named or otherwise, live somewhere on the Timeline. To tell it what to do, you have to *path* to it, which is geek speak for saying "Tell ActionScript where it is." When you path to something, you use a special notation called *Dot Notation,* which really means that you use "." characters instead of "/" characters to target an item. For instance, if you are in your living room, and you want your spouse to get your reading glasses from your desk in your upstairs bedroom (where he or she happens to be), the dot notation instruction to get your glasses when you shout to your spouse would look something like this:

```
this.upstairs.bedroom.desk.spouse.retrieveGlasses();
```

where this refers to your starting point, which is the living room, and upstairs, bedroom, and desk all refer to locations. spouse refers to an object that can do things (if he or she isn't too lazy), and retrieveGlasses() is the action you want him or her to take. retrieveGlasses() is also referred to as a *method,* which is something an object actually does. More on that in Lesson 9. If you don't have a spouse, you'll have to go get your glasses yourself:

```
this.retrieveGlasses(upstairs.bedroom.desk.glasses);
```

In this second example, `upstairs.bedroom.desk.glasses` refers to where your glasses are. The keyword `this` means you.

Keywords are special words reserved by Flash that have a particular meaning in ActionScript. When you are in the Actions panel and adding your own ActionScript instructions to control how an application works, you will see certain words change color. The color they change to depends on what the keyword is used for, but any time something changes color, it's because it's *reserved* by Flash for particular tasks. You should therefore be cautious not to name symbols or ActionScript objects with names that are otherwise reserved by Flash, such as `getTimer`. For now, don't sweat it too much. All your ActionScript in this lesson will be added with Script Assist and will be used to control buttons and movie clip Timelines.

There are many other aspects of ActionScript that you'll look at in Lesson 9. The ActionScript you add with Script Assist will let you test some of the features you added in the previous two exercises and will also provide the foundation for the interactivity used throughout the rest of the book.

Using Actions to Control the Timeline

ActionScript can be used to control many features in Flash. One of the more common uses of ActionScript is to control the Timeline of the main Flash document or the Timelines of movie clip symbols. In this exercise, you will add an action to control the main document Timeline with the Actions toolbox.

You should still be working with bookstore10.fla in this example.

1. Select the actions layer and then open the Actions panel.

If the Actions panel is not open in the layout, open it using Window > Actions panel. You can also open the Actions panel with the keyboard shortcut F9 on Windows and Option+F9 on Mac OS X. Expand the Actions panel. In the first exercise in this lesson, you created keyframes for each page of the Tech Bookstore. In this step, you will add a `stop();` action on each page.

2. Select each keyframe on the actions layer, starting with frame 1, and add the `stop();` action to each keyframe using the Actions panel.

If Script Assist is still turned on in the Actions panel, press the Script Assist button to turn it off. Because the `stop();` action doesn't require any special parameters to make it work, you will simply add it with the Actions toolbox.

At the very top of all the ActionScript in the Actions pane, make a blank line. Position your cursor in the blank line, and in the Actions toolbox, expand the Global Functions > Timeline Control categories. Double-click on stop to add the stop(); action to your Timeline. Select the next keyframe on the actions layer and add the same action. The stop(); action causes the playhead to stop once it reaches each of these keyframes, which is a navigation feature of the Tech Bookstore that will be put to good use in Lessons 9 and 10.

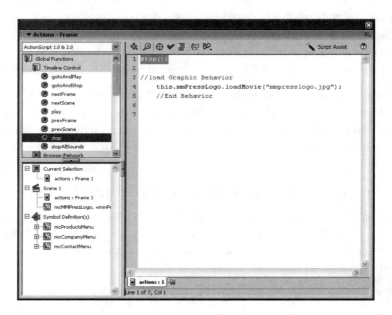

3. Test the FLA file and then save the changes you made to the file.

Press Ctrl+Enter (or Command+Enter on the Mac) to test the document in the testing environment. If you tested the bookstore before now, the SWF file played through each page. Now the document stops on Frame 1 (the home page). Each new page that you navigate to will stop when the playhead arrives at the frame, which will happen when you get the menu buttons working and you can navigate the site's pages. Also notice the JPEG image being loaded into the SWF file while in the testing environment. The JPEG is now dynamically loaded into the movie clip holder you created for it in the earlier exercise.

Note *You won't be able to navigate through each page yet. You can do so after you add the ActionScript that makes the buttons and menu system work in Lesson 9.*

Select File > Save to save the modifications you made to the FLA file.

Creating a Home Button

In this exercise, you will create a button to cause the SWF file to return to the home frame of the Tech Bookstore. You will duplicate your invisible button that you created in Lesson 4 and place it over a large logo so that it works like a hot spot. You have to duplicate the invisible button because there is a big hole in it which you will patch with the Merge Drawing model. You don't want to change the original invisible button because it won't work correctly if you do, so that means you have to duplicate and edit the symbol to minimize the amount of work you have to do.

1. Insert a new layer above the buttons layer and name it home button.

Select the buttons layer and insert a new layer called **home button** above it. The reason that you need a separate layer for this new button is so you can lock and hide it while not hiding the other buttons on the buttons layer. It's really just for organizational purposes and has no other hidden reasoning behind it.

2. In the library, Right- or Control-click the btnInvisible button symbol and choose duplicate from the context menu. Name the new button btnHotspot.

You'll remember from Lesson 4 that duplicating a symbol is a great way to speed up development. In this case, you have all the elements you need for an invisible button; you just need to get rid of the gap in it.

When you duplicate the symbol and rename it, double-click it to enter symbol-editing mode.

3. In symbol-editing mode, draw a rectangle the same color as the current fill over the gap in the button. Make sure that you are in the Merge Drawing model.

In symbol-editing mode, select the Hit frame of your button. Select the Rectangle tool and set the stroke color to No Color. Press the fill color control, and hover the eyedropper over the rectangle currently in the Hit frame. Click to set the color. Make sure that you are in the Merge Drawing model and draw a small rectangle big enough to patch the hole in the graphic.

Because the fill colors match, merge drawing will turn the whole graphic into one big rectangle. Click Scene 1 to return to the main document Timeline.

4. Drag an instance of btnHotspot into the home button layer and assign it an instance name.

Drag an instance of btnHotspot from the library and drop it over the top of mcLogo. Using the Free Transform tool, resize the button so that it just fits not only the logo in the upper-left corner but it also covers the "Tech Bookstore" text.

With the Selection tool highlighted in the Tools panel, click the invisible button you just created and expand the Property inspector, in which you can enter an instance name into a text input field where it says <Instance Name>.

Click your mouse in the <Instance Name> text field and type **btnHome**. Now you can use ActionScript to reference that particular instance of the button on the Stage and execute code used to manipulate the SWF file in a particular way when the button is clicked (also known as an event). In this case, when the button is clicked, you return to the Home page of the bookstore.

5. Use Script Assist to add the ActionScript that will return the playhead to the frame labeled home.

In this circumstance, you will add ActionScript directly to the button object using Script Assist.

Select btnHome, and open your Actions panel with F9 or Option+F9 (Mac). Switch to Script Assist mode by pressing the Script Assist button. In your Actions toolbox, select Global Functions > Timeline Control, and double-click goto. This will add a gotoAndPlay action to your button by default.

Change the action by selecting the Go To And Stop radio button. Change the type to Frame Label, and in the frame drop-down list, select "home." Script Assist automatically "sees" all your frame labels, which makes it easier to set the action. When you are finished, your Actions panel should appear the same as the following figure.

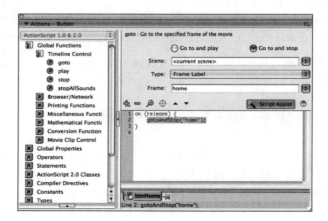

Tip *You will want to use frame labels instead of frame numbers whenever possible. When your FLA files get larger and more complicated, it is much harder to remember what content was on which frame number. Also, if you ever move content, you would have to change your ActionScript instead of just moving the frame label to a new location. Using frame labels allows you to simplify and give frames a logical name rather than just a number.*

6. Lock and hide the home button layer and clean up the library.

Lock and hide the home button layer by pressing the eye icon and lock icon beside the name of the layer in the Timeline, which prevents you from accidentally adding any instances or moving the invisible button. It also means that you can hide the teal blue appearance of the invisible button while you are working on the Tech Bookstore.

It is a good practice to keep the library clean as you work. Drag the btnHotspot symbol in the library into the buttons folder, move the mcMMPressLogo symbol into the movie clips folder, and move the Loader component into the components folder.

7. Save the changes you made to the FLA file.

As usual, save your changes using File > Save before moving on to the next exercise.

Removing the Hand Cursor

When you mouse over a button or hotspot in an SWF file, the hand cursor appears. This is typically what you want to have happen because it indicates what part of the SWF file is interactive and clickable. However, when you have invisible buttons that control whether or not a drop-down list appears, you don't want the button to have a hand cursor because the hand cursor is really a feedback mechanism letting a user know that if they click there, something will happen. In this case, they can click until their fingers turn blue—nothing will happen at all! Therefore, in this exercise, you will remove the hand cursor from the invisible button for the button surrounding the menus so users can't tell that it is there. You should still be using bookstore10.fla for this exercise.

1. Test the FLA file to see how the hand cursor looks.

Press Ctrl+Enter (or Command+Enter on the Mac) to test the FLA file. When you mouse over the upper area of the site, a hand cursor appears. This cursor can be rather distracting and it means that the button isn't really invisible at all to visitors to the website.

Because this button should not be known to the visitor at all, you need to change the button so the hand cursor does not appear when the visitor's mouse hovers over the area.

2. Select the `btnInvisible` symbol instance. Give the invisible button an instance name.

First, select the invisible layer button and unlock it. If it is hidden, show it. Make sure that your home button layer and your button layers are hidden.

With the Selection tool, select the invisible button instance on the Stage that will cause the drop-down navigation menus to return. Give it the instance name **btnReturnMenus**.

3. Add the ActionScript to hide the mouse cursor for `btnReturnMenus`.

Select Frame 1 of the actions layer. You will add the ActionScript to this frame. Launch your Actions panel if it is not already launched and temporarily turn off Script Assist. Script Assist can be a little funny to work with after you've already added a Behavior to a frame. You're shutting Script Assist off so that you can position your cursor at the top of the Actions window to make sure that whatever code Script Assist adds, it adds it in the right place instead of in the middle of something that might already be there.

Position your cursor so that it is blinking in its own line at the top of the Actions pane. You may want to press Enter to make a blank space and then put the cursor back at the top. Press Script Assist to turn Script Assist back on.

In the Actions toolbox on the right, select ActionScript 2.0 Classes > Movie > Button > Properties and double-click `useHandCursor`. In the Script Assist expression field, replace `not_set_yet` with `btnReturnMenus`. After the text `useHandCursor`, type = **false** to hide the hand cursor.

When you are finished, your Actions window should appear similar to the following figure.

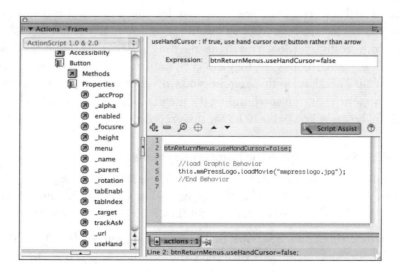

4. Test the FLA file to verify that the hand cursor is hidden around the menus.

Press Ctrl+Enter (or Command+Enter on the Mac) to test the FLA file. Mouse over the Stage where the invisible button is located and notice that your cursor no longer changes to a hand because of the ActionScript you added in the previous step.

5. Save the changes you made.

After you've saved your file, move on to the next exercise.

Making the Movie Clip Button Work

The movie clip button was built and then animated in the previous couple of lessons. You were even introduced to stop actions while building map.fla, so the animation did not continuously loop. In this exercise you will complete the movie clip buttons by adding some simple actions that make them animate properly when you click on the buttons themselves. You are still using bookstore10.fla for this example.

1. Open the library and find the movie clip buttons. Double-click the `mcSampleChapter` button so you can edit the movie clip.

The buttons you created say sample chapter and table of contents on the front of the buttons, and you will be able to find them in the library. Double-click the sample chapter button in the library so it opens in symbol-editing mode and then refamiliarize yourself with how you structured the button earlier.

2. Select Frame 1 in the actions layer and add a `stop();` action. Continue by adding the `stop();` actions on Frames 14 and 25.

Select Frame 1 and then maximize or open the Actions panel (F9). Turn off Script Assist by pressing the Script Assist button, and type **stop**(); into the Script pane. Select Frame 14 on the Timeline, press F6 to insert a keyframe, and then type **stop**(); into the Script pane.

Press F6 on Frame 25 to insert a new keyframe on the actions layer and then type **stop();** into the Script pane.

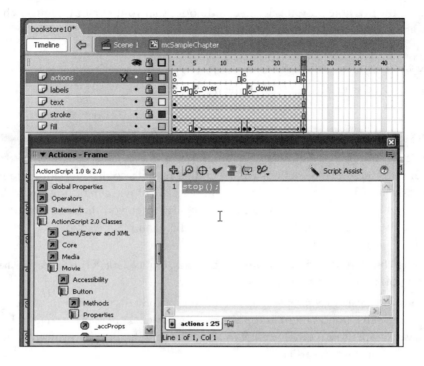

3. Type in **play();** for the _over state on the actions layer.

Enter new keyframes on the actions layer above the _over and _down states. Select the keyframe for _over and type **play();** into the Action panel's Script pane. This action tells the playhead to continue and play the next frame(s).

The reason you need to add play(); on the _over frame is because Flash is programmed to stop on each frame label when you create a movie clip button. If you were to allow Flash to just stop, the brightness tween animation would not play as a result. Therefore, you need to tell Flash to play the animation instead, which is why you add the play(); action on the frame.

4. Move the playhead to the _down frame and add the play(); action on the actions layer.

When the user clicks the button, you want another brightness tween to occur. Therefore, you need another play(); action so the button does not stop at this frame label.

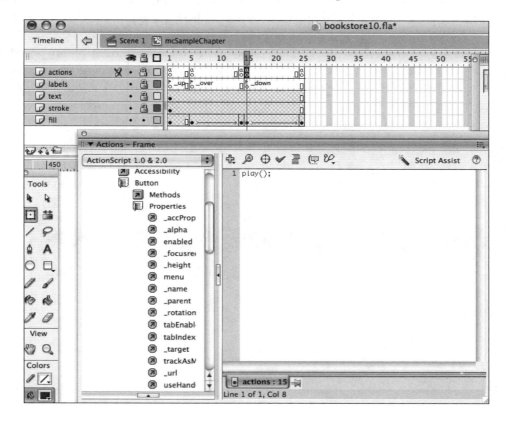

Add a blank keyframe on Frame 15 of the actions player by selecting it and pressing F6. Open the Actions panel and type **play();** into the Script pane.

5. Return to the main Stage by pressing Scene 1 on the edit bar. Repeat Steps 1 through 4 for the mcToc button.

Repeat the exact same steps from Steps 1 through 4 for the other movie clip button. When you are finished, return to the main Stage again using the edit bar.

6. Save the changes you made to the FLA .

After you are at the main Stage, choose File > Save to save the changes to your file. Make sure that you save the file in the TechBookstore folder. In Lesson 9, you will learn more about events that will be triggered when users roll the cursor on and off of the button.

Using the Script Navigator and Pins

Now that you added ActionScript in several different places in your FLA file, you should try using the Script navigator to find scripts that you have added to the document. Unfortunately you can't keep your ActionScript all in one place when you're using behaviors, so it is a good idea to familiarize yourself with these tools to help you find where scripts are placed when you need them in your FLA file. The Script navigator can be used to navigate through the scripts you have in a document. It contains a tree where you can navigate through all the different pieces of code in your FLA file. Frame and object actions are all represented in the Script navigator as part of the tree structure it uses to organize the code in.

You can also pin scripts in the Actions panel. If you select a piece of code in the Script navigator, you can either click a pin button to pin the script or double-click the code in the Script navigator. This means the code remains "open" in the Actions panel, like an open document with its own tab.

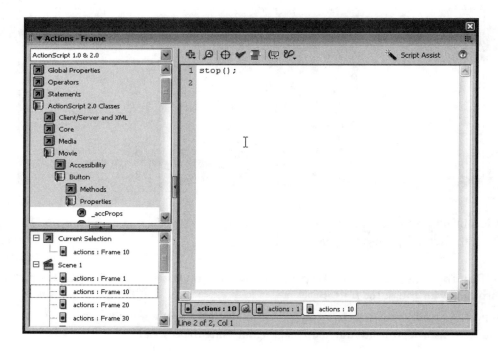

Then all you have to do is click the tab to access the piece of code for editing in the Actions panel. Script pins make it easy to navigate through and edit each piece of code by clicking on different tabs right below the Script pane. You'll find out how to use script pinning in the following exercise.

1. Using bookstore10.fla, expand or open the Actions panel by pressing F9.

The Actions panel opens with the Actions toolbox and Script navigator on the left, and the Script pane to the right. A bar separates the two areas, and it can be resized as necessary.

2. Move the bar between the Script pane and the Script navigator to resize each section of the Actions panel.

You can click and drag the bar between each area to resize the Script navigator section of the Actions panel. When you are editing code, you probably want to minimize the Script navigator and Actions toolbox section by clicking on the arrow button in the middle of the bar to close it completely.

3. With the Script navigator maximized, click actions: Frame 11 under the mcProductsMenu heading.

When you click each of these items, you can see the associated code appear in the Script pane. When you click an item in the Script navigator, the document's playhead moves to the frame that the selected script is on. The Script navigator helps you navigate throughout the code in a FLA file without too much effort. When you find code that you need to edit, you can pin these scripts, as seen in the following step.

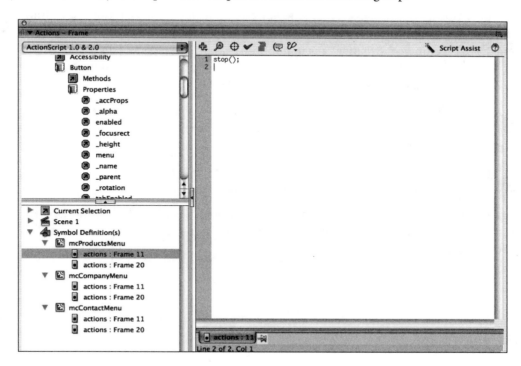

4. Select actions: Frame 11 in the Script navigator under the `mcProductsMenu` heading and click the Pin active script button below the Script pane. Then try pinning a second script in the document.

After you click the Pin active script button, which looks like a thumbtack, the code stays in the Actions panel until you close the pinned script.

Click actions: Frame 11 in the Script navigator and then click the Pin active script button. You can also select an instance or frame containing a script on the Stage and then right-click (or Control-click on the Mac) the script tab in the Actions panel and choose Pin Script from the contextual menu. This procedure pins the script in the Actions panel, and you see a new tab added underneath the Script pane as a result.

Tip *You can also double-click the code in the Script navigator to pin the script in the Actions panel.*

To close a pinned script, select one of the actively pinned scripts either by its tab or the pinned script in the Script navigator. When it is selected, the pinned script thumbtack changes; when you click the button, the script is unpinned.

5. Click through the script tabs for the pieces of code that you have pinned.

Use the script tabs below the Script pane to navigate through the pinned scripts. Navigating through the scripts does not move the playhead in the FLA file. Pinned scripts make it much easier to find code than having to hunt through the Flash document to find all the different places you might have placed code. If you use behaviors to place code on different instances, you will probably notice how useful this tool is!

Note: If you have too many scripts pinned that the Actions panel is not large enough to hold all the tabs, a double-arrow button appears to the right of the panel. If you click this button, a menu appears that shows the additional pinned scripts.

You do not need to save any changes that you made in this exercise, so just close the document and choose not to save changes when you're finished.

In Lesson 9, you will learn more about the ActionScript language and why it works the way it does. The more you know about ActionScript, the more you can ultimately make your Flash 8 applications do.

What You Have Learned

In this lesson, you have:

- Added behaviors to an instance and the Timeline in a FLA file (pages 159–164)
- Learned how to modify behaviors after they are added to a document (pages 164–166)
- Created basic server interaction by loading a JPEG into a Loader component (pages 166–169)
- Explored some of the basics of ActionScript (pages 170–171)
- Added `stop()`; actions to control the playhead in a SWF file (pages 171–172)
- Added a new home button to the bookstore (pages 173–175)
- Used Script Assist to remove the hand cursor from a button (pages 175–177)
- Added code so the movie clip button animates properly as a button (pages 177–179)
- Learned how to use the Script navigator and script pinning to find the scripts in your document and edit them (pages 180–182)

7 Adding Sound and Video

Once upon a time, sound was the sole citizen of the realm of CD-ROM. It was very lonely there, so it went abroad and soon found its way to the World Wide Web, where it promptly gummed up the works by being too big and making download times way too long. In an effort to make everyone happy, it changed its nature, became MIDI-formatted, and MP3-formatted, and stopped being annoying background music because now it was so much better to use, and instead started being used for feedback, learning, and enhancement. And the web was a happier place.

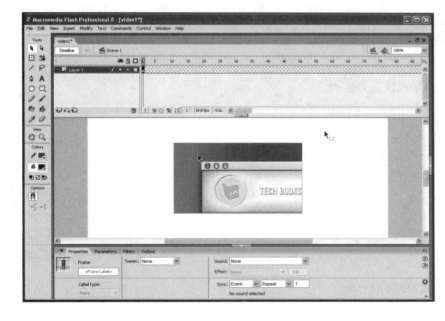

Video and sound make the Tech Bookstore website more engaging

Then came the much, much larger cousin of sound, which you all know as video. Video was big (and we're not talking popularity here, friends, we're talking *bandwidth*). Video was picky, too, because some video only worked with QuickTime, and other video only with Windows Media Player, and still others only with RealPlayer. For a web designer, video was a VNI (very neat idea) that just wasn't practical to implement unless there was a SGR (Super Good Reason). Now, however, that is no longer true.

All the time video and sound were busy trying to make footholds in the web, a tool called Macromedia Flash Player was very quietly finding its way to average home users. The Flash Player at first wasn't able to accommodate sound and video, but eventually, the genies at Macromedia waved their development wands and before you know it, Flash Player (now on nearly every computer in the world) could not only animate but also could handle sound in several sophisticated ways. What's more, it suddenly was able to handle video, too. And the web became a happier place all over again.

In this lesson, you will work with sound and video, covering only the most commonly used features for Macromedia Flash 8 Basic. You'll import sound and change its properties. to control how nice it sounds. You'll also import video to play in your document Timeline. Because you haven't got a magical development wand, you'll have to do customization of your sound and video the old-fashioned way, which is manually. You will also learn the do's and don'ts of sound and video because when it comes to using these two cousins, just because you can do it doesn't mean you should.

What You Will Learn

In this lesson, you will:

- Import sound
- Add sound to a button Timeline
- Add sound to the main Timeline
- Customize sound
- Import video
- Encode and compress video

Approximate Time

This lesson takes approximately one hour to complete.

Lesson Files

Media Files:

lesson07/assets/video1.mov
lesson07/assets/video2.mov
lesson07/assets/video3.mov
lesson07/assets/sound.mp3
lesson07/assets/click.wav

Starting Files:

lesson07/start/bookstore10.fla

Completed Files:

lesson07/complete/bookstore11.fla
lesson07/complete/video1.fla
lesson07/complete/video2.fla
lesson07/complete/video3.fla
lesson07/complete/sound.fla

Using Sound and Video

Sound and video have become almost indispensable to many applications these days. Sound is most often used as a feedback mechanism, indicating to a user that they can or have clicked on something, providing users with instructions on completing a task, or letting users know they've selected right or wrong answers in e-learning applications. Video is also used for similar purposes, although on the web you might see it used for everything from entertainment to videoconferencing (all of which can be done with Flash). Together, sound and video can take your applications to the next level, not only enhancing the end user experience but also providing information that otherwise couldn't be presented.

Adding sound can be extremely useful if your site caters to people who are visually impaired. It can be valuable to add audio cues to a SWF file, prompting key press actions or reading text aloud. Or, you can create an MP3 sampler for a freelance musician or add a company's jingle when its website loads. Adding tacky or annoying music is fairly easy to do, but detracts from the site. Getting your peers to test your site and provide feedback can help you avoid useless clutter and find subtle, creative, or diverse ways to use sound and video in your SWF files. Because sound and video add a lot of file size to a document, you have to make sure they're worth your bandwidth and the bandwidth of your visitor.

Editing Sound and Video

When practical, you can and should edit sound and video in external editors before you import them. Flash 8 has no sound-editing capability, other than volume control. Flash 8 is, however, capable of very basic video editing. When you import a new video file, you can edit and/or compress the video file at the same time. You can create shorter clips from the video, crop the size of the frames, color-correct the footage, and sew it all together. You cannot, however, create transitions or create other special effects that really require the use of a video editor such as Final Cut Pro, Adobe Premier, or Avid Express.

This doesn't mean there aren't cheap or free solutions to edit your videos in simple to very complex ways. Windows Movie Maker 2 allows you to quickly and easily edit your video files, and it's also free (but available only for Windows XP). QuickTime Pro is a very reasonable (and useful) piece of software that enables you to perform very simple video editing and compression. For those of you on OS X, there's iMovie. These free or nearly-free editors are all you need for fade ins and fade outs, cross-fades, simple filters, and basic color modification and correction. For more advanced or professional video editing and compositing, look to After Effects, Avid Express DV, or Final Cut Pro that allow you to perform detailed and controlled color corrections and compositing.

Assuming Responsibility with Your Media

You have to make some important decisions when you are adding sound and video. Consideration for your visitors is important! Some visitors might not want to be forced to hear the music that you are playing (if you are using a loop by the author, this is more often the case). Your visitor might be in a public setting that has other music playing already. Because of these reasons, you should at least always offer an "off" button for background sounds. Volume controllers or pause/play toggles also work very well. This kind of responsibility and usability offers a much better experience when someone visits your site.

Because sound and video files are often very large, you should try to communicate how much data need to be transferred to the end user by using something like a progress bar. If the file is large (like our video file), you should give some kind of indication that content is downloading so a visitor doesn't arrive at the page and think nothing is happening. Also, your video might also include an audio track. If so, you should offer the opportunity to control the audio using buttons or sliders.

Compression, Codecs, and Plug-ins

Compression reduces the size of a file by using complex mathematical equations that remove information from the content that is not necessary for hearing or viewing it. This means that the video, sound, or file you are working with will be quicker to download online, but you will always lose some quality in the process.

There are several software programs, other than Flash, which are made to compress video files in particular. You can use professional solutions such as Discreet Cleaner 6 (Mac) or Discreet Cleaner XL (Windows), or you can use a simple solution such as QuickTime Pro. Sorenson Squeeze, which has features that are created with Flash in mind, can compress videos directly into FLV (Flash Video) or SWF formats.

Other programs, such as Windows Movie Maker 2, allow you to compress video when you export a video project. This ability can be particularly useful if you need to edit video in ways that Flash cannot.

Tip *The most important thing you can remember about compression is to always try to avoid recompressing sounds or video after they haves already been compressed. Recompressing material leads to a significant loss in quality.*

Codecs are small pieces of software that are used to compress and then decompress files. The file is compressed for placing online and then it is decompressed by the codec again when viewed on the client's computer. Sorenson Video 3, Cinepak, QDesign Music 2 (audio), Mpeg4, and DivX are examples of codecs. If you compress a video using a particular codec, both you and those watching your video would need that codec installed to decompress the video again. Sometimes codecs are already installed into players such as the QuickTime player, but other codecs need to be installed separately by the end user.

Note *Flash uses On2 VP6 codec by default, which is a codec that is specifically for importing video into a Flash document. The codec is built into the Flash Video importer. Flash 8 can also use the Sorensen Spark codec.*

Delivering Media Online

When you are delivering media online, you have to think about what visitors need to view your files and how long what they need takes to download. File size and how long it takes visitors to download on different connections should be an immediate consideration when you are working with sound and video files.

You should note that SWF files actually *progressively* download, so a SWF file plays as it downloads into a visitor's computer. Streaming is a slightly different concept because streaming sound or video is not saved to the browser's cache, unlike a progressively downloaded file. The catch with streaming sound and video is that when the file is finished playing, it will begin to download the data all over again if you want the sound to loop. What's more, streaming sounds and video require a server application, such as Flash Communication Server MX, to do the streaming. Another issue with streaming sounds is that sometimes the SWF file will rush to keep up with the streamed sound, so it might start dropping frames to keep up with the sound or video being streamed. If there is ActionScript on those frames, your code will be lost. On the plus side, streaming sound and video are the only useful solution to delivering very large files, video- or audioconferencing, or simulcasts (such as Major League Baseball games).

File Size Considerations

Even though you are adding great and interesting content to your SWF files, it is important not to go overboard. Sound and video can very quickly fatten up the file size of your application. You have to make sure that you budget what media you add to the SWF file, and ask yourself whether the files are the best use of the file size and bandwidth you will need to devote to the presentation. It might be the best way of communicating a message, but there might be another similar way of getting the same job done that ends up saving you 800K, for example,.

Some video files are not practical to deliver over the Internet. The larger the frame size, the larger the file, and the larger the file, the longer the download. Please do bear in mind the old adage, *just because you can,* doesn't mean you should. To that end, if you must use video over the Internet, then you should control all elements you can control for that will keep file size down. One of those elements is *frame size.* Digital video with a frame size of 640 x 480 pixels delivered over the web is not unlike shoving an elephant through a hollow coffee stirrer. You very well may be able to do it, but it's going to take a long, long time. Something smaller, such as 320 x 240 pixels, might be a better move. If you have to deliver high frame sizes, you should consider deploying over CD-ROM. One day, these considerations will be vaporized, but until the technology brings us to that day, less is more. Unless it's peanut butter swirl ice cream. Then less is just wrong.

Importing Sound into a Document

There are many different kinds of files that you can import into Flash documents. If you are importing sound files, you can use MP3, AIFF (Mac), and WAV (Windows) files. If you have QuickTime installed on your Mac or Windows computer, you can also import additional file formats, such as Sound Designer II files and AIFF and WAV files on either platform. MP3 files can be dynamically loaded into Flash 8 Basic using ActionScript, or the MediaPlayback component in Flash 8 Professional.

You can import MP3s into a FLA file and place a sound in the Timeline or you can dynamically load an MP3 from the server when the SWF runs. You can set the MP3 to stream or load it into memory and play it when event occurs.

Many Flash designers and developers create or find loops to use in their SWF files. Loops are a good way to create the illusion of having a lot of loaded sound, but keep the content small and quick to download. You can find sound loops to download online that are free to use in your projects, or you can create your own loop using audio software such as ReCycle, Cakewalk Plasma, or Acid Pro. Don't forget GarageBand for those of you on OS X.

Note *You should make sure to create a loop that loops seamlessly. Loops must begin and end when the waveform crosses the "0 crossing" between the positive and negative waveform where there is no sound. If you trim your music exactly to the beat, so the waveform is crossing the 0 mark, you will not hear the distracting "pop" at the end of your loop. Also, make sure to remove any extra space at the beginning and end of the loop. It helps to create a loop that has an odd number of bars, which means that instead of 4 bars if you are using 4/4 time, create 5 bars of music. The uneven nature means that it will take the ear a longer time to recognize the sound is a loop.*

1. Create a new FLA document and call it **sound.fla**. Save the document in the TechBookstore folder on your hard drive.

You will use this file to import sound and experiment with it some. You will not use the file in your Tech Bookstore website, however.

2. Copy sound.mp3 from the lesson07/assets folder on the book's CD-ROM onto your hard drive.

You can copy the file anywhere you want on your hard drive, but be sure to remember where it is located so you can find it in the following step. This MP3 file will eventually play in the background of the tour you will create in the following lesson. It is approximately eight seconds long and will be dynamically loaded in as an event sound in the background.

3. Choose File > Import > Import to Library. Browse to find the **MP3** file on your hard drive. Select the file and click Open (or Import to Library on the Mac). Then open the Sound Properties dialog box.

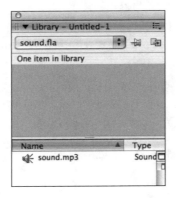

After you choose the MP3 file and click Open, the sound is imported directly into the library in Flash. Open the library and find the MP3 sound you just imported. Right-click (or Control-click on the Mac) the sound itself and select Properties from the contextual menu. The Sound Properties dialog box opens, in which you can modify the export settings for the sound.

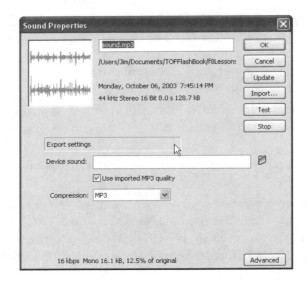

4. Deselect the Use Imported MP3 Quality check box above the Compression menu.

MP3 is Flash 8's default sound compression type, so it is selected in the Compression menu automatically. Because you imported an MP3 file, Flash assumes that you want to use the imported sound file's quality settings. Deselecting this check box gives you the ability to change the quality settings in Flash, so that you can have a higher- or lower-quality sound. The tradeoff to the higher quality sound, of course, is file size.

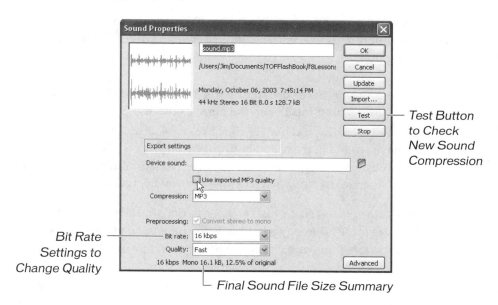

Bit Rate
Settings to
Change Quality

Test Button
to Check
New Sound
Compression

Final Sound File Size Summary

Take a few minutes to try different bit rates with the MP3 compression type. Press the Test button to hear what the new bit rate will sound like in the final SWF file. Notice that as you change the bit rate, the new resulting file size for the MP3 file is summarized at the very bottom of the dialog box.

When you are finished, click OK to exit the dialog box.

Note *You can set overall export settings in the Publish Settings dialog box (File ›
Publish Settings), but the properties for an export that you choose in the Sound
Properties dialog box override those settings. However, if you choose "Override
sound settings" in the Publish Settings dialog box, the settings in Sound Properties
are overwritten. You will learn more about Publish Settings in Lesson 11.*

5. Save the file before moving on to the next exercise.

Adding and Customizing Sound

You can change the sounds you are using in Flash right in the authoring environment! You should keep in mind that Flash is not an audio editor, and is mostly limited to volume and pan effects. It won't replace a dedicated audio editor like those mentioned previously in this lesson. However, for basic customizations and edits, Flash can help you change the sounds you import into the authoring environment without leaving the workspace.

In this example, you will create a fade in at the beginning of the sound you imported and modify it when the sound starts by trimming off the beginning. You are still working with sound.fla for this example.

1. **In sound.fla, select Frame 30 or greater on the Timeline and press F5 to insert a new frame. Then drag sound.mp3 from the library onto the Stage.**

You will see the waveform span across the Timeline because you added the frames. The waveform represents the sound in the MP3 file, because sound is not visually represented on the Stage. When you are working with a SWF file that has many different layers, make sure that you create a separate layer for a new sound so that you can find your sounds easily.

Note *Sound, like everything else, must be dragged onto the Stage with a keyframe selected. Because there is already a keyframe the beginning of the file, the sound file will be placed there (there are no other keyframes in the Timeline, after all).*

2. **Click a frame containing the waveform on the Timeline and change the Sync drop-down list in the Property inspector to Event. Then click the Edit button in the Property inspector.**

The sound is set to event in the Flash document after you change the Sync drop-down list. Stream means the sound will play as it downloads. When the sound is set to event, the entire sound has to download before the sound begins to play. When you click the Edit button, the Edit Envelope dialog box opens.

3. **In the Edit Envelope dialog box, click the Zoom Out button on the bottom of the dialog box so you can see more of the waveform.**

Zooming out from the waveform allows you to see more of the sound's waveform. You can use the Zoom In button to get a close up view of the waveform, which is useful when you need to accurately trim the beginning or end of the sound.

4. Add a Fade In Effect from the Effect drop-down list.

Edit Envelope allows you to do a number of things: First, you can select a prebuilt effect from the Effect drop-down list. Second, you can edit that effect, or create one of your own, in the *channels* in the Envelope. The channels represent speakers, really, with the top channel playing in the left speaker and the bottom channel playing in the right. The centerline of the channel is the average volume for the sound.

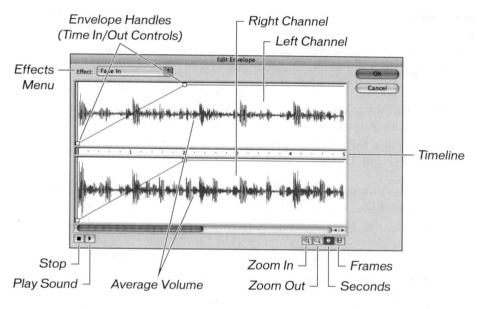

The little white squares are *envelope handles,* also called *Time In/Time Out* controls. You can drag these handles around to change at what point the sounds starts or stops, or to create fade and pan effects. You can add more envelope handles by clicking anywhere on the envelope lines in the channels, and you can remove them by dragging them away. Press the play button to hear any changes you make.

Because you already have what you want, which is a fade in effect, press OK to exit the Edit Envelope and return to the main document.

5. Save your changes before moving on to the next exercise.

Adding Sound to a Button

Most short sounds and many long sounds in Flash files are added directly to a Timeline, whether it is a symbol Timeline or the main document Timeline. When sound is added directly to a Timeline, though, it needs to be told how to behave. It can behave as an *event* sound, it can *start* or *stop* at given keyframes, or it can *stream*.

Event sounds must be completely downloaded before they start to play, and they must play independently of the Timeline after they are told to play. Because of this independence, every time some event causes the sound to play, such as a button being clicked or the playhead entering a keyframe that instructs the sound to play, the entire sound plays. Not only does the entire sound play but it also doesn't care whether it's already playing, it just makes a new instance of the sound and starts playing there, which means that two versions of the same sound are playing at different points in time. Yikes! For these reasons, event sounds are great for short sounds, but not good at all for very long sounds. Event sounds are perfect for button sounds and loops.

Streaming sounds are great for long sounds because they start playing before the file is completely downloaded. When a sound is in a Timeline and is set to stream, the sound must occupy an amount of frames equivalent to the total amount of time it will play over. Then, the animations and visuals on other layers must eventually occupy the same number of frames as the sound. This way, animations and sound can be synchronized.

Tip *Synchronization using streaming sounds forces the Flash SWF file to keep up with the sound because sound is processed on a board other than video. Flash accomplishes this task by kicking out frames to force the animations to keep up.*

In this exercise, you will import a sound file that will be used to add a click to the buttons. The buttons you want to add sound to reside in the Tech Bookstore itself. You will add sounds to `btnProducts`, `btnCompany`, and `btnContact`, which are present on all the pages.

1. Open bookstore10.fla from the TechBookstore folder on your hard drive and save a new version of the file as bookstore11.fla.

A new version of the bookstore FLA file is saved into the TechBookstore folder. You will make only minor modifications to the bookstore in this lesson. You can also open bookstore10.fla from lesson07/start.

2. Find click.wav in the lesson07/assets folder on the book's CD-ROM and save the sound file anywhere on your hard drive.

A WAV file is a commonly used uncompressed audio file format. You will import the WAV file into Flash, in which you can set compression settings for when you export the sound as part of the SWF file. Even though WAV is typically used on the Windows platform, QuickTime can be used to play and import click.wav if you are using a Mac.

Tip *You should always try to import uncompressed sounds whenever possible, such as a WAV or AIFF file, so the sound will not be recompressed when it's made into a SWF file.*

3. Import click.wav into Flash by choosing File › Import › Import to Library. Open the library and locate the sound file you imported (which is still called click.wav) and drag it into the library's media folder.

Choose File > Import > Import to Library from the main menu. Locate the WAV file you just saved from the CD-ROM on your hard drive and click Open (or Import to Library on the Mac). After you import the file, open the library in Flash, locate the click.wav file, and drag it into the media folder in the library.

4. Modify the sound properties by Right-clicking (or Control-clicking on the Mac) and choosing Properties from the contextual menu.

The Properties dialog box opens, in which you can choose how the sound is published when you create a SWF file that includes the WAV. Choose ADPCM from the Compression drop-down list. ADPCM is an excellent compression for playing short sounds on the web. Change the sample rate to **5 kHz**, and the ADPCM Bits to **3**. For this type of sound, these settings result in a high quality, and a .1K file size.

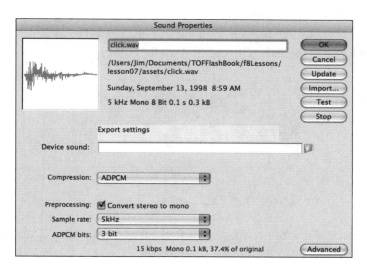

5. Select `btnProducts` from the library and double-click its icon to enter symbol-editing mode. Insert a new layer in the button Timeline and rename it **sound**.

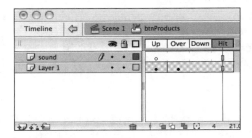

Double-click the button icon in the library so it opens in symbol-editing mode. The `btnProducts` symbol opens in symbol-editing mode so you can add the sound to the button. You will see one layer inside the button that has keyframes on each frame. You need to add a new layer to hold the sound for the button because it's always a good idea to keep sounds on their own layer in the Timeline. So click the Insert New Layer button, and then double-click the new layer's name and rename the new layer **sound**.

6. Add a new keyframe in the Down frame of the sound layer.

Add a new keyframe to the Down frame by selecting the frame and pressing F6. The down frame is "played" whenever the visitor clicks the button. This means the sound will play only when the button is clicked, not when the visitor rolls over the button.

7. Select the new keyframe on the Down frame and drag the click.wav sound from the library onto the Stage.

The sound, which is a subtle short click sound, is added to the Down state for the button when you drag it over to the Stage. This means when the button is clicked, the sound will play.

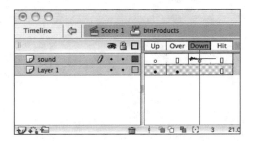

A waveform is seen in the frame, which indicates that a sound is located on the Timeline. You won't see a visual representation of the sound on the Stage, and if there are no frames after the keyframe the sound is in, you will barely see the waveform. This is one of the reasons it is a best practice to keep your sounds on their own layers; as was mentioned previously, it makes them easier to find!

8. Repeat the process, adding the same sound to the `btnCompany` and `btnContact` on the main Stage. When you are finished, lock the buttons layer again.

After you have added the sound to the `btnProducts` instance, press Scene 1 in the edit bar to return to the main Stage. Double-click each `btnCompany` and `btnContact` in the library, then add new layers and drag the click sound onto a new keyframe on the down frame, just as you did for `btnProducts`.

9. Test the sound with Enable Simple Buttons.

If you want to test the button to hear the sound you added play, select Control > Enable Simple Buttons. Make sure that the buttons layer is visible and then press `btnProducts`, `btnCompany`, and `btnContact`. Enable Simple Buttons will make your buttons behave mostly as they would in the final SWF, so this is an ideal way to test the button sound.

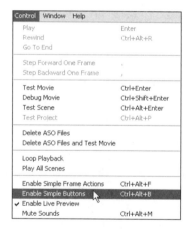

When you are finished, select Control > Enable Simple Buttons to turn the feature off. You cannot move or select your buttons when Enable Simple Buttons is active. Make sure to hide your buttons layer again.

10. Save your work.

You have now added the first sound effects to the bookstore.

Importing Video into Flash

Now that you have imported some audio into the FLA file, it's time to switch gears and add some video to a FLA file. Flash 8 Basic allows you not only to import and embed video but also to do some very simple edits to the video as you import it. You can edit the single video file into several smaller clips if you like or bring the whole thing in without editing. Either way, you have a lot of control over the compression (or export) settings for the video.

A critical thing to consider before you import video is how much control you have over editing and compression prior to or during import. The more control you have typically means the better compression you can manage to achieve while still balancing file size with an acceptable quality. However, even with adequate control over compression (and a good codec), video can still be very large because of the amount of data contained in every single frame. Consider the following points about video before you start to edit or compress it:

- *Trim your video.* Remember that blank areas at the beginning and end of the footage add to the file size, so make sure that you use Flash's editing features during the Video Import Wizard (used in the following exercises) to trim off any extra video at the beginning and end if you haven't already trimmed it prior to import.

- *Test your settings.* If file size is very important, you should try out different import settings and quality levels. All video footage is different; it compresses and decompresses differently, depending on factors such as color, movement, and effects. If your video looks great when you import it, try changing the settings and compress the original file a bit more (perhaps by using a lower-quality setting or fewer video keyframes). It might still look great, but can end up importing with a smaller file size.

- *Limit fading, noise, and movement if possible.* Fading includes fading in and out and also refers to one clip of video fading into another (known as cross-fading—something you might use if you have edited your video in another program). Noise refers to the speckles over each frame you might see if your footage is dimly lit, and movement (such as a tree blowing in the wind) similarly involves a lot of pixels moving. All these factors usually mean that the footage will be a larger file size. Two video clips that are the same frame size and length—and taken with the same camera—can be a different file size depending on these factors. The footage is also difficult to compress, usually meaning that you need to use more keyframes and a higher-quality setting.

If you cannot avoid using fades or movement, or are having a lot of noise in your footage, remember to add more video keyframes when you compress the clip (you'll notice a setting for keyframes when you work with compression later on). The more keyframes you add, the better appearance your video has. However, the clip will also be a larger file size after it's compressed.

Avoid recompressing video that has already been compressed. Every time you recompress your video, more artifacting occurs, and the quality decreases. Artifacting means you will see blocks and pixilation in the video, which looks bad and of low quality. Because your original footage is already compressed, it probably contains "residue" of blockiness, so this throws off the second compression, the quality level decreases, and more of this blockiness occurs. Always try to compress from a video file with the least amount of compression.

Tip *When you are working with video on a Timeline, remember that it is different from a Flash Timeline. If you're working with normal video imported directly into Flash, you cannot add code or keyframes within the video itself (although you can insert the video into a movie clip and add ActionScript to that).*

For this exercise, you will import a video that you will use for the Tour page of the Tech Bookstore site. Following this exercise, you need to import a few other videos, so you will need to revisit this exercise when you do so (unless you remember all the steps!).

1. Create a new file called video1.fla and save it in your TechBookstore folder on your hard drive. Change the Stage Size to 320 x 179.

You will embed videos into Flash and then publish them. In a later lesson, you will dynamically load the SWF files that you are producing, so you want the Stage size and the video dimensions to match. 320 wide by 179 high are the width and height of the MOV files you will import.

2. Find video1.mov in the lesson07/assets folder on this book's CD-ROM and copy the file into your TechBookstore folder on your hard drive. Change the fps to 15 in video1.fla.

You must have QuickTime 4 or greater on the Mac or DirectX 7 or greater on the PC to import video. Choose video1.mov from the lesson07/assets folder on the CD-ROM and copy it to your hard drive.

Note *This video file does not have any audio. You can expect to see a warning or alert in relation to this. You will be using the audio that was imported earlier to go along with the video files. If you were to import a video with sound, you could not hear it when working with your document in the authoring environment. You could hear it only when you test your document or publish the SWF file.*

Change the fps setting for video1.fla to 15 using the Property inspector.

3. Choose File > Import > Import Video and find video1.mov on your hard drive.

When you open the Import Video dialog box, you are placed in the Select Video section.

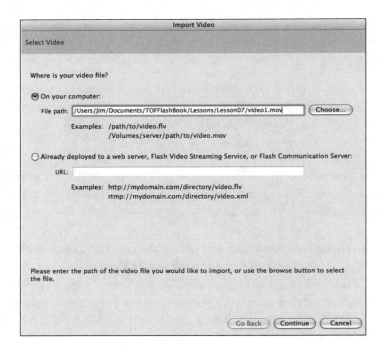

The Select Video section enables you to import a video file already on your computer or point to a video file already uploaded to a web server. The dialog box is more or less a wizard that, once you've chosen an import option, presents you with different steps and different choices to make about how you want to use video at each point. You will actually physically import video to the document Timeline, which embeds it in the final SWF file.

Note *This book does not treat the FLV format, because the book covers only Flash 8 Basic. Flash 8 Professional contains many components that are specifically designed to work with the FLV format for video.*

Press the Choose button in the Import Video dialog box, select video1.mov on your hard drive in the Import Video dialog box, and then click Open. Press the Continue button to move to the next option.

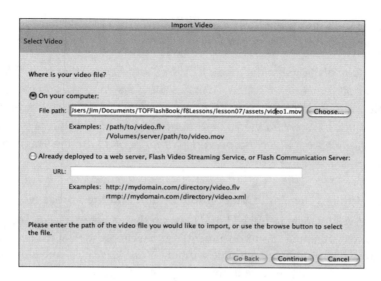

4. Choose to embed the video file in the Flash document and then click Continue.

After you have selected how to bring in your video, you are brought to the Deployment section, which allows you to choose how you will deliver the video file.

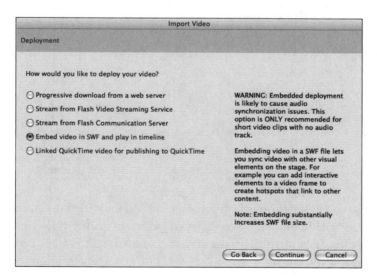

You have the choice to embed, progressively download, stream, or link the video to the SWF file you export. If you embed the file, you can edit the video and manipulate it with

ActionScript or add buttons that can be used to control the video. When you are finished, click the Continue button.

5. **Select the Embed the Entire Video radio button and then press Next.**

The section after deployment is Embedding. Here, you choose how you want your embedded video to be treated within the Flash 8 document. You can choose to treat the embedded video as either a movie clip symbol or a graphic symbol, or just leave it as embedded video. You can also choose to place an instance of the video on the Stage by default. If you deselect that option, be more selective about where the video will be placed within the document.

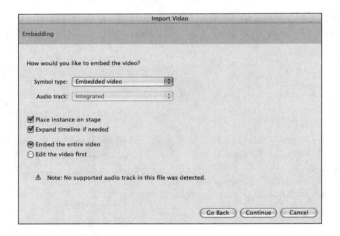

At this point, you can progress directly to compressing and importing the entire video or you can edit the video first. Editing the video allows you to create smaller video clips from a large video, which is incredibly useful. This means that you do not necessarily need to import the entire video and you can drop the footage you don't need and save on some file size.

Tip *In most circumstances, it is more sensible to edit the video before it is imported into Flash with a proper video editor because Flash video editing really is about trimming the video down into smaller pieces. You won't always have that option, though, so don't forget about this feature, even though you don't use it in the book.*

In the next exercise, you will look at Flash 8 Basic encoding settings, which control the file size of the video when it is imported, as well as its quality. Leave the wizard open because you aren't done yet!

Encoding the Video

You have some control over the video compression (or encoding) when you are importing video into a Flash document. Flash doesn't give you as much control as other software might allow you to have; for example, Sorenson Squeeze, which contains the Spark Pro codec, is a fantastic tool for compressing video. Flash uses the Spark codec (the basic version) within Flash, and when exporting video for Flash 8 Player, can use On2 VP6 (which is the default). On2 Technologies produces the codec and has the advantage of having alpha channel support.

> **Tip** *Flat areas of color are more difficult to compress well. These areas are typically the first area of a video clip to go blocky when you encode a video because they are difficult areas to compress. Adding a greater number of keyframes and setting the Quality to a high setting will help, but will have a more dramatic impact on your overall file size.*

1. In the Encoding Section of your Import Video dialog box, press the Advanced button to show encoding options.

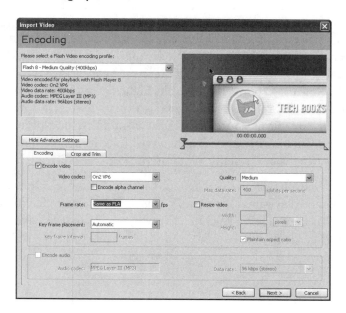

The advanced section gives you more control over how the video will be encoded when it is imported. You have options to change your video encoder, as well as to set keyframe intervals and quality.

2. Select the On2 VP6 video encoder if it is not already selected. Set your frame rate to match the source file and set the keyframe interval to Automatic.

Part of compressing video is determining frame rate and the keyframe interval.

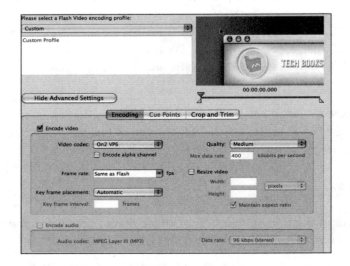

By default, Flash 8 sets the frame rate of the video to be encoded to the same frame rate as the source video you are actually encoding. This is considered the best practice. The frame rate is more of a performance issue than a file size issue because the video must move along its own Timeline based on CPU usage. The higher a frame rate, the more CPU is consumed; however, unless you have a very good reason to do so, it is not recommended to change the frame rate during encoding because it could have unexpected consequences with the final file. If you have plenty of experience with video, you'll know the pitfalls and change the frame rate at your discretion. For our purposes, we will leave it to its default.

The keyframe interval you will set to automatic. In video, keyframes are video frames that contain data. The more keyframes there are in a video file, the more file size you wind up with. By default, Flash will insert a keyframe for every two seconds of video, which is more than ample for this particular file.

3. Set the Quality to Medium.

The quality determines not only the appearance of the video during playback, but also the end file size and playback performance. Generally, the higher the quality, the larger the file, and the more system resources are consumed on the end users computer.

Tip *You have the option of changing the quality to a custom setting by choosing Custom from the drop-down list, and changing the data rate. The lower the data rate, the lower the quality of the file, but also the smaller the file size will be. Experiment. It can't hurt anything!*

4. Press Continue.

At this point, you are brought to a summary page that gives you information about the choices you made. If you change your mind about anything, now is the time to press Go Back and change things.

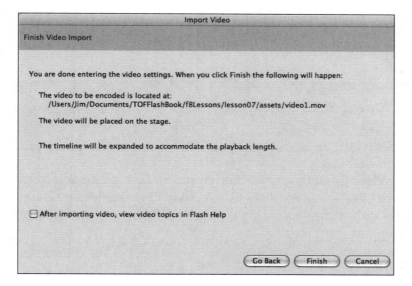

5. Press Finish to import and encode the video. Place the video instance at an *x* and *y* of **0** using the Property inspector.

Because you chose to embed the video and place an instance of it on the main document Timeline, your Timeline is expanded so the video has enough frames to play through. In this way, embedded video is very much like a graphic symbol. If the parent Timeline (in this case, the main document Timeline) isn't moving, the video isn't playing.

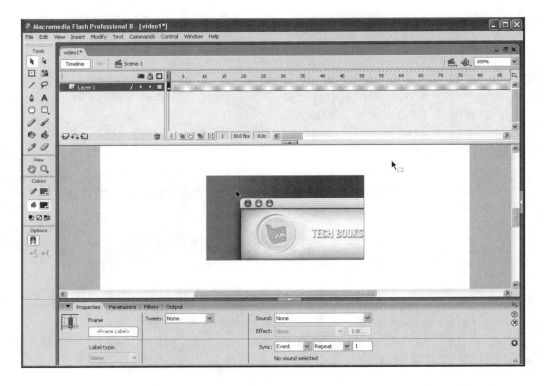

Because your video is now on the main document Timeline, you can control it almost as if it were a movie clip. You can add ActionScript that jumps to labeled frames if you want users to skip ahead to "chapters," or create Stop, Start, Pause functionality using Buttons.

Select the video instance on the Stage, and place it at an *x* and *y* of **0** so that it occupies the entire Stage.

6. Publish the document by selecting File > Publish Settings.

Publishing the file produces a SWF version that contains the video. You will use this SWF file in a later lesson to load the video dynamically.

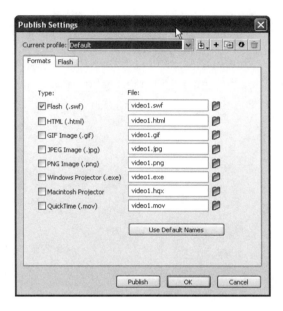

Select File > Publish Settings and then deselect the HTML box in the Formats tab. Publish the file by pressing the Publish button and then press OK. Save and close the file.

7. Repeat the steps from the previous two exercises to produce video2.swf and video3.swf.

Create two new FLA documents, and name them **video2.fla** and **video3.fla** respectively. Import video2.mov and video3.mov into their corresponding files using all the steps in this exercise. Be sure to publish each file and then save and close it before moving on to the next.

What You Have Learned

In this lesson, you have:

- Learned about using media assets on the web (pages 187–190)
- Found out how to import sound files (pages 190–193)
- Customized the sound in Flash (pages 194–195)
- Added sound to three buttons (pages 196–199)
- Imported a video using the Import Video dialog box (pages 200–205)
- Learned more about compression settings in Flash (pages 205–209)

8 Creating Forms Using Components

Macromedia Flash components are small applications that are created using Flash and compiled into SWC files, and there is a large set of them included out of the box. Components range from simple interface elements, such as drop-down lists, to robust and complex applications such as photo galleries, polls, charting engines, or even text editors. Components are very useful because they can be dropped into a Flash document and instantly add functionality to a website merely by changing parameters and sometimes using only a small amount of ActionScript.

This lesson shows you how to use many of the components included in Flash 8 Basic to build forms in which users can enter feedback and fill out a survey. The default UI (user interface) components installed with Flash 8 Basic are extremely useful for building forms quickly. You will learn how to use these components to construct a form in which users can select options and enter data that will be sent to a server.

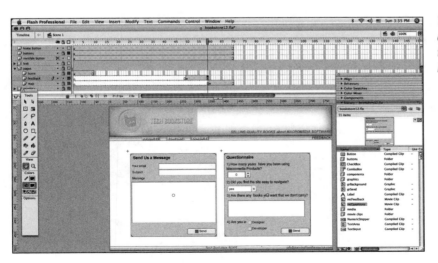

Two forms using components for the Tech Bookstore

What You Will Learn

In this lesson, you will:

- Learn about forms and data
- Discover Flash components
- Create a feedback form
- Add an icon to a Button component
- Use Focus Manager for tabbing

Approximate Time

This lesson takes approximately one hour to complete.

Lesson Files

Media Files:

None

Starting Files:

lesson08/start/bookstore11.fla
lesson08/start/mail_icon.fla

Completed Files:

lesson08/complete/bookstore12.fla

Introducing Forms and Data

Forms are typically a kind of application, sometimes a series of pages, which allow you to collect information from a user. You are probably familiar with forms found on the Internet. You might have filled out a registration form when you activated Flash or given detailed information if you are applying online for a job. You have probably filled out forms to become a member of an online forum. These forms gather the data you enter and submit this data to a server when you click a button indicated for that purpose (think "submit").

Because of the addition of components and server integration, Macromedia Flash 8 Basic enables you to create forms easily and quickly, including search forms, feedback forms, and polls, which ultimately enhances your application (as long as you don't go form crazy that is). You can even build complete website administration sites, as an example, in which you can add, modify, and delete items like news events, or manage your other content. Using a few short lines of ActionScript and components, you or a developer can easily integrate a Flash application with a server-side language, such as ColdFusion, PHP, ASP, or JSP. Server-side languages help you integrate your website with an application server. You might want to integrate with a database, XML, or other forms data (such as a Web Service) that is then used and displayed by the website.

Note *This book is designed to cover only the features found in Flash 8 Basic. However, if you are using Flash 8 Professional or upgrade to Flash 8 Professional at a later date, it is even easier to integrate Flash with these technologies using the Flash Data components. One of those components makes it easier to work with a technology called Flash Remoting, which allows you to pass data back and forth between ColdFusion, ASP, or Java by using ActionScript to enable this data transfer. Flash 8 Professional makes this kind of data transfer easier by allowing you to exchange data with the server without having to write large amounts of ActionScript. Flash Remoting is fast, beautiful, and a wonderful thing. You should check it out!*

Macromedia Flash 8 Basic provides a few other technologies that allow you to easily talk to a server-side language such as XML. XML is a markup language that you use to format data (for example, names, addresses, and phone numbers) and transfer it to other computers, operating systems, or applications such as Flash—where it can be used in various ways. It is a very simple and intuitive way to organize data, although there are simple to very complex ways used to format and use it online. Flash has excellent XML support, meaning that a SWF file can read and parse (turn into an ActionScript data structure that is) XML documents and send XML data to a server, although Flash 8 Professional also offers the option of using a special XMLConnector component to make the communication easier. Flash 8 Basic also comes with a special class called the LoadVars class, which is used to load and send data. You will use the LoadVars class in Lesson 9 to load information and in Lesson 10 to send information from the feedback and questionnaire forms you set create in this lesson.

Introducing Flash Components

You've already learned a little bit about components earlier, and learned that components can help designers add functionality in the SWF file that they might not want to or be able to program using ActionScript. Designers can simply drag and drop components onto the Stage, change a few parameters in the Property inspector, and write a small amount of ActionScript to make the component work in rather complex ways if needed. Components can speed up application development or create elements that can be reused with relative ease.

Note *Components are compiled into SWC files and can be purchased or downloaded for free from the web. Distributing components is quite popular, and you will have no problem finding many to work with by searching online. There are many websites devoted to distributing components. A database of files is available on the Macromedia Exchange, and there are a number of books aimed solely at Flash components.*

The components found in Flash 8 Basic (and additional components in Flash 8 Professional should you upgrade to it) are excellent to use when you are building applications using multiple instances of certain components, like a Button component, throughout the application. If you are using only one component in a specific context and not reusing it after that, know that components add at least 25K of file size when you first drag one in to your interface. This is because the ActionScript necessary to include with any component must be included with the SWF file when it is published. However, because this ActionScript is the same for many of the components in the V2 set, it needs to be included only once, so adding additional kinds of components might not bulk up your SWF at all. This is why it's advantageous to include many components, but not as advantageous if you use only one or two. Some components do not include the same architecture, so additional file size might be added, depending on what components you use. So essentially, when you use one component, you get them all. Take advantage of it!

Flash 8 Basic includes many components with the software, including Button, CheckBox, ComboBox, Label, List, Loader, NumericStepper, ProgressBar, RadioButton, ScrollPane, TextArea, TextInput, and Window.

Flash 8 Professional has additional components, including the Accordion, Alert, DataGrid, DateChooser, DateField, Menu, MenuBar, and Tree components. Flash 8 Professional also has several components for connecting to Web Services and XML files, and Media components allow you to play back and control streaming FLV (Macromedia Flash Video) or MP3 files.

The following list outlines some of the components that are included with Flash 8 Basic. Maximize the Components panel to view a list of the UI component set.

Button: This component is a customizable button that allows you to define a label (the text that is shown on the button's face) and icon (a small graphic). This component is similar to using HTML's input type of Submit or Button, and has a number of built-in visual effects, such as rollover and click effects. Because this component is part of the much broader component class, it can also be bound to other Flash components to make interface elements functionally dependent on each other.

CheckBox: Similar to a check box in an HTML page, this component allows an end user to select an item of information in a form that will ultimately be stored in a database somewhere. The idea behind it is to allow users to select more than one option in a grouping of options (such as asking users what their interests are, what newsletters they want to subscribe to, and the like). You can customize the placement of the label and check box control. It also allows a value of either `true` or `false`.

ComboBox: This component allows users to make a selection from a drop-down list. You can control the list and what each menu item associates to, as well as how many items will display in the menu before it begins to scroll. The drop-down list feature along with the scrolling list feature are the "combo" that makes this component what it is.

Label: This component is a single-line static text field. The text can be changed at runtime using ActionScript. At first glance, it seems to be the least useful of the components; however, it is very important in ensuring that the font used in your labels matches the font used in the drop-down list and text areas of the other components you use.

List: This component is similar to the ComboBox component, except it displays multiple lines of data at once, rather than in a drop-down list that scrolls after a fixed number of lines. The List component allows multiple items to be selected at once so that users can make more than one selection.

Loader: This container component can be used to load SWF files or JPEG, PNG, and GIF images. It can be customized to allow you to easily resize the content that is being loaded to fit the size of the component. Or you can have the component resize itself to fit the contents being loaded. The Loader component itself is not actually visible on the Stage; it's really more of a shell, and its presence is otherwise unknown by the end user.

NumericStepper: You can use this component to select number values. The component is similar to a text input field, but it is restricted to numbers. It also comes with a couple of arrow controls that increment and decrement the current value by a certain number. You can specify minimum and maximum values and also change the increment for the number so that it increases by something like 2's or 5's rather than incrementing by 1.

ProgressBar: This component displays a preloading bar for content that you are loading into a SWF file. It has a built-in feature that tracks the download progress of files loading into something like the Loader component.

RadioButton: This component is similar to radio buttons that you might see on an HTML page; it is used to force the end user to select only one piece of information in a related group. You can group radio buttons so only one button can be selected at one time.

ScrollPane: This component allows you to easily scroll content within a window using horizontal and/or vertical scroll bars. It is useful when you want to load a large amount of content to a small space and help you show a greater amount of content in a limited space.

TextArea: This component is a text field that includes scroll bars. This component is a multiline editable text field, and can be used either to display information or to collect information from an end user. You can load plain or formatted text into this field, which will show scroll bars when the text exceeds the display area.

TextInput: This component creates a single-line text field. A user can type text into the field, which can be collected and used in a document or sent to a server by using ActionScript. You can specify the Text Input component as a password field that replaces the characters the user types with dots, so that someone looking over their shoulder doesn't actually see the text they are typing.

Window: This component is a draggable floating window that includes a title bar and button that is used to close the window. It is designed to work much the same way as an HTML pop-up window, with similar controls.

The following exercise will explore a few of the more common UI components. You will also learn how to change component parameters using both the Property inspector and the Component inspector panel.

Building the Feedback Form

In this exercise, you will create a new movie clip that adds a feedback form to the Contact page of the Tech Bookstore website. The feedback form gathers information from a visitor and then sends it to a server, which will email the information to you. That part of the feedback form will be covered in Lesson 10. Here, you create the visual part of the feedback form.

1. Open bookstore11.fla from the TechBookstore folder on your hard drive and save it as bookstore12.fla. Create a new movie clip by choosing Insert > New Symbol and call it mcFeedback. Rename Layer 1 to background.

Alternatively, you can open bookstore12.fla from the lesson08/start folder on the CD-ROM. Insert a new movie clip symbol. After you create the new movie clip called mcFeedback, rename Layer 1 to **background**.

2. Draw a rectangle on the Stage with a fill color of #E7E7E7 and a one-pixel black stroke. Add some text to the background. Lock the background layer.

Select the Rectangle tool from the Tools panel, set the Fill color to #E7E7E7, and set the Stroke color to #000000 (black). Set the drawing model to Object drawing. Press the Set Corner Radius button in the options area of the Tools panel and set the corner radius to **5** points. Draw a rectangle on the Stage and resize it by using the Property inspector.

Double-click the rectangle to select the fill and stroke and maximize the Property inspector. Set the width to **300** px and the height to **300** px. With the object still selected, press F8 to convert the object to a graphic symbol and name it **grBackground**. Move the rectangle to the *x* and *y* coordinates of **10, 10**.

Finally, add a title at the top of the form on the background layer. Select the Text tool and set the Text type to Static, choose Arial for the font, select a black fill color, select a font size of 14 points, select Anti-alias for readability as the font-rendering method, and make the text bold.

Click the Stage and type **Send us a message**. Position the text field near the upper-left corner of the rectangle on the background layer. When you finish changing the coordinates and adding the static text, the Stage will look similar to the figure following. Lock the background layer when you're finished.

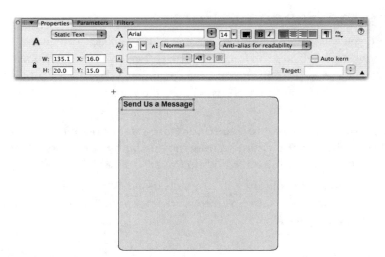

3. Insert a new layer and then drag the Label component onto the Stage.

The Label component allows you to add captions to text fields. Although you can create labels using the Text tool, using Label instances allows you to keep a consistent look among your components and you can make your application accessible to visually impaired visitors.

Create a new layer and rename the layer **form**. Open the Components panel and locate the Label component from the UI Components folder. Drag three instances of the Label component onto the Stage near the left edge of the rectangle you created in Step 2.

4. Add custom text for each Label instance on the Stage.

Select the first Label instance on the Stage and open the Property inspector. In the Property inspector, make sure the Parameters tab is active and click on the text parameter. Enter **Your email** for the text parameter and press Enter or Return. The Stage immediately updates the component's appearance.

Tip *You can also maximize the Component inspector panel and change the label's text in the inspector. It contains options that are not available in the Property inspector and are only otherwise accessible using ActionScript.*

Select the second Label instance, change the text parameter to **Subject** and press Enter. Then change the third Label instance's text parameter to **Message**.

5. Change the *x* and *y* coordinates of the `Your email`, `Subject`, and `Message` Label instances on the Stage using the Property inspector.

Select the `Your email` Label instance on the Stage and use the Property inspector or Info panel to change the *x* coordinate to **13** and the *y* coordinate to **44**. Select the Label instance for `Subject` and change the *x* coordinate to **13** and the *y* coordinate to **66**. Change the `Message` label to an *x* coordinate of **13** and a *y* coordinate of **88**.

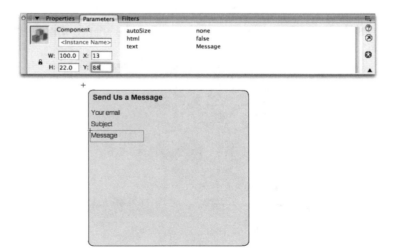

6. Drag two instances of the TextInput component onto the Stage. Then change the width of both instances using the Property inspector.

The TextInput component is similar to using the Text tool and setting the Text type to Input Text. It replicates a text input form field on an HTML page or on your operating system. Each kind of text input field allows a user to input values and data that can then be used in your application.

The TextInput component is limited to displaying only a single line of text. Using the Property inspector, you can set whether or not the text in the component can be modified, whether it is a password (the characters are replaced by symbols such as dots), or whether default text is entered into the field when the page loads. If you maximize the Component inspector panel, you will see additional parameters that can be used to modify the component. By using the Component inspector panel you can set a maximum number of characters that can be entered into the component instance, whether or not certain characters are accepted, and whether the component is enabled or even visible on the Stage.

Drag two instances of the TextInput component onto the Stage. Maximize the Property inspector and enter **tiEmail** into the <Instance Name> field. Resize the component's width by entering **200** into the width field. You can maintain the default instance height of 22 pixels.

Select the second copy of the TextInput component on the Stage and type in an instance name of **tiSubject**. Change the instance's width to **200**, as you did with the previous instance.

7. Position the TextInput instances on the Stage.

With the Property inspector still maximized, select the tiEmail instance on the Stage. Change the *x* coordinate to **108** pixels and the *y* coordinate to **44** pixels, which will align the TextInput instance with the Your email label that was created earlier. Change the *x* coordinate of tiSubject to **108** pixels and the *y* coordinate to **66** pixels so it is aligned with the Subject label.

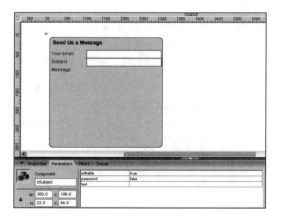

8. Add an instance of the TextArea component to the Stage, change its dimensions, and position the instance among the other elements already on the Stage. Give the new instance an instance name of **taMessage**.

The TextArea component is a multiline (more than one line of text) version of the TextInput component, and it has a few features that are quite useful. First and foremost, you have the ability to format text that is displayed in the component using Cascading Style Sheets (CSS), which allows you to display text that is much nicer than was possible in previous versions of Flash. Flash has HTML formatting support built into the text area component as well, and there are more tags now supported than there used to be. Most notably, HTML support also includes embedded JPEG, PNG, and GIF images by using the <img> tag. Because TextArea is a multiline component, you can also control word wrapping. But the best thing about the component is this: when there is more text than there is component to display it, a scrollbar appears! This is enough to make many designers and developers weep with joy.

Drag an instance of the TextArea component onto the Stage. Position at the *x* and *y* coordinate of **13** and **110** pixels, respectively, using the Property inspector. While you're at it, set the width of the component to **295** pixels and the height to **150** pixels so the Stage matches the following figure. Then type in an instance name of **taMessage** into the Property inspector.

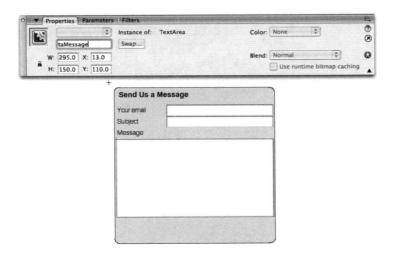

Note *You may have noticed the naming convention you are using prefixes each instance name with ti for Text Input and ta for Text Area. This convention makes it easy to identify which kind of component you are referencing when you are writing or viewing ActionScript. Very often, when you are working with ActionScript, you don't see the objects on the Stage. This naming convention makes it easy to figure out what they are.*

Select the TextArea component on the Stage and open the Component inspector panel. The Parameters tab in the Component inspector panel allows you to modify additional properties of the TextArea component which the Property inspector doesn't display. The Component inspector panel allows you to limit the total number of characters that can be entered into the TextArea by entering a number into the maxChars parameter. You can also disable word wrapping, restrict which characters can be entered into the TextArea, mask the text input as a password, or disable the TextArea so that users cannot enter any text.

You do not need to modify any of these parameters; however, it helps to remember what parameters are available because you will work with and modify them in upcoming lessons.

9. Save the changes you made to the file.

You will continue building the form in the following exercise, except that you will be working exclusively with the Button component in the next steps. Make sure that your changes are saved before moving on.

Using the Button Component

You can use the Button component in Flash for anything you can image buttons to do, such as to submit form data when the button instance is clicked, among other things. Button component instances can be used to trigger events written with ActionScript just like button symbols, such as opening a new browser window and web page. So why use a Button component? Well, first of all, you don't have to build it…it's ready-made. Second of all, there are many properties of the Button component that you can control using ActionScript, when you've finally been converted to a script-nerd (evil laughter here), such as the label text or its rollover color. You cannot programmatically control these properties with button *symbols*.

This exercise continues where you left off in the previous exercise.

1. In bookstore12.fla, open `mcFeedback` in symbol-editing mode, and then select Frame 1 of the form layer.

You probably still have bookstore12.fla open in Flash. Find `mcFeedback` in the library, and double-click the movie clip to open in symbol-editing mode. Then select Frame 1 of the form layer inside the movie clip.

2. Add a Button component to the Stage by dragging it from the Components panel and dropping it onto the Stage. Change the text label on the Button instance.

With the form layer still selected, drag an instance of the Button component from the Components panel on to the Stage. Select the instance you just added, maximize the Property inspector, and type **bSend** into the `<Instance Name>` field. Then select the Parameters tab.

Change the text on the button from the default Button to **Send** by typing in the new value of the label parameter. The Button instance's label (the text on the Button's face) changes after you change the value in this parameter and press Enter.

3. Change the position of the Button instance on the Stage to the lower-right corner of the rectangle graphic.

Move the Button instance to an *x* and *y* coordinate of **207** and **280** pixels, respectively. Use the W and H text fields in the Property inspector to change the location of the instance. The position of the instance is moved to the lower-right corner of the rectangle graphic on the Stage. Leave the dimensions of the button at 100 pixels wide by 22 pixels high.

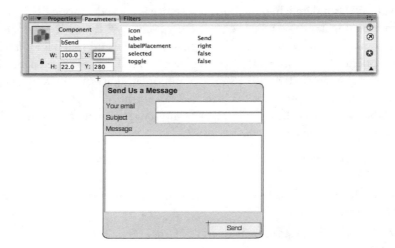

4. Import an icon graphic for the Button instance into a new graphic symbol.

You can customize the Button component by linking an icon to the instance. The icon will be displayed on the face of the Button instance, which allows you to add a nice personal touch to the form and make the form a bit more usable. The icon must be a graphic or movie clip symbol in the library, and it must have a *linkage identifier*, which you need to link to the Button component instance.

Tip *Included on the CD-ROM in the finished bookstore12.fla file is an icon that you can use with the Send button. Alternatively, you could create your own custom graphic or movie clip in Flash that could be used instead.*

Open mail_icon.fla from the lesson08/start folder on the CD-ROM by selecting File > Import > Open External Library, and drag the send_gr graphic symbol from the external library into the bookstore12.fla library. The drawing that is made inside this graphic has its *x* coordinate and *y* coordinate set to 0 and 0, respectively.

5. Rename the symbol to **grSend** to be consistent with your current naming convention, and add a Linkage Identifier to the **grSend** symbol in the library.

Many problems that people experience in Flash are due to two things: lack of planning and lack of consistency. In this circumstance, we are importing a graphic symbol created by a different designer who is using a naming convention other than what you are using. Changing the symbol's name in the document library ensures that your naming conventions are still consistent. Change the symbol's name by double-clicking the name send_gr in the library, and typing **grSend** in its place.

Second, before you can use the symbol as a Button icon, you have to assign it a name so Flash can link it to the Button component instance. By using the Linkage Properties dialog box, you can assign a Linkage Identifier to the symbol, which allows Flash to uniquely identify the symbol so you can use it in the SWF file.

In the document library for bookstore12.fla, locate the grSend symbol you just renamed. Right-click (or Control-click on OS X) the grSend symbol in the library and select Linkage from the contextual menu. The Linkage Properties dialog box opens.

In the Linkage Properties dialog box, select the Export for ActionScript check box in the Linkage section of the dialog box, which allows you to enter an identifier in the text fields at the top of the window. grSend should show in the Identifier field by default. If not, enter **grSend** into the Identifier field and leave the AS 2.0 Class field empty. Click the OK button to return to the Stage.

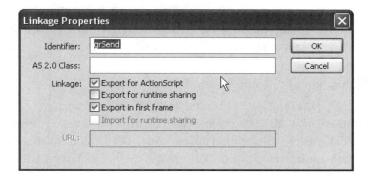

6. Add an icon to the Button component instance.

Select the Button component instance in the lower-right corner of the Stage and maximize the Property inspector. Enter the Linkage Identifier, **grSend**, into the icon parameter in the Parameters tab of the Property inspector. The Linkage Identifier is what ActionScript uses to find objects from the document library when the SWF file is running. It is case sensitive, so it's important to type the name into the icon parameter exactly the same way as it appears in the Linkage dialog box. When you finish, you will notice a grey box on the left side of the Send label of the Button instance.

This is where the icon will be located when you publish the SWF file. The icon will not show up in the authoring environment. You need to test the SWF file to view the icon on the instance, but because you do not yet have an instance of this movie clip on the Stage, you will not see anything relating to the form if you test now.

7. Modify the position of the icon on the Button instance.

If you want to change the location of the icon on the Button instance, you can modify the value for labelPlacement in the Property inspector. By default, the value for labelPlacement is set to right, which means that the label appears on the right side of the icon. If you set the labelPlacement parameter to top or bottom, you might need to resize the button's dimensions on the Stage in order to see both the icon and the label.

8. Insert a new layer above the form layer and call it **labels**. Then insert a new layer above labels and rename it **actions**. Select Frame 20 and press F5 for all the layers so they extend to Frame 20. Then insert a keyframe on the actions and labels layer at Frame 10, and add frame labels at Frames 1 and 10.

Select the form layer and click the Insert Layer button in the Timeline to insert a new layer, and rename it **labels**. With the new labels layer still selected, click the Insert Layer button again, and rename the new layer **actions**. When you have the new layers created, press F5 on Frame 20 for all four layers. Then insert a new keyframe on Frame 10 on both the labels and actions layers. Press F6 to insert new keyframes.

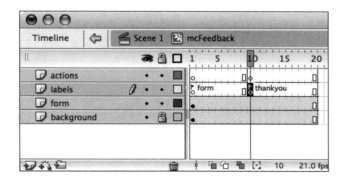

Select the keyframe on Frame 1 of the labels layer and type **form** into the <Frame Label> field in the Property inspector. Then select the keyframe on Frame 10 and type **thankyou** into the <Frame Label> field.

9. Insert a blank keyframe at Frame 10 on the form layer. Add some text somewhere within the grBackground graphic that says "Thank you for your feedback" or similar. Drag a Button component and place it below the text.

Select Frame 10 and then choose Insert > Timeline > Blank Keyframe from the main menu. Select the Text tool, set the text to static and whatever font you choose, and enter a message saying that the feedback has been sent. When you're finished, open the Components panel and drag an instance of the Button component onto the Stage. Change the button's label to **Back** using the Property inspector, set the Instance name to **bBack**, and position the button at **207** *x* and **280** *y*, so that it matches the position of the Send button.

With the Button component instance still selected, expand the Actions panel and switch to Script Assist mode if you are not already in it. In the Actions toolbox, expand Global Functions, Timeline Control, and double-click the goto action. In the parameters, choose the Go to and Stop radio button. From the Type drop-down list, select Frame Label. In the Frame drop-down list, select form.

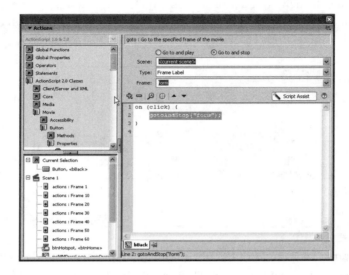

You will not add the ActionScript for the instance bSend yet. You will add that ActionScript in the next lesson.

Note *The triggering event in your Actions panel is* on(click)*. Button components have different events that they can respond to, another thing that separates them from Button symbols. A Button symbol would have had a triggering event of* on(release)*, which is the same thing as* on(click)*. Both events mean that someone has clicked and let go of the mouse button.*

10. **Save the changes you made to the feedback form and return to the main Stage.**

Save bookstore12.fla in the TechBookstore folder after you finish positioning elements on the Stage and you are pleased with the way the icon looks. You will continue working with this file in the next exercise that builds a second form using more components.

Building a Questionnaire Using Flash

In the following exercise, you will create a questionnaire that users will fill out and send to the server by clicking a button. This questionnaire uses several new components not yet covered in this lesson. Because Flash installs many default user interface components, it is very easy to create forms such as these and have them working in no time. You will add ActionScript in Lesson 10 that will collect and send the information out to a server.

The NumericStepper is a cool little component that allows your visitors to click through an ordered set of numbers so they can do things like specify how many giant cookies they want to add to their shopping cart (if you're building a website that sells cookies of course. You should. Cookies are delightful). The component is a text field showing a number in a text field that's next to small arrowed buttons. When these buttons are clicked, the numbers either step up or down through the set of numbers. You can set the minimum, the maximum, and the interval amount between each number. The NumericStepper handles only numeric data.

The ComboBox allows users to make a selection from a drop-down list (Chocolate Chip, Sugar, or Peanut Butter cookies? Oh to decide.). You can set a ComboBox to editable, which means that instead of making a selection from the menu, a user can type a selection into a text field first or select an option from the menu instead. You can set the text that is displayed in the drop-down list and the associated data for that text and write ActionScript so something occurs when a selection is made.

1. Open bookstore12.fla if it isn't already open. Duplicate the symbol mcFeedback and name the new symbol **mcQuestions**. Double-click its type icon in the library to enter symbol-editing mode.

mcQuestions will have the same general structure as mcFeedback. Its Timeline will be the same, its background will be the same, and it will have a send and back button with the same ActionScripts attached to them. Duplicating a symbol creates an exact copy of the symbol in the library. You can edit that copy to focus only on what will change inside the symbol definition and leave the unchanging parts alone. In short, you're saving yourself some time, so you can get back to whatever hokey movie you were watching on television as quickly as you can. Lazy bones.

Duplicate the mcFeedback symbol by right clicking (Control-clicking on OS X) the symbol and choosing Duplicate from the context menu. In the Duplicate Symbol dialog box, name the new symbol **mcQuestions**. Double-click mcQuestions to enter symbol-editing mode.

2. Change the text Send Us a Message to **Questionnaire** and delete all the components but the Button component from the Stage.

With the Selection tool, double-click on the text "Send us a message." Change the text to read **Questionnaire**. Remove the Label, TextInput, and TextArea components from the Stage. Leave the Button component instance where it is.

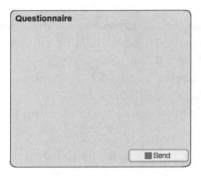

3. Add text fields to the form layer.

Right-click (or Control-click on OS X) the form layer and choose Lock Others from the context menu. Select the Text tool from the Tools panel and change the text type to Static Text in the Property inspector. Choose Arial for the font, a font size of 12 points, black for the fill color, and set the font rendering method to Anti-alias for readability. With the Text tool still selected, click and drag on the Stage to create a fixed-width text box just under the width of the grBackground graphic symbol. Type in the following text: **1) How many years have you been using Macromedia Products?** Don't worry about the position of the text on the Stage right now because you will modify the layout later in this exercise.

Add three more Static text fields to the Stage with the following text: **2) Did you find the site easy to navigate?**; **3) Are there any books you want that we don't carry?**; and **4) Are you a:**

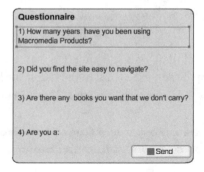

4. Select the form layer and add the NumericStepper, ComboBox, TextArea, Button and CheckBox components to the Stage.

Select the form layer and maximize the Components panel. Add one instance of the following components to the Stage: NumericStepper, ComboBox, TextArea, Button. Then add two instances of the CheckBox component. Just drag the component from the Components panel onto the form layer, as you did in the previous exercise.

Arrange the component instances so that they appear roughly the same as in the following figure. Resize your text fields if necessary.

Note *Resizing the text field by using the Info panel or Property inspector can lead to text that is distorted. You must use the drag handles for the text field to resize the text field properly.*

5. Modify the parameters of the NumericStepper component using the Component inspector panel.

Select the NumericStepper component on the Stage using the Selection tool. Position it near the bottom-left corner of the first question. Using the Property inspector, you can modify the following: the maximum and minimum range that can be used in the NumericStepper, the stepSize that controls the amount that the current value will be incremented or decremented when the user presses the up or down button in the component instance, and the value parameter that defines the current or starting value of the component.

Maximize or open the Property inspector, and make sure you have the Parameters tab selected. Set the minimum parameter to **0** and the maximum value to **10**.

6. Modify the parameters of the ComboBox component instance on the Stage.

With the ComboBox component selected on the Stage, maximize the Property inspector. Double-click on the data parameter in the Property inspector, and the Values dialog box appears. This is where you can enter new values for the ComboBox component.

Click the plus (+) button at the top of the dialog box twice to add two new values. Change the first value to **1**, change the second value to **0**, and then press OK to close the dialog box and return to the Stage.

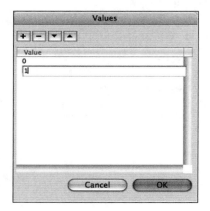

This time, double-click the label parameter in the Property inspector to open the Values dialog box again. You are adding labels that will correspond to the data values you added earlier. Add two values, change the top value to **Yes**, change the bottom value to **No**, and click the OK button to return to the Stage.

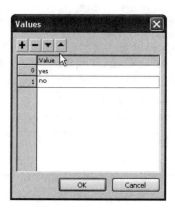

Tip *When you are adding values, you must be careful to make sure that the values in the data property correspond to the values in the labels property or your users may experience unexpected results.*

7. Change the parameters of the CheckBox component instances on the Stage.

Select the CheckBox component on the Stage and change the label parameter to **Designer** in the Property inspector. Move the second CheckBox component to the right of the Developer check box and change the label to **Developer** in the Property inspector. If you want to move the label on the other side of the check box, you can use the Property inspector and change the label Placement from right to left.

Note *Now that you have placed all the questions on the Stage, you might want to select all the instances along the left side of the rectangle and use the Align panel to line them up with precision. Make sure that the To Stage button is deselected first, so they align to the other instances and not to the left side of the Stage.*

8. Save your changes.

Because you duplicated the mcFeedback symbol, you do not need to do anything further. The mcFeedback and mcQuestions forms both have send and back buttons that work with the exact same ActionScript. You've already got it from the duplication process, so you don't need to go back and add it again.

In the next exercise, you will set a tab order for the components in the mcFeedback form, and you will also set keyboard focus to tiEmail by default when the form first appears.

Using the Focus Manager

All the components in Flash 8 Basic automatically support the FocusManager class, which can be used for specifying a tabbing order for components, or to disable the capability to tab to a form object altogether. Tabbing is very useful for visitors who prefer to navigate forms by tabbing, and vital for visually impaired users who partially rely on tabbing through forms as their primary or only mode of navigation. The FocusManager class is all ActionScript, which means that you will have to write some of your own script to use it. Not to panic, it's really not so tough, once you get used to it. The script you write works in conjunction with a property of most user interface components called tabIndex. With this property, you specify numbers in the order you want the keyboard to jump to when a user hits the tab key.

Note *It is important to remember that there is no user interface control used to define the properties and methods of the Focus Manager, so you have to enter ActionScript in the Actions panel in order to set tab order or disable tabbing to items.*

In this exercise, you will add tabbing to the bookstore12.fla file you created earlier.

1. Open bookstore12.fla, which is located in the TechBookstore folder. Double-click mcFeedback to enter symbol-editing mode and select Frame 1 of the actions layer inside the movie clip.

Open the bookstore12.fla document saved in the TechBookstore folder and select Frame 1 of the actions layer after you have double-clicked mcFeedback and entered symbol-editing mode.

2. Define the tabbing order using ActionScript.

The feedback form has four primary elements in it: the From email address, the Subject, the Message TextArea, and the Send button, which sends the feedback to the server. You will define the tabbing order of the text fields and button from top to bottom, so the tiEmail instance will have a tab index of 1, tiSubject will have a tab index of 2, taMessage will have a tab index of 3, and bSend will have a tab index of 4.

Maximize or open the Actions panel (F9). You will not use Script Assist for this exercise, so turn it off by pressing the Script Assist button. Add the following code in Frame 1 of the actions layer:

```
tiEmail.tabIndex = 1;
tiSubject.tabIndex = 2;
taMessage.tabIndex = 3;
bSend.tabIndex = 4;
```

When you test the code in a browser later on, you must test the document in a web browser by pressing F12 on your keyboard.

Note *You can't test the FocusManager quite yet—until you add the scripts to enable the navigation in Lesson 10. You can however, copy and paste this ActionScript and your components into a new Flash document if you want to test this out now.*

When you press Tab a few times, the cursor will tab through each of the instances on the Stage. After the focus reaches the bSend Button component, if you press Tab again it sets the focus to the tiEmail instance because there are no items with a higher tab order than the bSend, so it returns to the first item in the tab index.

Tip *Tabbed movie clips and button symbols display with a yellow box around the instance. Components display the halo color. Remember that the halo is the green (default color) glow around the components that you see when you mouse over them.*

Note *To use tabbing, the SWF file must be viewed in a browser window. Tabbing does not work with movie clips or buttons in the testing environment or in a SWF file playing in a stand-alone Player.*

3. Set a default form button using ActionScript.

You can also set a default button instance, which simulates being clicked if a user presses the Enter or Return key while filling out the form (unless you are within the TextArea component). Being able to press the Enter key is similar to a behavior in HTML when you are filling out forms. In the Actions panel, add the following line of code to the bottom of the existing ActionScript:

```
focusManager.defaultPushButton = bSend;
```

This snippet of code sets the default push button to bSend (which happens to be the only button in the document). If a user presses Enter while they are filling out a form, the click event handler will be triggered for the sent_btn button instance. Clicking the Send button will have no effect on the SWF file until some ActionScript is added to the FLA file in the next lesson.

4. Set form focus on the tiEmail instance.

Imagine that you wanted to set the focus to a certain form instance when the Flash SWF loads into the Tech Bookstore. This is a little bit more user-friendly for your visitors because they won't have to reach for the mouse and click a form field before being able to type in their e-mail address.

Add the following line of ActionScript below the existing code into the Actions panel:

```
focusManager.setFocus(tiEmail);
```

This line of code sets the current focus to the tiEmail instance on the Stage. This method could also become extremely useful if you had form validation in the SWF file and wanted to set the form focus to a TextInput field that was left blank or wasn't a valid value. You could then send the user an alert and also set the focus for the empty text field that needs their attention.

5. Clean up the Library.

You have added a lot of new symbols to the bookstore, so you should take a moment to open and re-organize the Library. Move all the components you added into the components folder. You will also have a graphic, movie clips, and sounds in there. Move the movie clips into the movie clip folder and the sounds into the media folder.

6. Place the new movie clips on a new layer on the Stage. Give each of the movie clips instance names of **mcFeedbackForm** and **mcQuestionForm**.

Insert a new layer on the Timeline above map and rename the new layer **feedback**. Insert a new keyframe on the feedback layer below the feedback label (Frame 50) on the Timeline. Remove all the frames on the layer greater than Frame 60 by selecting them, Right-clicking (or Control-clicking) and choosing Remove Frames from the contextual menu.

Open the library, locate the mcFeedback and mcQuestions symbols, and drag them onto this new layer. Place the two symbols on the empty part of the Stage and align the two instances horizontally, similar to the following figure:

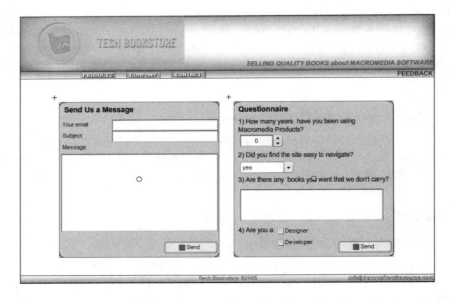

Select the feedback form and enter **mcFeedbackForm** into the Property inspector for its instance name. Select the questionnaire and type in **mcQuestionsForm** into the Property inspector.

7. Save the changes you have made to the document.

Choose File > Save to save all the changes you have made to the FLA file. In Lesson 10, you will work more with ActionScript to send information out of the forms and into an server.

What You Have Learned

In this lesson, you have:

- Learned more about forms and data (pages 212–213)
- Discovered the Flash UI component set (pages 214–217)
- Created a feedback form (pages 217–222)
- Used the Button component (pages 223–228)
- Created a questionnaire (pages 228–233)
- Discovered how to use the Focus Manager (pages 233–236)

9 Learning ActionScript Basics

Just because you have Macromedia Flash 8 Basic doesn't mean that you don't have access to one of the most powerful features of Flash. ActionScript is what you use to "make things go," and without it, well, your Flash applications aren't really applications. They're more like pictures at an exhibition: Very nice to look at, but what do they do? Well, if they had ActionScript, they would be calculating sales tax, or reading in information from text fields, or streaming MP3 files from some other location through the Flash Player, and any number of super-cool things that go beyond the scope of just looking pretty.

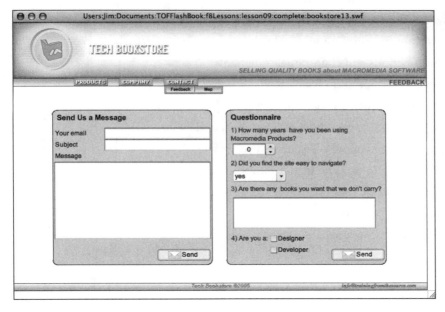

ActionScript adds life to the Tech Bookstore!

If the term ActionScript makes you tremble, fear not. ActionScript really is about bossing things around. You use it to tell movie clips what to do, to call that neighbor-kid LoadVars and tell him to go get some things for you at the local text file. It's about organizing things. In short, it's nothing radically different from what you do when you give your spouse a shopping list before you send him to the store (men, we know that means us because we can't be trusted at the store alone without a list). You're telling things what to do, in what order, and how. So if you're bossy, ActionScript will be a breeze.

In this lesson, you'll use ActionScript to load in external data. You'll use ActionScript to send data out of Flash as well. What's more, you'll finally get to animate your menus. You won't be using Script Assist in this lesson, so warm up your fingers; you'll have to type ActionScript on your own. In every circumstance, though, you'll see that most tasks are very similar to one another, and you should get the hang of it in no time.

What You Will Learn

In this lesson, you will:

- Learn about ActionScript 2.0
- Learn about objects, methods, and properties
- Learn how to use strict typing with variables
- Learn how to use code hinting to speed up writing ActionScript
- Learn about functions and conditional statements
- Learn about using scope and variables
- Learn more about _root, _parent, and levels
- Work with the LoadVars object to send and retrieve data
- Use events, event handlers, and listeners in your code
- Add CSS formatting to text and load it into a document
- Build the Catalog, Reviews, News, and Home pages
- Make the Tech Bookstore menu animate
- Make the Tech Bookstore menu work

Approximate Time

This lesson takes approximately three hours to complete.

Lesson Files

Media Files:

lesson09/assets/catalog01.png
lesson09/assets/catalog02.png
lesson09/assets/home01.jpg
lesson09/assets/home02.jpg

Starting Files:

lesson09/start/bookstore12.fla

Completed Files:

lesson09/complete/bookstore13.fla
lesson09/complete/reviews.fla
lesson09/complete/news.fla
lesson09/complete/catalog/catalog01.fla
lesson09/complete/catalog/catalog02.fla
lesson09/complete/reviews/0321213408.txt
lesson09/complete/reviews/0321219198.txt
lesson09/complete/home.fla
lesson09/complete/home.txt
lesson09/complete/styles.css

Learning about ActionScript 2.0

ActionScript 2.0 is an object-oriented scripting language. Object-oriented languages are designed to make the lives of scripters and programmers as easy as possible by taking certain types of functionality and organizing them into these things called *classes*, which then serve as templates more or less for items that need to use all that functionality. When you want to use a class, you make an *instance* of it, which is also referred to as an *object*. The object inherits all the instructions in the class, so it more or less knows what it is and what it can do out of the box. Objects have *methods*, which are things that objects *do*, *properties*, which more or less define the object, and events that they can either *broadcast* or respond to. More on that stuff a little later. Right now, we just need to know that this is part of how ActionScript 2.0 works.

ActionScript 2.0 is *case-sensitive*, which means that when you create things like *variables*, *functions*, and *instance names* with uppercase and lowercase letters, all your references to those items have to match exactly for them to be recognized. What's more, the methods, properties, and events used by ActionScript objects have to match exactly, too. The method getURL() is not the same thing as getUrl(). If you don't capitalize the R and the L, Flash will have no earthly clue what you're talking about and what it is you are trying to accomplish. It is case-sensitive.

Lastly, ActionScript 2.0 is *extensible*. What that means in human language is that you can make it do things that it doesn't do out of the box. Flash 8 Basic comes with only so many classes and capabilities. Fancy-pants functionality such as complex employee data management needs to be created by some very brainy developer who understands these things. The developer can create his or her own classes, objects, methods, and events to handle data in Flash in whichever way that individual wants to handle it. This isn't to say that you can make ActionScript 2.0 do *everything*, but you sure as heck can come close. Not only that, but he or she can turn their ActionScripts into behaviors, components, or menu commands that can be installed with Extension Manager (see Appendix A for more on the Extension Manager).

> **Tip** *The creation of classes, methods, properties, and custom objects is beyond the scope of this book, although we do cover the concepts here. Please see Macromedia Flash 8 ActionScript: Training from the Source, ISBN 0-321-33619-4 to learn how to make your own classes, methods, and properties.*

Learning About Classes, Methods, and Properties

ActionScript 2.0 and Flash 8 Basic are both based on a functional model that involves *classes*, *objects*, and *instances of objects*. While you don't have to know everything about how this model works, it certainly helps to have an understanding of the concepts behind it, because it touches nearly every aspect of how Flash 8 and ActionScript 2.0 work (and work *for* you). Besides, the more you know about it, the easier it is to boss your application around!

First, you need to understand a *class*. A class is a collection of scripts that define common capabilities and properties. Classes are important, because they prevent developers from having to recreate lines of code every single time they need to do the same thing in the same or different applications. You can think of them as templates for functionality, and everything around you, in programming, Flash, and real life, belongs to a class of some sort or another.

For example, if you're a dog lover, you might have gone out one day and adopted a puppy. Puppies belong to the Dog class, which is the master template for every dog ruining flower beds on the planet Earth. You know a dog is a dog because all dogs have similar properties and behave in a particular way, from smallest to biggest. When you go and get a puppy from a breeder or a pet store, you have *instantiated* the dog class (that is to say, made an instance of it, although technically 'twas the momma dog that made the puppy instance), and therefore have a dog object. The puppy is built from the dog template, or dog class, and inherits all of the methods and properties that dogs come with at birth. And you just thought you were getting an enthusiastic friend!

All dogs have *methods* in common, such as bark() and slobber() and run(). A method is what something does. They also have similar *properties*: coatType, size, weight, gender, name, and so on. Properties describe the physical structure of an object. When you train a dog, you are adding methods to it; when you groom a dog, you are altering its properties. However, calling methods and changing properties don't change the fundamental structure of the dog, so no matter what you do to it or what you teach it, it is still and always will be a dog. Got it? Good. Because if you want to start changing the fundamental nature of objects like dogs, you'll have to start creating your own classes; fortunately, however, in Flash, you won't have to go to that extreme, because chances are Flash already has classes that handle the tasks you want to accomplish.

> **Note** *If you want to create your own classes, they must be created in external files with an .as extension that are compiled into the SWF file when you publish it. You won't create any classes for this book, but instead just use what are called "built-in classes" that are included in ActionScript itself. All those classes are also stored externally in .as files in Flash's install directory. Feel free to look at them, but don't change anything!*

ActionScript 2.0 includes a number of built-in classes, such as the Math class, Button class, and Date class. You have already used the MovieClip class, and some of its methods and properties, which include methods such as stop, and gotoAndPlay. The MovieClip class also has properties you can change or set for an instance, such as _visible, _width, and _height. Heck, your Stage is actually an instance of the MovieClip class. You will look at how to use a built-in class shortly.

Objects based on the MovieClip, Button, TextField, and Component classes that come with Flash can be created (otherwise know as *instantiated)* visually. However, many Flash classes, such as LoadVars and Sound, must be instantiated using ActionScript. When you create a new instance of a class using ActionScript, you are really calling a constructor function, which is a special kind of function defined in a class that assembles the object and sends it out into memory. Kind of like an assembly line in an automobile factory. To create a new object instance using ActionScript, you write a line of ActionScript similar to the following:

```
var rockinSound:Sound = new Sound();
```

In this example, you are creating (or constructing) a new instance of the Sound class giving it the instance name rockinSound, so that you can refer to it when you need it. The Sound instance is stored in memory, so to use it, you have to call it by its name. If you went to pick up your kids from day care, you wouldn't walk into the building and shout "Hey kid, let's go!" because you might wind up with more kids than you bargained for. Or a few kids. Or no kids at all. You have to shout "Hey Cheyenne!" to gather your unruly child (or niece in this case) and hurry along your way. Unpredictable results when gathering children from day care are bad results, and likewise just as bad in ActionScript. "Hey Sound!" has no meaning to Flash. So you name the instance of the Sound class, then call it by name when you want it to do something. Just like a movie clip on the Stage is an instance (or copy) of a movie clip symbol in the library, rockinSound is an instance of the Sound class, only in memory, waiting to do your bidding.

The Sound class is an example of a built-in class. "Built-in" means that the class shipped with Flash, was installed on your computer, and is written with the ActionScript language. The class also has predefined methods and properties that create the class itself, produced by the kind programmers at Macromedia, so you have one less thing to worry about.

Looking at Methods and Properties

A class consists of methods and properties, you saw in the previous section. Again, methods are functions associated with that object's class, such as the Sound class, and are used to do something with the object. There are built-in methods in the ActionScript 2.0 language for the built-in classes you learned about earlier. For example, setRGB() is a built-in method of the Color class. This method sets the hexadecimal color value for an instance you have in your SWF file.

Properties are also built into the classes that come with ActionScript 2.0 and Flash 8 Basic. Properties are like variables or data used to define the physical structure of an instance, a lot like the variables you use in your SWF file. Take, for example, the code you looked at in Lesson 6:

```
myMovieClip_mc._visible = true;
```

In this code, `_visible` is a property that is used to define whether an instance is visible (`true`) or invisible (`false`). As you can tell, the visibility property is being defined for the `myMovieClip_mc` instance on the Stage.

> **Note** Events and event handlers are discussed later in this lesson in the example called "Using Events and Handlers."

Learning How to Use Strict Data Typing

Strict data typing means that you explicitly tell Flash what data type a variable can hold when you create it or what kind of an object an item is if it's constructed from built-in or custom classes. If you create (or declare) a new variable and strict type it to a particular class (data type), the rules of that class apply. Flash expects only that kind of data to be stored in that variable, such as the String class expecting a string to be contained in the variable. You use strict type to protect yourself from your own mistakes; if you accidentally try to send number information into something that can only hold characters, you'll get an error message long before you try to deploy the application. You have to fix things before you can make them work. For example, if you declare a new variable as in the following code, you are telling Flash to create a new variable called `myString` that stores only characters:

```
var myString:String;
```

You only need to tell Flash what data type to use when you declare the variable; meaning that you only need to strict type initially for each variable you declare. If you try storing a different data type in the variable created with strict typing, such as in the following code, an error occurs when you publish the document:

```
var myString:String;
myString = 15;
```

An error occurs because you are trying to store a number to that variable, which is not accepted by Flash because you told Flash that you'd only be using that variable for characters. Kind of like trying to convince the guy you rented a garage from (which stores cars) that the alligator you're trying to house is okay. In the above example, Flash is expecting a string of characters, not numbers. Therefore, to fix it, the following code would work:

```
myString = "15";
```

The number 15 is now the characters 1 and 5, so you don't throw an error.

Using Code Hints in the Actions Panel

Code hinting is a feature found in the Actions panel when you are typing out your own ActionScript. Code hints can really save time when scripting and even helps reduce many of the typos and errors that might break your scripts.

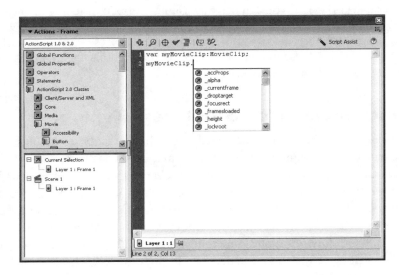

Code hints can be invaluable if you are trying to enter text into a text field and can't remember which property to use. There are two ways to open the drop-down menu: strict typing the variable or adding suffixes to the variable. You've already seen examples of using suffixes throughout this book.

To get code hints to appear, you must name your variables, objects, and symbol instances in particular ways, or—barring that—data type your objects. When you create a variable name, it's just a variable name that stands for anything from a number that's a score in a game to XML data. Strict data typing or suffixes tell Flash what data type (class) the variable belongs to. If you specify what kind of data that variable is for, the code hints show the correct methods and properties for that class. You've seen data typing earlier in this lesson, and the previous figure shows an example of code hints appearing when referring to a data typed object in the script.

The second way to specify the type of variable is to use suffixes. This procedure isn't as flexible as data typing because the suffixes have to refer to ActionScript objects (classes) such as the Sound class or the MovieClip class. By ending instance names for objects in your FLA file with suffixes such as _mc (MovieClip), _btn (Button), _txt (TextField), _str (String) or _lv (LoadVars), Flash provides the proper code hints for that instance. Although not every one of the suffixes provides code hints (notably _gr because you cannot write ActionScript for a graphic), one of the other major benefits of following this naming scheme is that it makes it much easier to remember what data type each symbol is within the library of the FLA file. An example of variable suffixing follows:

```
var homeContent_lv = new LoadVars();
homeContent_lv.load("home.txt");
```

Remember that each time you refer to the `homeContent_lv` variable in the ActionScript, the `lv` suffix should be appended because it is part of the variable name. Not every data type has an associated suffix (for example, `Object` has no suffix). Therefore, it might be necessary to use a couple of the methods listed in this section to provide code hints for each of your different variables.

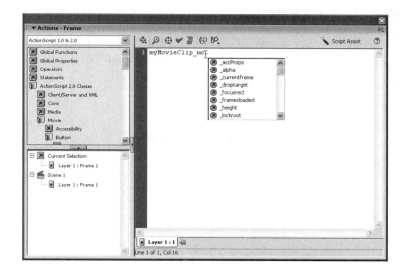

There is a third way to get Flash to display code hints: by typing the data type (the kind of data the variable holds, such as a String, Number, Movie Clip, LoadVars, and so on) and variable name within a comment, such as:

```
// LoadVars homeContent;
homeContent.load("home.txt");
```

A *comment* is a message that you type within the ActionScript code, usually to tell yourself or others what is happening in the code at that point, or as reminders of things to do. Comments do not actually execute any code. However, when you use a comment in this way, you are effectively data typing the ActionScript object (in this case, a LoadVars object).

Therefore, as soon as the dot is typed after the variable name, the Actions panel opens a list of available methods and properties for the LoadVars object, just as in the preceding example.

Whatever way you choose is completely up to you. If you can't make up your mind, you can even combine the methods, as in the following code:

```
var homeContent_lv:LoadVars = new LoadVars();
```

This code has the advantage of using a suffix that can help you remember what the variable is throughout your code, and it also uses strict data typing that makes sure you don't accidentally try setting the variable to the wrong data type such as a Number or String.

Using Functions and Conditional Statements

Functions are blocks of code that are typically reused many times in a FLA file. Functions can *return* a value when they're done doing what they do and have parameters passed to them to modify how they execute. *Parameters* (sometimes called arguments) allow you to pass an unchanging (or static) value or variable into a function. Then the value(s) can be used and manipulated in your function's code. Parameters, then, change how your function executes.

When you're cooking dinner at home, you're executing a function. It's a function because you weren't born knowing how to cook. You had to be taught by your father or grandmother or Julia Childs (how we miss her). The parameters that modify your cooking function might be what, when, how long. If you were to write your cooking function, it would probably look like the example below:

```
cookYummyFood=function(what,when,howLong)
{
    you.prepare(what);
    placeInOven(howLong);
    cookIt=when
    return what


}
```

In this example, cookYummyFood is the name of the function. What is the dish you are going to prepare, when is what time you're going to put it together, and howLong is the amount of time it will be in the oven. When you call the function, it would look like the example below:

```
Self.cookYummyFood(chicken, 5:00,1hr);
```

When it's finished executing, it *returns* the chicken. That is to say, the chicken is removed from the oven. Mmm…chicken.

Note *You might notice that components also have parameters. This means that the parameter values that you enter or set using the Property inspector or Component inspector panel are setting particular values within the ActionScript used by the components. ActionScript in each component recognizes what to do, based on the values you set in the Flash authoring environment.*

Functions are used all throughout Flash and ActionScript. Many are built in, but you can actually make your own to suit your specific needs. You've already seen several examples of functions—from the simple stop to the onLoad method of the LoadVars class. When you find yourself writing the same scripts over and over, changing similar code blocks into a single function with parameters that stand for the few things changing helps you manage your ActionScript code.

A conditional statement is different from a function and executes if a particular condition evaluates to true. A condition evaluates to a Boolean: either true or false. Depending on what value is the outcome determines whether code is executed or not, or sometimes what code is executed. In the following example a conditional statement is used to determine if dark chocolate is good for your health. If the doctor says it is, then you can eat it. Otherwise, you're out of luck:

```
if (darkChocolate == healthy) {
 //if this statement is true, do this
     self.eat(darkChocolate);
} else {
 //if dark chocolate isn't healthy, do this
    self.weep();
}
```

So you see, you use conditional logic in your everyday life, when you're at the candy counter trying to choose between dark chocolate and something good for you (blech). In ActionScript, as in life, you have to evaluate, then execute.

Note *The double equals seen in the previous code means you are comparing two values. Essentially, you are seeing if one thing equals something else. Think of it as matching.*

Understanding Scope

In Lesson 6, you learned about some of the things that make up ActionScript, such as variables, keywords, and data types. You also learned about how dot notation works and a bit about how dot notation is used to construct lines of ActionScript. Now you will take a look at where ActionScript lives in a FLA file.

One of the most important and sometimes confusing parts of ActionScript is getting a good grasp of how variable scope works and how it is used when you are writing code and working with Flash files. A *scope* is the area of your FLA file in which a variable can be referenced. That means if a variable exists in a certain place, such as within a function or on a particular Timeline, that is where its scope is. Understanding how scope works (and where your variables are) can take some practice and patience, and a certain amount of experience. As you test many different scenarios with your own personal projects, you quickly get a good grasp about how scope affects a Flash file. It might take some practice to get the hang of scope and see how it affects your code firsthand, so don't worry if it doesn't make sense right away.

In Lesson 6, you found out that variables are similar to containers that hold a piece of data, and you learned a bit about how to name them. A very important rule to remember is that two variables cannot have the same name. However, a variable can have the same name if they are in a different scope. This indicates how the code lives in different areas of your SWF files. There are three available scopes within Flash, as discussed in the following sections.

Local variables: These variables are available only when a function is called. Local variables are those inside the two curly brackets of a function, as you just saw in an earlier exercise. Outside of this function (when it's not being called), these variables do not exist.

Local variables are defined within a function using the var keyword and no longer exist when the function exits (when it's done). This means that the variables you use inside the function cannot be used in other places on the Timeline or in your code, which is a good thing most of the time because you won't have conflicts in other pieces of ActionScript with variables that might use the same name. Another benefit is that Flash uses fewer resources because it doesn't have to keep track of a large number of variables, which are no longer being used in your application. The local variables exist only for the life of the function and then disappear.

An example of a local variable is as follows:

```
function myVariable() {
 var myNum:Number;
 //myNum variable exists here
}
//myNum no longer exists.
trace(myNum); //undefined
```

When you trace the myNum variable outside of the function, undefined is returned because the variable no longer exists outside of the myVariable function. Remember that the trace statement can be used to test your code and send messages to the Output panel when you test a document.

Note *Although it is possible to use the same variable names in functions and in other scopes without naming conflicts, this isn't always advisable. You should avoid using the same names whenever you can because the practice can lead to confusion when editing your code at a future date if you have similarly named variables all throughout your FLA file in different scopes.*

Timeline variables: These variables are available to any script only within the same Timeline. Remember that your SWF file can have more than one Timeline because a Timeline can exist on a different level or in a movie clip or component. Levels will be defined in the following section. If you have more than one Timeline, there can be different Timeline variables in each of these areas—and all have the same name without running into conflicts.

When a variable is defined in a Timeline, that variable is available on frames after the variable has been defined. For example, if the following code were placed on Frame 10, it would create a variable named numUsers in the main Timeline. That variable exists throughout the Timeline after Frame 10. Before Frame 10 plays, that variable is not available in the SWF file.

```
var numUsers:Number = 5;
```

Global variables: These variables are available to any of the Timelines, scopes, or functions within the SWF file. Therefore, you can declare a global variable and then use the variables in other SWF files that are loaded into the main SWF file, and throughout the entire main SWF file without making any changes to your ActionScript or file structure. Global variables are slightly different from the first two scopes because they are not defined with the `var` keyword and are prepended with the keyword `_global`, as follows:

```
_global.numUsers = 5;
```

Because you cannot use the keyword `var` when defining global variables, you cannot use strict data typing with global variables. If you want to take advantage of code hinting with global variables, you must use the suffix method (appending `_mc` or `_lv` onto the end of the variable) or the comment method.

Using `_root`, `_parent`, `this`, and Levels

You might want to target a variable that exists in a different scope or Timeline in your SWF file. If you are writing code that is nested within a movie clip (or a component) and you want to access something on the main Timeline, such as a button, you need to use `_parent` to access the other Timeline. You use these scopes to tell the SWF file where to go to access those variables. When using the `this` keyword, you're referring to the current object in the current scope. For example, when you're within a movie clip and refer to `this`, you're telling the movie clip to look at itself. The `_parent` keyword references the parent item of the current object. For example, if you have a movie clip instance on the Stage and within the movie clip object are references to `_parent`, you are referring to the Timeline that the movie clip is on. You can combine the use of `this` and `_parent` to reference objects all throughout your SWF files. If you are in a nested movie clip, you can always use code similar to the following to navigate through the hierarchy of the SWF file to control other movie clip instances or component values:

```
this._parent._parent.otherMovieClip_mc.stop();
```

Another tricky concept to grasp can be the use of the `this` keyword. Depending on the exact context, it can refer to different things. If you use `this` within a movie clip instance, `this` refers to the Timeline of the movie clip. If you are using `this` in a button function, the `this` keyword refers to the Timeline containing the button instance rather than inside the button itself. If used with an `onClipEvent()` handler attached directly to a movie clip, the `this` keyword refers to the Timeline of the movie clip.

Consider the following code. If you place the following similar code on the main Timeline, it does very different things. Perhaps you have an SWF file playing, and there is a movie clip called `myClip` on the Stage that's also playing some content. You can treat movie clips like buttons using ActionScript (which you will do to the movie clip buttons that you created earlier) by giving them the onRelease event handler.

```
myClip_mc.onRelease = function() {
 this.stop();
};
```

This ActionScript stops the myClip_mc instance itself if it were animating. The ActionScript inside the function targets the movie clip's Timeline using the this keyword. However, if you use the following ActionScript instead, the ActionScript stops the main Timeline instead of the movie clips Timeline:

```
myClip_mc.onRelease = function(){
 stop();
};
```

The movie clip is being treated like a button, and buttons are made to target the Timeline they are sitting on, not the Timeline of the button itself (unless, of course, you use the this keyword).

You will encounter the frequent usage of _root when you use Flash and study other people's ActionScript. When users use _root, it means they are targeting the main Timeline. It's kind of like your root directory on a hard drive (for example, C:) or the root folder for a website. This is generally referred to as absolute referencing. Just as absolute referencing is not always the best idea to use in a website (it's hard to transfer your site to another domain if you use absolute referencing), it's also not a great idea to use in Flash in many circumstances because it's hard to move your ActionScript somewhere else. It can also cause problems when you load SWF files into other SWF files.

What causes problems when you are using _root is straightforward. When you refer to _root in an FLA file, you are referring to the SWF file's main Timeline when the document has been published. However, when you load that SWF file into a different SWF file, root means the SWF file that you're loading *into*. You can control for this by using a special property called lockroot, which tells a movie clip or a SWF file that references to root shouldn't go beyond that SWF file or movie clip. You're telling movie clips and SWF files then to behave as though *they* were the main document Timeline. It's a "you're the man" kind of property, and it's very, very useful. It has true or false values, and is also outside the scope of this book, but you can learn more about it in other books from the *Training from the Source* series.

In the application you are building, nested within the movie clips on the Stage are code or elements that the code targets. If those movie clips were empty, you would be able to load a SWF file into any of them, and that SWF file could target objects on the main Timeline.

If you have code within the SWF file loaded into the movie clip, you can use _parent to target the main Timeline or objects out on the main Timeline. Another way of loading SWF files into your application however is to use *levels*.

Levels belong to the Flash Player, sort of like floors with invisible planks. The first SWF file to load into a level provides the foundation for the rest of the house, more or less, and loads into level 0. It determines the width and height of the Flash Player object in the HTML page, as well as the background color and the frame rate. From there, you can load other SWF files into other levels; those SWF files will inherit the background color and frame rate determined by the first SWF file, and will match their upper-left corners with the upper-left corner of the first SWF file. The SWF files stack one on top of the other like floors in a building or like pancakes in a stack. Well, pancakes without the butter and syrup, anyway.

The first document to load in the Flash Player occupies _level0. From there, levels progress from _level1 to some very large theoretical number (last this author heard, it was in excess of 2 million). You don't have to load SWF files into levels in sequence, however. You can load the first SWF file into the Flash Player, load a navigation bar SWF file into level150, and all the content in-between (so the navigation bar is always above everything else). It's all very relative. You can also load the SWF file onto _level0 and replace the main Timeline's content instead, although this may not be such a great idea if the original clip contains variables and features that you need throughout the life of your application.

Tip *When you load a SWF file into a movie clip or a component (such as the Loader), it is not being loaded onto a new level, but instead into the movie clip or component instance itself. Then the content is contained within the movie clip and should be treated like any other movie clip on the Stage. This has the advantage of making it easier to handle data such as variables.*

If you need to target something on a different level of a loaded SWF file, you would use the following ActionScript:

```
_level2.myMovieClip_mc.gotoAndPlay(3);
```

Tip *Before you call any code targeting a SWF file that is being loaded, you should make sure that the content has completely loaded beforehand, or else the code you are executing will not work properly.*

Understanding LoadVars

You will be using the LoadVars class throughout the Tech Bookstore. Now that you have a better understanding about classes, objects, methods, properties, functions and conditional statements, you will look at the LoadVars class as an example of how to start putting these concepts together in a workable form.

LoadVars is a simple way to build dynamic websites that are easy to update. LoadVars can load variables defined in an external text file into Flash on the fly. Those variables then become properties of the LoadVars object that you're using to load data and can be references as such throughout the rest of your ActionScript. Because the LoadVars object is loading data from a text field when the SWF file runs in the browser, any changes to the data can be made in the text file itself to update the Flash file. No need to republish! Another benefit of using LoadVars is when you're using any server-side language—such as ColdFusion, PHP, ASP or Java—it is possible to have your server-side language query a database and write the latest news articles to a text file that can then be loaded by an SWF file.

There are three different ways of using Flash and LoadVars: send, sendAndLoad, and load. send simply sends data to a server where it can be processed by server-side scripts and entered into a database, appended to an XML document, sent as an e-mail, or used however you design the server-side solution to work. Using sendAndLoad sends the data to the server, but also accepts a response from the server and places the result in a LoadVars object, in which the variables can be manipulated or displayed using Flash. Loading and using variables can be useful for the Tech Bookstore if you want to send an ISBN number to a template on your server and have the server-side software query a database, grab a book review or information based on that book, and return the result to Flash to be displayed in the SWF file. The final method, load, is what you'll mainly be using throughout the Tech Bookstore site. The load method loads variables from a text file, and you'll display the variables in TextArea component instances or elsewhere throughout the Tech Bookstore application.

A sample text file, which can be used by Flash, could look similar to the following listing:

```
&name=Sue&
```

By loading in the previous simple text file using the sendAndLoad or load method, Flash creates a new variable in the target LoadVars object named name and gives it a value of Sue. You can add as many other variables to the text file by separating each name/value pair with an ampersand (&) and an equals sign (=), as in the following example:

```
&name=James&
&position=mentor&
&manager=Nate W&
```

The code here creates three separate variables in Flash: name, position, and manager. The value of name is set to James, the value of position is set to mentor, and the value of manager is set to Nate W. To load these values into Flash using the LoadVars class, save the listing into a text file, in this case named testfile.txt, and add the following ActionScript code to a blank Flash document:

```
var test_lv:LoadVars = new LoadVars();
test_lv.load("testfile.txt");
test_lv.onLoad = function(success:Boolean) {
    trace(this.name);
};
```

Because you're using LoadVars for this example, you have to save the Flash document to the same folder as the testfile.txt document before you test the sample code.

> **Tip** You can place the text files in a directory different from the SWF file that will load them. You just have to make sure that you reference the file correctly in the load method: `test_lv.load("textFiles/testFile.txt")`, and so on.

The code creates a LoadVars object named test_lv. You load in the external file using the load method in the LoadVars class, which happens in the second line of ActionScript. The method takes a single parameter, which is the path to the file that you want to load. In this case, you're loading in a file named testfile.txt, which is in the same folder as the current Flash document.

The next piece of code might be a little tricky to understand. The LoadVars class also has a couple of events that Flash triggers when certain things occur. In the code, the event that is being triggered is onLoad, which Flash triggers when the text file defined in the load method has been *completely* loaded into Flash. The code simply says when the specified text file has finished loading, execute the following code. After the file has been completely loaded and the onLoad event triggers, your three variables defined in the testfile.txt file are stored in the test_lv LoadVars object. You can now trace the value of test_lv.manager and see the value Nate W in the Output panel. In the previous code listing, you are using what is known as an inline, or anonymous, function, which is simply a function that hasn't been given a name.

An inline function does the same thing as named functions. There are some differences, and one is that they're usually attached to a specific object and perform a specific task. Another is that they don't hang around in memory waiting to be called. The function is created when an event happens, executes in response, and then is removed from memory until the next time it is needed.

Creating the Reviews Page

Now it's time to start working with Flash and add some ActionScript to make the FLA files do something useful. In this exercise, you will look at how to write a custom function that loads text into a TextArea component. This page creates the Review page containing a List component, which you can click to choose a review to look at. When you click the review's title, it appears in a TextArea next to the List. You will be using components to set up the structure of the Review page. You create a brand new FLA document to form the body of the review and then publish a SWF file that will be loaded into the Tech Bookstore later on.

Before you start writing any ActionScript, open the Actions panel in Flash (F9). Click the Options menu in the Actions panel and choose View Line Numbers from the drop-down list.

Line numbers help you find any ActionScript errors that appear in the Output panel when you test the document because the Output panel tells you the line number containing the error. The error is a lot easier to find when you have line numbers turned on in the Actions panel!

1. Create a new Flash document, resize the Stage to **720** pixels wide by **345** pixels high, and add some metadata. Rename Layer 1 to **form**. Open Publish Settings and deselect the HTML check box in the Formats tab. Save this document as **reviews.fla**.

Create a new Flash document and change the size of the Stage by clicking the Size button in the Property inspector, or by pressing Ctrl+J (or Cmd+J on the Mac) to open the Document Properties dialog box. Enter **Tech Bookstore Reviews** in the Title field and add a brief description in the Description field. In the dimensions text input fields, enter **720** pixels for the width and **345** pixels for the height and then press OK.

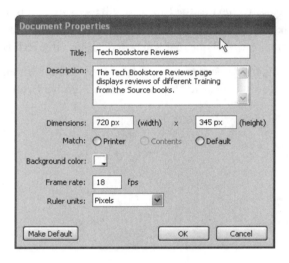

In the main document Timeline, rename Layer 1 to **form**, which sets up the dimension and the first layer of the FLA file.

When you publish the document, you don't need to generate an HTML page. You only need the SWF file, which you'll load in to the Tech Bookstore. Therefore, choose File > Publish Settings. Deselect HTML under the Formats category and press OK. Then choose File > Save to save the new file as **reviews.fla** in the TechBookstore folder on your hard drive.

2. Drag a List component instance onto the Stage, resize it, and enter a new position for the instance using the Property inspector.

The List component is used much the same way as a list in HTML: It displays labels for the user to interact with, and associated with each label is usually some kind of data. The List component allows a user to make multiple selections if you want to provide them with that ability.

Open the Components panel and drag a copy of the List component onto the Stage. With the List component still selected on the Stage, open the Property inspector and change the component's width to **200** pixels and change the height to **325** pixels. Enter a value of **10** pixels for both the *x* and the *y* coordinates to position the component near the upper-left corner of the document. Give the component instance an instance name of **reviews_ls**.

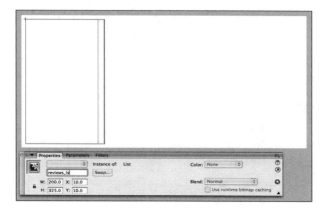

You'll use the List component to ultimately list the reviews available for a book and allow users to change to the review that they want to read.

3. **Copy the two review files onto your hard drive. Configure the List component using the Property inspector. Add data and labels for two reviews to the List component using the Values dialog box.**

To keep the reviews organized, create a new folder inside the TechBookstore folder on your hard drive called **reviews**. Save the two sample reviews that are provided on the CD-ROM in the lesson09 folder into this new folder. They're titled 0321219198.txt and 0321213408.txt, respectively, and are titled based on the ISBN numbers for the book. In a database type search, you might create a script that searches for ISBN numbers rather than titles because each ISBN number really only refers to one and only one book, whereas there may be several books floating around with the same title. You will use the LoadVars class to load the information from these text files into your Flash SWF file.

Tip *You want to place all the reviews inside a dedicated folder because if you add dozens of reviews in the root folder, it would be messy and difficult to navigate through. All these reviews are simple text files. You could create more reviews if you want and then add them to the reviews folder. You could even add your own by opening up one of the text files in question and copying the format of the simple HTML formatting. Organization is the key to any successful venture, Flash applications included. Don't believe it? Ask The Donald.*

There are a few different ways to populate the List component, but perhaps one of the simplest is to manually enter the information into the component using either the Property inspector or the Component inspector panel. You already saw how to do this in a previous lesson when you created the survey, although you populated a ComboBox in that lesson. Populating the List component is for all intents and purposes the same.

In the Property inspector, switch to the Parameters tab, select the *data* row, and then press the magnifying glass button on the far right of the row to open the Values dialog box.

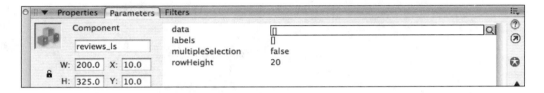

Click the plus (+) symbol twice to add two values. To keep the reviews organized, we decided to name each file after the ISBN number of the book. This way, if you need to locate a specific book in the list at a later date, you have to search only for its ISBN instead of scanning through each text file looking for the specific book. In the first value, change the value to **reviews/0321213408.txt**. Note that the directory name is appended to the file so that Flash knows that the file is not in the same directory as the SWF file. Click the second value and enter **reviews/0321219198.txt**. Click the OK button to close the dialog box and return to the Property inspector.

Click the labels row and again on the magnifying glass on the far right of the row to open the Values dialog box again for the labels in the List component. Click the plus symbol two times to add two values, just as you did for the data parameters. In the top value, change the default value to Fireworks: TFS, which is the title of the book. In the second value, change the value to Dreamweaver: TFS. It is very important that you pay special attention to enter the values in the same order when adding data and labels; otherwise, a user clicks one book title, and the bookstore returns the review of a completely different book. Click the OK button to close the Values dialog box when you are finished.

4. Add a TextArea component to the Stage and position the component using the Property inspector.

Drag an instance of the TextArea component onto the Stage and align its top-left corner near the List component's upper-right corner. With the TextArea component still selected on the Stage, go to the Property inspector, change the width to **490** pixels and the height to **325** pixels, and give this instance an instance name of **review_txt**. Set the *x* coordinate of the TextArea component to **220** pixels and the *y* coordinate to **10** pixels. In either the Property inspector or Component inspector panel, set the editable property to **false** so users can't change the review text and set the html property to **true** so you can use text with embedded HTML tags.

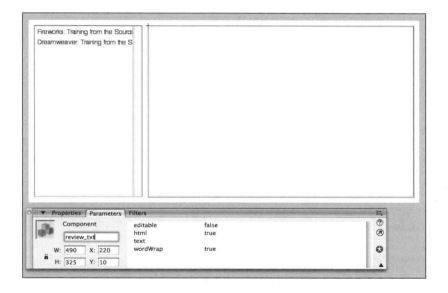

5. Insert a new layer on the Timeline and rename it **actions**. Write a function to load the selected book's review.

Insert a new layer on the Timeline and rename it **actions**. Expand the Actions panel. If Script Assist mode is on, turn it off now by pressing the Script Assist button so that it is not highlighted. Select Frame 1 of the actions layer and then add the following function into the Script pane in the Actions panel:

```
function loadReview(evt) {
    var review_lv:LoadVars = new LoadVars();
    review_lv.load(evt.target.selectedItem.data);
    review_lv.onLoad = function(success:Boolean){
      if (success)
      {
         review_txt.text = this.content;
      }
      else
      {
         trace("unable to load text file.");
      }
    };
}
```

Here, you are creating your own reusable function by using the function keyword followed by the name you want the function to have. After you define the function's name, which in this case is loadReview, you define any *parameters* that your reusable function will accept inside the brackets. This function takes a single parameter named evt. Everything between the { curly brace and the } curly brace is considered the function's body; these lines are the instructions that will execute when the function is actually called.

The first thing this function does is to create a LoadVars object in memory and gives it the name review_lv. The next line of code is another example of a built-in function within Flash. The load function takes a single parameter, which is the URL of the file to load. In this case, the value is taken from the data field of the selected item in the reviews_ls List instance. The value of evt.target is the path to the reviews_ls instance, as you will see in the following exercise.

Tip *Any time you click or interact with a component, button, or movie clip, the object you're interacting with broadcasts an event. Sort of like screaming when someone drops a frozen turkey on your foot. Flash captures that information about who is broadcasting the event and stores it in an object with properties of target and type. Type is the event. Target is the path to the broadcaster. So, when you have a frozen turkey dropped on your foot, evt.target would be: theKitchen.jim. The type would be screamInPain. The object storing this information would be mysister, in this case, who can then relay information to people who ask why my foot is broken....*

The `review_lv.onLoad` is an example of a different type of function. The `onLoad` function is actually an event that is triggered when the file has been completely loaded by Flash. Flash executes the function listed after the `review_lv.onLoad` code when the event triggers. This is what is known as an *inline function* (or *anonymous function*—same thing) because it doesn't have a function name and can be triggered only when the `onLoad` event is triggered.

The inline function takes one attribute called `success`, which tells you whether the file was successfully loaded. If the value of the `success` attribute is `true`, the file has been loaded. Therefore, Flash sets the `text` property within the `review_txt` TextArea to the value of the content variable within the `LoadVars` document. However, if the value of success evaluates to `false`, the file was unable to load, and therefore you display a message in the Output panel.

This example code has several different function types defined in only a few lines, but understanding how methods and events work is imperative when developing applications using LoadVars, XML, Web Services, or Flash Remoting.

6. Press the Check Syntax button in the Actions panel toolbar and check that the syntax of your ActionScript does not generate any errors. Save the changes you made to the file.

Click the Check Syntax button in the Actions panel to see whether there are any syntax errors in the code you just wrote.

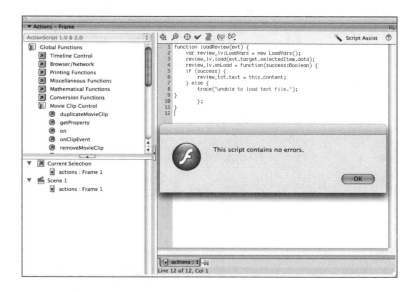

If everything works correctly, save the changes you made to your FLA file by choosing File > Save. You will continue working with this file in the next exercise.

Using Events and Handlers

The previous exercise looked briefly at an event in Flash. Events are like flags that are raised when something happens within Flash. An *event* is an action that occurs at runtime in a SWF file. When the SWF file is playing, events occur when a movie clip or an XML file loads, a button is clicked, and so on. Event handlers and listeners are actions that help manage those events. You've seen a couple examples of events already with the LoadVars class. When the file has been loaded by Flash, the onLoad event is generated by Flash, and any function defined for that event is then executed. A simple example of this happening is when a button is clicked (the event): The SWF file goes to and plays a designated frame.

An example of what you've already seen is when a file is loaded, either successfully or not. LoadVars triggers the onLoad event—telling Flash that the operation has completed. This is necessary because Flash continues processing code instead of halting the SWF file to wait for the operation to complete. This is what is known as *asynchronous communication*. In the previous exercise, you ask the SWF file to load the contents of a text file. When the SWF file receives a result, the SWF file either displays text in the TextArea component or displays an error in the Output panel (if you are in the test environment). Because trace statements are not sent to the user when you publish the FLA file, users do not see the contents of any trace statements in your SWF file.

There are all sorts of different events for many items within Flash. If you are loading an MP3 at runtime using Flash, for example, three different events can occur: onID3 triggers when the ID3 data (information about the MP3 file) is available, onLoad triggers when the MP3 has finished loading, and onSoundComplete triggers after the MP3 has finished playing. When something triggers, it means that Flash executes any function that might be defined in the event handler for these three events. You can see an example of this happening in the following code:

```
var intro_sound:Sound = new Sound();
intro_sound.loadSound("Tool - disgustipated.mp3", true);
intro_sound.onID3 = function(success:Boolean) {
        trace(success);
};
intro_sound.onSoundComplete = function() {
        trace("sound has completed");
};
```

This script first defines a new instance of the Sound object and then loads in an MP3 into the Sound object instance using the built-in loadSound method. The true after the MP3 filename tells the SWF file that you want to *stream* the MP3 rather than waiting for the entire MP3 to load before beginning playback. Then you create event handlers for the onID3 event and for the `onSoundComplete` event. As each of these events occurs, the SWF file executes each function that's defined in the *event handler* automatically. The event handler are the instructions that execute when the event occurs. That means that when any sort of ID3 information is available in the SWF file, the `onID3` event triggers, the function executes, and the SWF file traces the value of the success attribute. The trace tells you whether the sound was successfully loaded into the SWF file.

When the MP3 finishes playing, the `onSoundComplete` event triggers, and the SWF file displays a message in the Output panel in the testing environment. The `onSoundComplete` function can be very useful if you want to load a new MP3 when the current MP3 finishes playing.

Using Listeners

You use *listeners* frequently in this lesson when you are using components in the interfaces. Listeners are used frequently in Flash, and are objects that do something based on who is *broadcasting* an event. Listeners are very similar to event handlers because they both wait for events to happen in a SWF file and then perform an action when the event occurs. There are two important distinctions between events and listeners: Listeners are caught by *listener objects*. Listener objects are objects with instructions that execute when a broadcaster object sends an event to the listener. Which brings you to the other difference and that is you must associate a broadcasting object (like a button) and a listener object using ActionScript. Essentially, you are telling your broadcaster to let your listener know when something happens. The listner then executes instructions from there. When you use components, you use the `addEventListener` method to do that and specify the event to broadcast and the listener object that will handle that event. You can see an example of listeners in the following code:

```
var listenerObject:Object = new Object();
listenerObject.click = function(evt) {
  trace("you clicked the button.");
};
myButtonComponentInstance_btn.addEventListener("click", listenerObject);
```

The first thing that happens here is you create an object to receive the events. Then you define a function handling the event and optionally assign it to the `evt` object as an argument. Flash uses the name of the event that the function catches as a property of the function. By doing this, you can have a single object catch several different events.

The last thing you do is add the event listener to a button on the Stage with an instance name of `myButtonComponentInstance_btn`. Then you tell the SWF file which event you are listening for (in this case, click, which triggers when the user presses and releases the button) and then pass the `listenerObject` as a parameter.

Adding a Listener to the Reviews Page

The LoadVars class has two events available: onData and onLoad. The onData event triggers when a result has been returned from the server, but before the results have been parsed by Flash. The onLoad event triggers if you call the load or sendAndLoad method of the LoadVars class, but it triggers after the results have been parsed by Flash. Each event is useful in different circumstances, and they each take different parameters.

Note *It is important to remember that if you are using the onData event in your code, the onLoad event no longer triggers unless you specifically call it from within your code.*

The following exercise focuses on handling an event that is triggered when the user changes the value of the List component. You should still be using reviews.fla for this example.

1. Add an event listener to the List component instance using ActionScript.

Select Frame 1 of the actions layer, and open the Actions panel. Add the following code to the Script pane, below the function that's already there:

```
reviews_ls.addEventListener("change", loadReview);
```

This code adds an event listener to your reviews_ls List component instance, which triggers when the user clicks a new book title. The addEventListener method takes two parameters: the event that it listens for (in this case, change) and the function to trigger when the event is triggered (in this case, the loadReview function you defined in the previous exercise). There is another option for the addEventListener method, allowing you to specify an object containing a function that is used to handle the event.

2. **Ensure that the document works properly by choosing Control › Test Movie. Then save and publish the document.**

Test the FLA file by selecting Control > Test Movie. Each time you click a book title in the reviews_ls component on the left of the Stage, Flash calls the loadReview function, which in turn loads that book's review into the TextArea instance. You also should notice that when the contents of the external text files display in the TextArea instance, the external files containing HTML formatting such as bold (using the <b> tag), italics (<i>), and images (<img>) affect the look of the text. If the TextArea component displays the actual HTML source code, including tags, check that the html parameter is set to true in the Component inspector panel. If you look at the contents of the text files, you'll see that the images are actually loading from the Amazon.com servers for this exercise. In reality, you would want to load images from your server locally instead of from the servers at Amazon.com. You could save the image files locally and change the URL in the text files in which you're loading.

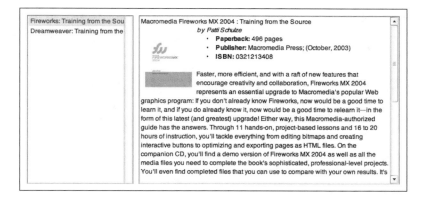

Return to the authoring environment and save the changes you made to reviews.fla. Publish the FLA file by choosing File > Publish to generate the SWF file. You will load this file into the main Tech Bookstore SWF file in a later lesson.

The file is generated in the TechBookstore folder. If you want to add more reviews, you can copy the text within an existing review and make changes as necessary. Save the new file into the reviews folder after you have finished editing them. Remember that you'll also need to modify both the data and labels parameters in the Property inspector for the list component and add new values similar to Step 3 of the previous exercise.

Adding Cascading Style Sheet Formatting to the Reviews

Cascading Style Sheets (CSS) is a method to define styles that can be applied to text and other elements within an HTML page. CSS documents contain rules defining which fonts a block of text should use, what kinds of spacing should be around certain elements such as images or table cells, or which colors are used with particular elements. When you use a style sheet, you can apply a single set of rules to every page within your site and have the site look consistent while maintaining the ability to change the rules and have the changes appear on every page you have applied the style sheet to immediately.

Flash boasts support for the original CSS1 specification as a way to format HTML-formatted dynamic or input text within a SWF file.

> **Note** *There are different versions of CSS. CSS2 has additional properties for formatting, although Flash does not support CSS2. Refer to* `http://www.w3.org/TR/REC-CSS1` *for the CSS1 specification.*

Although Flash supports only a subset of CSS1's properties, it is an excellent feature to use, because it allows you to easily format a block of HTML tagged text and have it look consistent with the rest of the site. There are two ways of adding style sheets to your Flash document: loading in a style sheet at runtime and defining the style sheet using ActionScript. Because you'll be using the same styles throughout the entire Tech Bookstore application, which is contained within several different SWF files, it is easier to use an external style sheet and load it into each of the separate SWF files. You can also use the same style sheet in the HTML pages you might also create, to help maintain consistency throughout your site, regardless of whether the page contains a SWF file or is only HTML code.

1. Open the reviews.fla document again from the previous exercises and lock the form layer.

Open the reviews.fla document you worked on in previous lessons and lock the form layer. Select Frame 1 of the actions layer, in which you will add ActionScript in the following step. In the third step, you will create the external style sheet file that styles the text.

2. Add ActionScript to reviews.fla, which will load a CSS file into reviews.swf at runtime.

In Frame 1 of the actions layer, add the following code before the existing code:

```
var flash_css = new TextField.StyleSheet();
flash_css.load("styles.css");
flash_css.onLoad = function(success:Boolean) {
    if (success) {
        review_txt.styleSheet = flash_css;
    } else {
        trace("Error loading CSS file.");
    }
};
```

The code listed is similar to using LoadVars in earlier exercises. The first thing you do is create a new Timeline variable named flash_css to contain the new style sheet and then load an external CSS file called styles.css. You haven't created styles.css yet, so if you were to save and test this, you would see "Error loading CSS File" in the Output window. The next block of code triggers when Flash receives an onLoad event and takes a single parameter (success), specifying whether or not the style sheet has successfully loaded. If the style sheet loads, the code assigns the style sheet to the reviews_txt TextArea instance. If it wasn't loaded successfully, an error is sent to the Output panel, notifying you that it has failed.

If you test the SWF file now by pressing Ctrl+Enter (or Cmd+Return on the Mac), you see that Flash displays the error message in the Output panel, saying that the SWF file couldn't find the CSS file. This occurs because you currently don't have the style sheet in the TechBookstore directory yet.

3. Create a Cascading Style Sheet file called styles.css to define the text styles. Save the file into the TechBookstore folder.

Open any text editor on your computer, or even an editor such as Dreamweaver that has specific support for CSS. If you are using a PC, you probably have Notepad installed; if you are on a Mac, you should have TextEdit installed. Enter the following code and save the file as **styles.css**:

```
p {
  font-family: Arial,Helvetica,sans-serif;
  font-size: 11px;
  color: #000000;
}
.headline {
  font-family: Arial,Helvetica,sans-serif;
  font-size: 24px;
  color: #999999;
}
```

The style sheet defines two styles. One style applies to the <p> tag, and another style is a custom style called headline, which you will apply to the book's title in each review. The headline style will be grey text and 24 pixels in size to help differentiate the headline from the rest of the text making up the review. Save the file into the TechBookstore folder on your hard drive and close the text editor.

4. Test reviews.fla again. If everything works correctly, save the document and publish the FLA file to generate an updated SWF file.

Test the Flash document by pressing Ctrl+Enter (or Cmd+Return on the Mac). Now if you click on the title of a book, Flash loads in the book's review and applies the style sheet to the TextArea. Save the file and republish the Flash document to update the SWF file in the TechBookstore folder.

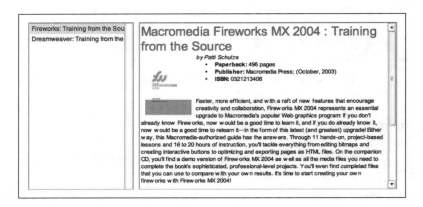

Creating the Catalog Pages

In this section, you create two new catalog pages that will import into the catalog.fla file you will create in the following exercise. The catalog pages are fairly simple pages that contain information on each book that is sold in the Tech Bookstore. You need to make only a couple of books for the catalog, but you can make many more if you want to.

Each catalog page uses a couple of buttons to open additional pages: One button opens a table of contents, and the second button opens a sample chapter. You created these buttons earlier in this book out of movie clips. The catalog pages also include an image of the book's cover and a short description of its contents. You can add whatever graphics you want to make the catalog pages look and feel customized.

1. Create a new folder in the TechBookstore folder called catalog. Open bookstore12.fla and save a new version of the file as bookstore13.fla.

First, create a new folder called **catalog** on your hard drive that's inside the TechBookstore folder. This is where you will save a couple of new FLA and SWF files you create in this exercise that will ultimately be loaded into the main Tech Bookstore application.

Open bookstore12.fla, either from the TechBookstore folder on your hard drive or from this CD-ROM's lesson09/start directory. Select File > Save As to save a new version of bookstore12.fla as **bookstore13.fla** into the TechBookstore folder on your hard drive.

2. Create a new document called catalog01.fla and save it in the catalog folder within the TechBookstore folder. Open the Publish Settings dialog box and turn off the HTML check box under the Formats tab. Resize the Stage.

When you publish the document, you don't need an HTML page generated. You only need to use the SWF file that is created when you choose to publish the document because eventually the SWF file will be loaded into another SWF file. Therefore, choose File > Publish settings, deselect the HTML option in the Formats tab, and click OK when you're done. Using the Property inspector, resize the Stage to **490 x 325**.

3. Drag the two movie clip buttons from the library in bookstore13.fla into the library of catalog01.fla.

In catalog01.fla, launch your document library if it is not already open. Press the New Library Panel button and select bookstore13.fla from the library drop-down list in the new panel. Drag an instance of mcSampleChapter and mcToc from the bookstore13.fla library and into the catalog01.fla library.

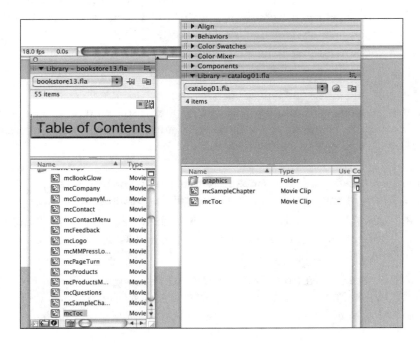

4. Delete the Table of Contents and Sample Chapter buttons from the Tech Bookstore library and close the FLA file.

When the mcSampleChapter and mcToc symbols are in the catalog01.fla document, you can delete them from bookstore13.fla's library by selecting each symbol and dragging them over the trash can icon located at the bottom of the library.

Tip *You always want to delete any symbols that are not being used in an FLA file so you can attempt to keep the FLA file size to a minimum. Deleting symbols does not affect the size of the published SWF file because any unused symbols are not compiled into the SWF file when you publish the Flash document. This is not true, however, of components. Components will be published with the SWF unless you specifically delete the unused components from your Library.*

5. Copy catalog01.png and catalog02.png from the lesson09/assets folder on the **CD-ROM** onto your hard drive.

Located within the lesson09/assets folder on the CD-ROM are files called catalog01.png and catalog02.png that contain images of *Training from the Source* book covers. Copy both files onto your hard drive.

6. Rename Layer 1 to **pages** and drag an instance of the Loader component into the layer. Change its contentPath parameter to **catalog01.png**. Insert a new layer above pages and rename the new layer **buttons**. Select the buttons layer and drag the two buttons onto the Stage. Add a layer called **static text**. Using the Text tool, create a new static text field on the Stage and then lay out all the items on the Stage.

First, rename Layer 1 **pages**. Expand the components panel and drag an instance of the Loader component onto the Stage. Position it near the upper-left side of the Stage similar to the following figure, and give it a width of **120** and a height of **150**. Set its contentPath parameter to **catalog01.png**, and set its autoScale property to **false**.

Tip *When you click away from the Loader component, it appears to disappear. To see its position when it is deselected, turn on the View Outlines option on your Layers pane.*

Create a new layer above pages and rename it **buttons**. With the buttons layer selected, drag the two movie clip button instances from the library onto the Stage. Position the two movie clip buttons under the Loader component instance on the Stage. Position the second movie clip button underneath the first button.

Finally, click the Text tool in the Tools panel and open the Property inspector. Set the Text type to static and the font to Arial 10 pt black. Select Anti-alias for readability as the font-rendering method. Select the static text layer and create a text field on the Stage that is the correct width of the field by clicking and then dragging. When you enter text into this field, it will create additional lines vertically. Type some text into the static text field you created. It doesn't matter what you type—you can use lorem ipsum text as placeholder text, open the completed catalog01.fla, and use the text you find in the finished FLA file, or find the actual book description online.

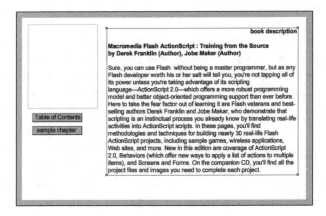

7. Give the two movie clip buttons new instance names. Then insert a new layer called **actions** and add functions to make the two buttons work.

Using the Selection tool, click each of the buttons near the top of the Stage and give them instance names. Enter an instance name of **toc_mc** for the table of contents button. Then enter an instance name of **samplechapter_mc** for the sample chapter button. Select the top layer in the FLA file and insert a new layer. Rename the new layer **actions**, expand the Actions panel, and add the following ActionScript to the Script pane:

```
stop();
samplechapter_mc.onRelease = function() {

getURL("http://www.trainingfromthesource.com/flashTFS/samplechapter.html", ¬
  "_blank");
}
toc_mc.onRelease = function() {
    gotoAndStop("toc");
}
```

This ActionScript stops the playhead on the current frame and defines two functions. One moves the playhead to a specific frame label, and the other opens a browser window. If the user clicks the sample chapter button, the browser opens and goes to a page containing a sample chapter; if the user clicks the table of contents button, the playhead moves to the frame that will be labeled toc in the following step.

8. Insert a new layer and rename it **labels**. Then add frame labels **toc** on Frame 5, and **home** on Frame 1. Insert new blank keyframes on the pages and actions layers under the frame label, and add a stop action on Frame 5 of the actions layer.

Insert a new layer and move it directly below the actions layer. Rename the layer **labels**. Right-click (or Control-click on the Mac) on Frame 5 of this new layer in the Timeline, select Insert Blank Keyframe from the contextual menu, and give that frame a label of **toc** using the Property inspector. Select Frame 1 on the layer and add a frame label of **home**.

Insert a new blank keyframe (F6) on Frame 5 in the actions layer and type **stop();** into the Actions panel. Add a new keyframe on Frame 5 of the pages layer by pressing F6. The text field from Frame 1 is copied onto Frame 5.

Note *You don't need to extend the buttons layer to Frame 5 because you are making a page that's exclusively used to display the table of contents, not necessarily to open the sample chapter.*

By adding a keyframe on this layer instead of a blank keyframe, you can change the text in the static text field on the Stage and be able to maintain the same positioning of the text field. It also allows you to keep all the elements in exactly the same place so the items don't shift when visitors navigate to the second area. Modify the text fields, so now it displays a table of contents instead of a book description. Finally, add a back button on the Stage onto the toc keyframe on the pages layer. Either create your own button or drag a Button component instance from the Components panel onto the pages layer.

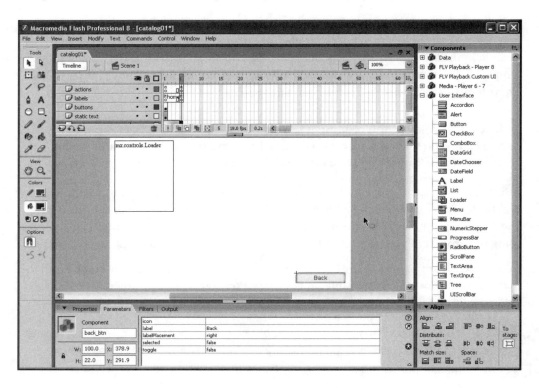

If you use a Button component instance, change the label parameter to **Back** and the instance name to **back_btn**. Select Frame 5 of the actions layer and type the following code into the Actions panel.

```
back_btn.onRelease = function() {
    gotoAndStop("home");
}
```

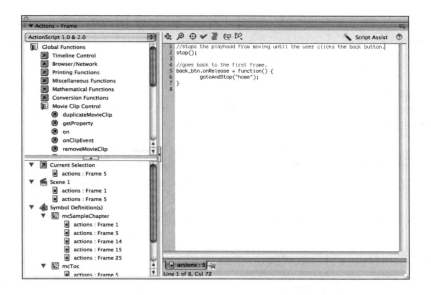

9. Test catalog01.fla and then save and publish the file if there are no problems. Save a new version of catalog01.fla by selecting File › Save As and name the new file **catalog02.fla** and make sure it's saved in the catalog folder. Change the contentPath parameter of the Loader component to **catalog02.png** and modify the catalog's text fields.

Test catalog01.fla to make sure that the document works as expected. If there are no problems, save the file, and publish it by choosing File > Publish. After you have saved a new version of catalog01.fla as **catalog02.fla**, you need to make only a few minor modifications (detailed as follows) to the FLA file and then republish it.

Note *If you don't want to create a second catalog page, you can always save catalog02.fla from the lesson09 folder on the CD-ROM into the TechBookstore folder on your hard drive and publish that file instead. But then everyone will call you lazy, and besides, you won't get any practice that way.*

Usually, the quickest way to rebuild any file (such as the catalog01.fla) while maintaining a consistent layout and feel is to save a new copy of it and change only what needs changing. It's the same principle as duplicating a movie clip symbol, really. This way, you can save a few steps by not having to re-create the entire file from scratch and then worry about positioning each element the same way.

Select the Loader component on the pages layer and change its contentPath parameter to **catalog2.png**. You'll need to do this at keyframe 5 of the pages layer as well. Lastly, change the text if you like in Frame 5 of the pages layer.

10. Test catalog02.swf in a browser window. If the page works correctly, return to the authoring environment, save the FLA file, and publish it to create catalog02.swf in the catalog folder.

Test the catalog02.swf file in a browser window by pressing selecting File > Publish Preview > Default in the authoring environment. If everything looks OK and you can navigate to the different sections of the SWF file and open a new browser window, save the file and publish the FLA file to generate the new catalog02.swf file. You should now have two SWF files in the catalog folder that you will import into the Tech Bookstore later in this book.

Building the Main Catalog

The Catalog section of the TechBookstore is very similar to the Reviews section built in the earlier exercises. The main catalog file has a List component with the names of several books. When you click one of the books in the List, it updates content on the Stage by loading in the catalog pages you created in the previous exercise. The main difference between the Catalog section and the Reviews section is that the Catalog page loads an external SWF file into a Loader component instead of using LoadVars and a TextArea component that the Reviews section used to display content.

1. Create a new Flash document and resize the Stage to **720** pixels wide by **345** pixels high. Open the Publish Settings dialog box (File > Publish Settings) and deselect the HTML check box under the Formats tab. Then save the file as **catalog.fla**.

Create a new Flash document by choosing File > New and selecting Flash Document. Resize the Stage to **720** pixels by **345** pixels using the Property inspector. When you publish the document, you don't need an HTML page generated. You need to use the SWF file that is created only when you choose to publish the document. Therefore, choose File > Publish settings. Deselect HTML under the Formats tab and click OK.

When you are finished, save the FLA file as **catalog.fla**.

2. Rename Layer 1 to **form** and add a List component to the Stage on the form layer. Resize the List instance to **200** pixels wide by **325** pixels high using the Property inspector and move the instance to the upper-left corner of the Stage. Give the List an instance name of **catalog_ls**.

The catalog section has a List component that includes names of books in the catalog that will update content on the Stage when they are clicked. Change the name of Layer 1 to **form**, open the Components panel, and then drag an instance of the List component onto the Stage.

Change both the *x* and *y* coordinates of the List instance to **10** pixels in the Property inspector. Change the width of the instance to **200** pixels and the height to **325** pixels, and type in an instance name of **catalog_ls** for the component instance.

3. Set the values and labels for the List component using the Values dialog box.

With the List component still selected on the Stage, open the Property inspector or Component inspector panel and click the data row. Click the magnifying glass to the right of the data row to open the Values dialog box. Add two new values by clicking the Add (+) button twice and enter **catalog/catalog01.swf** for the top value and **catalog/catalog02.swf** for the bottom value. Note that each of these values is prefixed with catalog/, which tells Flash that it should look for the SWF file in a subfolder named catalog.

Click the OK button to close the Values dialog box and select the labels row in the Property inspector. Click the magnifying glass again for labels to open the Values dialog box and enter values for the List component. Add two new values, setting the top value to **Flash ActionScript: TFS** and the bottom value to **Dreamweaver: TFS**. When adding values, you always have to exercise caution that you add the data in the same order as you add the labels; otherwise, your users click a title and receive information on a different book.

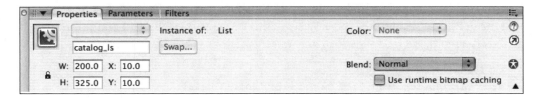

4. Add an instance for the Loader component to the Stage, and then position and resize the instance using the Property inspector.

Expand the Components panel and drag an instance of the Loader component onto the Stage. Set the width of the component to **490** pixels and set the height to **325** pixels, and then position the component at an *x* coordinate of **220** pixels and a *y* coordinate of **10** pixels. Give the Loader component an instance name of **catalog_ldr**. Use either the Property

inspector or Component Inspector panel to set the autoLoad parameter to **false** and the
scaleContent parameter to **false**.

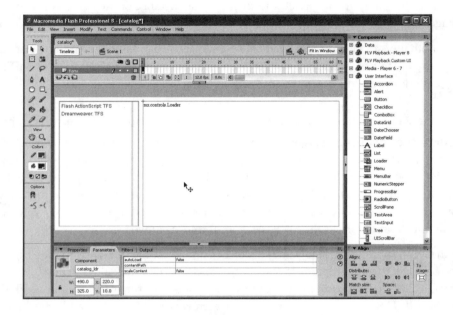

5. Create an actions layer and add ActionScript to load a catalog SWF file based
on the currently selected book in the List component.

Insert a new layer in the Flash document and rename the new layer **actions**. Make sure
that the new layer is above the other layers in the Timeline stack. Select Frame 1 of the
actions layer and add the following code into the Actions panel:

```
function loadCatalog(evt) {
    catalog_ldr.load(catalog_ls.selectedItem.data);
}
catalog_ls.addEventListener("change", loadCatalog);
```

This code defines a function named loadCatalog. The function loads the value of the
currently selected item's data property, which is the location to a SWF file. The function
loads that particular SWF file into the Loader component instance on the Stage.

The component's instance name is catalog_ls. You add a listener at the end of this
ActionScript that waits for the catalog's List instance to be clicked by the visitor. When
an item in the List is selected, the loadCatalog function is called. The function tells the
catalog_ldr to load the value of the currently selected item in the list. The value is
defined in the Values dialog box and contains the path to the SWF file.

6. Test the FLA file to make sure it works correctly. If so, save the changes you have made to catalog.fla. Then choose File > Publish to publish the SWF file into the TechBookstore folder.

In the previous exercise, you created a subfolder called catalog inside the main TechBookstore folder where you saved catalog01.swf and catalog02.swf (also provided in the lesson09/complete folder on the CD-ROM). So when you test the file, it should load those two SWF files from the catalog folder into catalog.swf. If the files don't load, open the catalog folder and make sure that the SWF files (and the folder itself) are there and named correctly. Ensure that you added the values correctly into the Values dialog box in Step 3.

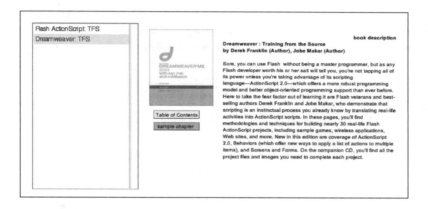

When everything works correctly, save the FLA file and then publish the file so an SWF file is generated in the TechBookstore folder.

Note *The path to the PNG images in the solution file is different from the path you set in the exercises in this lesson. The paths are produced to work with the directory structure of the solution files, so if you copy and paste any of the completed files into your own TechBookstore folder, be sure to change its directory references to match your own file structure.*

Creating the News Page

The News section of the Tech Bookstore is straightforward because it is very similar to the Reviews page you have already created. The News page consists of a TextArea component, CSS-formatted text, and a LoadVars statement to load the text content from a remote file. You use some text files that are provided for you on the CD-ROM.

1. Create a new document and resize the Stage to **635** pixels wide by **345** pixels high. Open the Publish Settings dialog box and deselect the HTML check box. Click OK, return to the main document, and save the file as **news.fla**.

Create a new Flash document and resize the Stage by opening the Property inspector. Set the new dimensions of the Stage to **635** pixels wide by **345** pixels high. Save the Flash document to the root of the TechBookstore folder and name the new document **news.fla**.

When you publish the document, you don't need an HTML page generated. You need to use the SWF file that is created only when you choose to publish the document. Therefore, choose File > Publish settings, deselect HTML under the Formats tab, and click OK.

2. Drag an instance of the TextArea component onto the Stage and resize it to **615** pixels wide by **325** pixels high. Position the TextArea instance on the Stage.

Drag an instance of the TextArea component onto the Stage from the Components panel. Expand the Property inspector. Resize the TextArea component instance to **615** pixels wide by **325** pixels high. Position the instance on the Stage at an *x* and *y* coordinate of **10** pixels. This should give the component a 10-pixel border on every side of the Stage. Give the TextArea an instance name of **news_txt**. Don't worry about setting the editable or html parameters in the Property inspector. You'll set those manually using ActionScript in a later step.

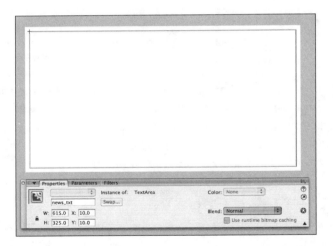

3. Rename Layer 1 in the Timeline to **form** and add an actions layer.

Double-click Layer 1 in the Timeline and rename the layer to **form**. Insert a new layer above the form layer and name it **actions**. Lock each of the layers to prevent accidentally adding any symbols to either layer. Because you won't be adding any more symbols to the Stage, you can lock layers and still add ActionScript.

4. Add ActionScript to import the cascading style sheet into the SWF file.

You learned how to import style sheets in an earlier exercise (CSS). By using an external style sheet, you can reuse the same style sheet throughout each of your Flash documents and maintain a consistent look. Select Frame 1 of the actions layer and add the following code into the Actions panel:

```
var flash_css = new TextField.StyleSheet();
flash_css.load("styles.css");
flash_css.onLoad = function(success:Boolean) {
    if (success) {
        news_txt.styleSheet = flash_css;
    } else {
        trace("Error loading CSS file.");
    }
};
```

This ActionScript is exactly the same as in the previous exercise, but with one exception. Instead of binding the style sheet to the `review_txt` instance, you're assigning the style sheet to the `news_txt` instance.

5. Load the news text file and set the `TextArea` properties.

Add the following ActionScript below the style sheet code on Frame 1 of the actions layer. This code is used to load in an external text file using LoadVars:

```
var news_lv:LoadVars = new LoadVars();
news_lv.load("news.txt");
news_lv.onLoad = function(success:Boolean) {
    if (success) {
        news_txt.text = this.content;
    } else {
        trace("unable to load text file.");
    }
};
```

This ActionScript should also be familiar from earlier exercises.

6. Set the `html` and `editable` properties for the TextArea instance using ActionScript.

Instead of setting the `html` and `editable` properties using the Property inspector, you will set them using ActionScript. Use the following code, which can be placed below the existing `LoadVars` code:

```
news_txt.html = true;
news_txt.editable = false;
```

The first line sets the `html` property value to `true`, enabling you to display HTML-formatted text in the TextArea instance `news_txt`. The second property, `editable`, ensures that the user can't modify the text and change the content in the TextArea. Even if you set `editable` to `true` (or if you left the line out altogether), and the user did change the content within the field, it wouldn't ruin your site. The changes would display only on his or her computer screen and not be visible to anybody else.

7. Test news.fla and make sure that the SWF file works properly. If so, save the FLA file and then go to the Publish Settings dialog box and uncheck the HTML option for publishing. Publish the document so news.swf is generated in the TechBookstore folder.

Test the SWF file using Control>Test Movie to make sure that the text loads properly. When you are satisfied that everything is working, save the document (name the document **news.fla** if you didn't already save the file in Step 1) and publish the FLA file so the SWF file can be loaded into the main Tech Bookstore website.

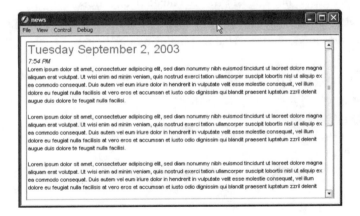

Building the Home Page

The Home section is also a block of formatted text that loads into the Tech Bookstore using LoadVars. The text is loaded into a TextArea component instance. In this section, you create a SWF file that loads into the front of the Tech Bookstore website. You reuse some of the content that you already created in earlier exercises. Because reusing assets makes for fast development, it is easiest to simply make a copy of the News section and modify it as needed rather than starting from scratch. So, in this exercise, you duplicate the News page and convert it into the Home page.

1. Open news.fla (created in the previous exercise). Save a new version of the file as home.fla in the TechBookstore folder.

By using news.fla as a starter file, you can skip a lot of steps while you create the new file, and you save having to retype out the ActionScript code from scratch. All you need to do is resize the Stage and TextArea component and modify the instance names and ActionScript slightly, thus saving some time.

Open up the copy of news.fla you created in the previous exercise. Choose File > Save As from the main menu. Enter **home.fla** as the new filename for the document and then click the Save button. Save this file into the same TechBookstore folder as the previous document.

2. Resize the dimensions of both the Stage and TextArea instance in the document.

Because the Home page on the Tech Bookstore site already has a featured book module, it is necessary to resize the home.fla document so it fits the bookstore properly. Using the Selection tool, click the TextArea component instance on the Stage and use the Property inspector to set the width of the component instance to **570** pixels. Leave the height at **325** pixels and the *x* and *y* coordinate at **10** pixels. Click on the Stage and change the dimensions of the document to **580** pixels by **345** pixels.

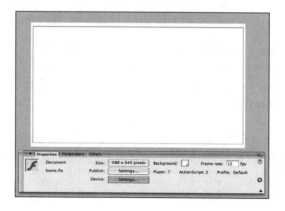

3. Enter a new instance name for the TextArea instance and change the ActionScript on the actions layer.

Select the TextArea component instance on the Stage and enter a new instance name of **home_txt** into the Property inspector. Because you changed the instance name for the component instance, you have to change the references to the TextArea in your ActionScript. You also have to change any references to news_lv to **home_lv**. Your finished modified code should look like the following:

```
var flash_css = new TextField.StyleSheet();
flash_css.load("styles.css");
flash_css.onLoad = function(success:Boolean) {
        if (success) {
               home_txt.styleSheet = flash_css;
        } else {
               trace("Error loading CSS file.");
        }
};
var home_lv:LoadVars = new LoadVars();
home_lv.load("home.txt");
home_lv.onLoad = function(success:Boolean) {
        if (success) {
               home_txt.text = this.content;
        } else {
               trace("unable to load text file.");
        }
};
home_txt.html = true;
home_txt.editable = false;
```

This ActionScript is almost identical to that of the news.fla. The only thing that needed to be changed was the instance names and the filename of the external text file being loaded.

The second-to-last line of ActionScript makes sure that the home_txt instance on the Stage displays HTML-formatted text correctly. This allows you to use images, bold text, italics, and bulleted lists to give your text some extra formatting. The final line of code sets the editable property to false so that users can't modify the text on their screen.

4. Copy home.txt, home01.jpg, and home02.jpg from the lesson09/assets folder on the CD-ROM to the TechBookstore folder.

Before you can properly test your Flash document, you need to either copy or create a text file that can be loaded in using LoadVars. A text file is adequate for the front of the Tech

Bookstore and can be found on the CD-ROM, so you don't have to type in a whole bunch of content for the front page. Naturally, you can create whatever it is you want for the front of the Tech Bookstore if you so choose and want to type in the text. Or you can use the home.txt file from the CD-ROM. Locate the lesson09 folder on the CD-ROM and copy the home.txt file and the two images home01.jpg and home02.jpg into the TechBookstore folder on your hard drive. Open the text file and look at the HTML markup.

Note *The two image files are used within the HTML formatted text and are loaded into the SWF file using the <img> tag in the home.txt file.*

If you're creating your own text file to load into the Tech Bookstore, you can make the HTML and formatting as simple or as complex as you like. Flash supports a small subset of HTML version 1.0 tags that include the following:

Anchor `<a>`: Allows you to add links to your Flash text fields. The <a> tag also supports the use of the target attribute, which allows you to specify the frame or window in which the link should open. If you're using a style sheet, you can also specify colors and attributes for `a:link, a:hover`, and `a:active`.

Bold `<b>`: Displays the text in bold.

Break `<br>`: Adds a line break at the specified point.

Font `<font>`: Allows you to change the current font, size, and color. This tag is very useful if you're not using style sheets and want to add some formatting to your text.

Image `<img>`: Allows you to add images to your text fields. This tag supports loading local or external image files, SWF files, or even symbols from the library (by assigning the symbol a Linkage Identifier).

Italics `<i>`: Displays the text in italic.

List Item `<li>`: Slightly different from HTML, the `<li>` does not appear between a pair of `<ol>` (ordered list) or `<ul>` (unordered list) tags. Flash's `<li>` tag allows you to easily create bulleted lists.

Paragraph `<p>`: Allows you to add a new paragraph.

Span `<span>`: Allows you to assign styles to a block of code.

TextFormat `<textformat>`: Allows you to build simple tables in Flash.

Underline `<u>`: Underlines a section of text.

Although Flash supports only about a dozen tags, combining them with Flash's built-in CSS support can lead to some fairly impressive results when it comes to formatting text for your sites.

When you load an image only into the TextArea, and the image is larger than the TextArea instance dimensions, scrollbars do not appear. You must have some text following the image for the scroll bars to activate. When you're loading large images and you want to scroll through them, you must use the ScrollPane component instead. Or write your own ActionScript with a movie clip that does the same thing.

If you want to use this file as is, close it. Otherwise, make any modifications to this file now that you know how it is being formatted.

5. Make sure that everything works properly in the Flash document. Save the file and then publish home.fla so an SWF file is generated in the TechBookstore folder.

Make sure that the FLA file works properly by selecting Control > Test movie to test the file in the testing environment.

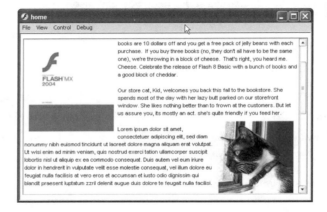

After you confirm that everything works in the SWF file and your formatting works correctly, return to the authoring environment and then save and publish the FLA file. A SWF file generates into the TechBookstore folder.

Animating the Menu

In this exercise, you will animate the menus that slide down in the Tech Bookstore when each button is clicked. You can see the functionality of them at the sample website at http://flash.TrainingFromTheSource.com. When a button is clicked, the menu slides down, and when the visitor rolls off the menu, the menu slides up. You created the animation that the menu actually uses earlier in this book. Now you will write the ActionScript that causes the animations to play when a visitor clicks the three buttons or rolls off the menu.

1. **Open bookstore13.fla from the TechBookstore folder on your hard drive, if it isn't already open.**

The file should have the edits that you made earlier in this exercise when you deleted the mcSamplechapters and mcToc from the library.

2. **Name all the instance names in the menu so you can control the buttons and movie clips using ActionScript later in this exercise.**

You have to add instance names for the three main buttons in the navigation bar and then the three menus sitting behind them.

Name the three buttons at the top of the main Stage, unlocking the buttons layer if necessary. Enter an instance name of **products_btn** to the Products button, **company_btn** to the Company button and **contact_btn** for the Contact button. Lock the buttons layer when you are finished.

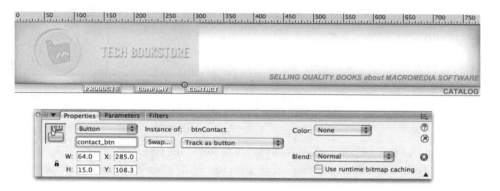

Now you need to give instance names to the three menus that are sitting behind the three buttons. It might be helpful to make the buttons layer hidden. The menus themselves are on the menu layer in the graphics layer folder. Right- or Control-click on the menu layer and choose Lock Others from the context menu. Make the mask layer hidden. Click the menu behind the Products button and give it an instance name of **productsmenu_mc**. Then give the menu behind the Company button an instance name of **companymenu_mc** and the menu behind the Contact button the instance name of **contactmenu_mc**. Note the suffixes that have been added to each of the symbol instances, so you can use code hinting when you start writing ActionScript.

Inside of the menu movie clips is another movie clip that you have to name. Double-click productsmenu_mc and select the menu inside that movie clip. Expand the Property inspector and give that clip an instance name of **menu1_mc**. You might first have to unlock the layer that the instance is on. Then select the second instance on this layer in the menu tween. Give it the same name: **menu1_mc**. Repeat this for the third and final keyframe in this tween.

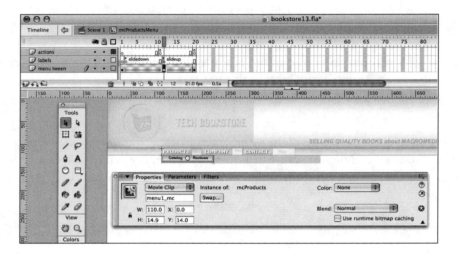

Use the edit bar to click back to the main Stage. Double-click companymenu_mc and give an instance name of **menu2_mc** to the clip inside companymenu_mc. Use the edit bar to navigate back to the main Stage, and repeat the process for the final menu, entering an instance name of **menu3_mc** into the Property inspector. Lock the menu layer when you're finished.

3. In Frame 1 of the actions layer, add the following ActionScript into the Actions panel. This code initializes the menu's variables. You also want to add a line of ActionScript removing the menu when the visitor Right-clicks on the Stage.

You should already have a stop action entered on this frame. Following this action, you need to add the following three lines of code. These three variables are flags that you use to track which of the three menus are currently open (if any). If the value is set to 0, the sliding menu is up or closed (inactive); if the variable is set to 1, it tells you that the menu is currently down or open (active) and visible on the Stage.

```
var prodmenu:Number = 0;
var compmenu:Number = 0;
var contactmenu:Number = 0;
```

Then add the following line of ActionScript after the variables:

```
Stage.showMenu = false;
```

When you add this ActionScript to the document, visitors will not see most of the Flash Player menu options when they Right- or Control-click on the SWF file after the file is published.

The contextual menu that opens typically includes a number of options such as zoom and play. However, all these options are removed from the menu if you add this ActionScript—except for Settings (which allows the visitor to control their Flash Player settings).

4. **In Frame 1 of the actions layer, enter the following code that closes any menus that are open when the mouse rolls out of the menu's area.**

The invisible button closes all the menus when a visitor rolls over it. Earlier in the book, you created an invisible button around all the menus when they are open.

You need to add some ActionScript that tells the SWF file when to call the function to close the menus whenever the mouse rolls over this invisible button. When the mouse rolls over the button, ActionScript is used to close any open menus.

Note *The following code in this example could be replaced by something in ActionScript called a* for..in *loop. Although this goes beyond the scope of the book, if you continue on in ActionScript, you might want to investigate and update this ActionScript accordingly. What happens is that you could place the three variables defined in the previous step into an object. Using the* for..in *loop, you can loop over each item in the object and execute a block of code. This would allow you to shorten the amount of code necessary and also make the ActionScript more flexible.*

Because the ActionScript you are adding to the Tech Bookstore is not major, it is okay to use repetitive ActionScript. Right now, learning how to properly use these few parts of the language is the most important part of the process.

```
//invisible button
this.btnReturnMenus.onRollOver = function() {
    if (contactmenu == 1) {
        contactmenu_mc.gotoAndPlay("slideup");
        contactmenu = 0;
    }
    if (compmenu == 1) {
        companymenu_mc.gotoAndPlay("slideup");
        compmenu = 0;
    }
    if (prodmenu == 1) {
        productsmenu_mc.gotoAndPlay("slideup");
        prodmenu = 0;
    }
};
```

This function is placed within an onRollover event handler for the btnReturnMenus instance, which means that it executes every time a user moves the mouse onto the btnReturnMenus instance (the invisible button on the Stage). The code looks at each of the menus and checks if the value is 1 (meaning that the menu is open in the SWF file). If the value of the variable is 1, the menu is open (has fully animated downward) and needs to be closed (animated upward). Therefore, you change the playhead of the corresponding movie clip (productsmenu_mc, companymenu_mc, or contactmanu_mc) to the frame labeled slideup to animate the menu so it is closed.

Also, note the path to the nested movie clips that are being closed in the previous code. Because the code is being written for the btnReturnMenus instance, the menu movie clips can be addressed contactmenu_mc.gotoAndPlay("slideup"). This is a button code referencing the Timeline that it is placed on, which is the Stage. From the Stage, you can directly reference the contactmenu_mc instance and its gotoAndPlay method.

5. **Now that the invisible button code has been added, follow it with the code for all the menus themselves.**

Now that you have the menus closing when you roll over the invisible button, it is time to add the ActionScript that animates the menus when you click the main navigation. The code is very similar to the code for the btnReturnMenus instance, except now you will be closing two of the menus if they are open and open the one that was clicked.

```
//products menu
this.products_btn.onRollOver = function() {
    if (contactmenu == 1) {
        contactmenu_mc.gotoAndPlay("slideup");
        contactmenu = 0;
    }
    if (compmenu == 1) {
        companymenu_mc.gotoAndPlay("slideup");
        compmenu = 0;
    }
    if (prodmenu == 0) {
        productsmenu_mc.gotoAndPlay("slidedown");
        prodmenu = 1;
    }
};
```

(code continues on next page)

```
//company menu
this.company_btn.onRollOver = function() {
    if (prodmenu == 1) {
        productsmenu_mc.gotoAndPlay("slideup");
        prodmenu = 0;
    }
    if (contactmenu == 1) {
        contactmenu_mc.gotoAndPlay("slideup");
        contactmenu = 0;
    }
    if (compmenu == 0) {
        companymenu_mc.gotoAndPlay("slidedown");
        compmenu = 1;
    }
};
//contact menu
this.contact_btn.onRollOver = function() {
    if (compmenu == 1) {
        companymenu_mc.gotoAndPlay("slideup");
        compmenu = 0;
    }
    if (prodmenu == 1) {
        productsmenu_mc.gotoAndPlay("slideup");
        prodmenu = 0;
    }
    if (contactmenu == 0) {
        contactmenu_mc.gotoAndPlay("slidedown");
        contactmenu = 1;
    }
};
```

Although the code looks very overwhelming at first, it is actually quite simple because it is very repetitious. There are three menus in the navigation: products, company, and contact. For each menu item, you have to check to make sure that the other two are not already open, which you can tell because of the three variables you set earlier (prodmenu, compmenu, and contactmenu). If the values of these variables equal 1, you know that the menu is already open and therefore needs to be closed before you can display the menu that needs to open.

The code is broken down into three major sections, one for each menu item. When the products_btn is pressed, Flash executes the inline function, checking whether the compmenu variable or contactmenu variable equals 1, meaning that the menu is already open. If a menu is already open, the variable is set to 0 and the menu is closed, similar to the code for the btnReturnMenus.

Finally, you check whether the menu you need to open—in this case, products—is open or closed. If it is closed, you animate the menu opening up. This code doesn't need any else statements because if the menu you want is already open, the work is done and you can just go to the next menu item to check if it's open or closed. The logic is the same with the company_btn, except you're making sure that prodmenu and contactmenu are closed.

> **Note** *Again, for the sake of simplicity, you aren't using the most elegant code possible for the menus. What is most important to take away is not only the process but also how the menus are being targeted and the general idea of if statements. This code could be shortened, although the complexity would increase accordingly and it would be more difficult to understand how it works. Perhaps one of the best ways to simplify the code is to create a function that takes two parameters: a menu item to expand and an array of menu items to hide. By converting the logic into a function, you would be able to reuse the code for all three cases and have to adjust only the parameters that get passed into the function.*

6. **Check the syntax of your code and format it in the Actions panel. Then test the menu animation in the testing environment.**

Press the Check Syntax button at the top of the Actions panel. If there are problems with your ActionScript, such as a missing bracket, a message will be displayed in the Output panel and you'll have to return and check your code against the ActionScript in Steps 3 to 5. When there are no errors, click the Auto Format button in the Actions panel toolbar, which formats the ActionScript with proper indentation and adds any missing semicolons at the end of a statement.

Press Ctrl+Enter (or Cmd+Enter on the Mac) to see whether the menus animate properly in the SWF file. If you run into problems, you want to first double-check that the ActionScript matches the code in Steps 3 to 5. If it seems to be related to the masking or invisible button, ensure that the mask is properly covering where the menu drops down and that the invisible button is properly surrounding where the menu drops down.

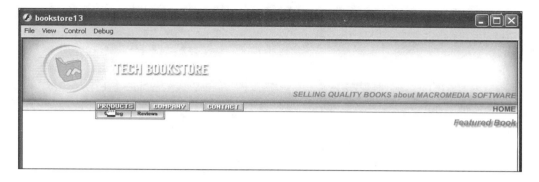

Tip *When you test the menu, you might find that the masking is slightly out of place. If the menus exceed the mask, you need to return to the mask and resize it appropriately so it doesn't obscure the menu. You might also find that the invisible button's hit area (the one that closes the menu) does not quite work properly. That means that you need to slightly resize the menu.*

7. **If the menu animation is correct, save the changes you made to the FLA file.**

Save the changes you made to bookstore13.fla and then move on to the next exercise, in which you add code so the buttons inside the menu work.

Controlling the Menu's Buttons

Compared with the previous exercise, the menu's buttons are a walk in the park. Remember that a button's scope means that event functions affect the Timeline the button is on, not the button's Timeline. That means that the buttons control the main Timeline unless you specify otherwise. In this exercise, you will need to specify otherwise because you want to control the main Timeline from a Timeline that is nested inside a couple of movie clips. That's about as tricky as it gets for this exercise, and it really isn't too bad at all if you remember the section on scoping that was covered earlier in this lesson.

When one of the buttons in a menu is clicked, a message goes back through a couple of Timelines to the main Timeline. Then the playhead moves to a new page.

1. **Add instance names for each of the buttons inside the menu using the Property inspector.**

These buttons need instance names so you can target them with your ActionScript. Each of the menu's buttons, as you might remember, are nested inside the movie clip menu that's nested inside the main menu movie clip. So click productsmenu_mc and then menu1_mc, and inside you find two buttons. Select the button that says catalog and enter the instance name **catalog_btn** into the Property inspector. Then click the button on the right and enter the instance name **reviews_btn**.

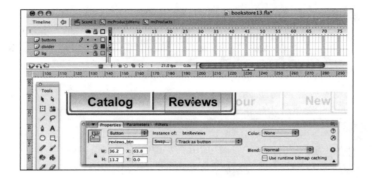

Navigate back to the main Stage using the edit bar, and repeat this process for the other two menus. The names you are giving them should be fairly intuitive. Give the buttons inside menu2_mc the instance names **tour_btn** and **news_btn**. Then give the menu3_mc buttons the instance names **feedback_btn** and **map_btn**.

2. Add ActionScript that is used to control the six buttons you find in the drop-down lists you just created. Enter this code following the code you added in the previous exercise.

You initially created these buttons to help visitors navigate throughout the Tech Bookstore, and you just gave them instance names so you can target them using ActionScript. The ActionScript targets the button so the function is called when the button is clicked; then the function tells the playhead on the main Timeline to move to the correct page in the Tech Bookstore.

Note *Remember that wherever a button is placed, the Timeline that the button is placed on is affected. Therefore, even though you are writing code for a button that is nested way inside a movie clip, the function you are writing affects the current Timeline. So you need to tell Flash where to look for the button, but you do not need to scope back to the correct Timeline to move the playhead.*

Select Frame 1 on the actions layer of the main Timeline. Expand the Actions panel and enter the following ActionScript into the Script pane.

```
this.productsmenu_mc.menu1_mc.catalog_btn.onRelease = function() {
    gotoAndStop("catalog");
};
```
(code continues on next page)

```
this.productsmenu_mc.menu1_mc.reviews_btn.onRelease = function() {
    gotoAndStop("reviews");
};
this.companymenu_mc.menu2_mc.tour_btn.onRelease = function() {
    gotoAndStop("tour");
};
this.companymenu_mc.menu2_mc.news_btn.onRelease = function() {
    gotoAndStop("news");
};
this.contactmenu_mc.menu3_mc.feedback_btn.onRelease = function() {
    gotoAndStop("feedback");
};
this.contactmenu_mc.menu3_mc.map_btn.onRelease = function() {
    gotoAndStop("map");
};
```

You should recognize button functions from code that you already entered for other buttons in the FLA files you have created. Although the structure might be familiar, targeting the button might not be. In this context, the this keyword refers to the current Timeline, which is the main Stage. Although this code works without it, it can be useful if you are moving your ActionScript around. Following this, you target contactmenu_mc, which is sitting on the main Stage and then inside this clip target menu3_mc. Inside menu3_mc is the button, so continue with the instance name map_btn. Because you have now targeted the instance you want to manipulate, you can enter the onRelease event handler and the rest of the inline function.

You already have labels on every frame in which a new page begins. These frame labels are used to navigate throughout the Tech Bookstore. The gotoAndStop action targets "map" (which is the name of the frame label). Frame labels must be placed within quotation marks (which mean a string).

Amazingly, you have now finished the main bulk of ActionScript that you find in the Tech Bookstore. The remainder of the work involved on the Tech Bookstore is integrating the FLA files you built in this and previous lessons into the main site. You will also optimize the Flash site, which is described in Lesson 10.

3. Test the buttons by selecting Control › Test Movie to see if the buttons work correctly.

When you click a button to open a menu, it animates downward. When you roll off the menu area onto the invisible button, it should then animate upward to "close" the menu. If you click a button in the menu, it should take you to a new page in the Tech Bookstore and stop. If the menus don't animate properly, go back and double-check your instance names and quickly check the code in this lesson. Make sure that each button in the three menus takes you to the correct page as well. If you still cannot get the menu working, locate the finished file on the CD-ROM and compare your file against what you find in the completed FLA file.

Right now, the content for these pages doesn't load. You will address that in the next lesson. Right now, just be sure that the pages are changing by looking at the title at the far right of the Stage.

4. Save the changes you made to the FLA file.

You can find copies of the finished products—called bookstore13.fla, catalog.fla, home.fla, and news.fla—in the lesson09/complete folder on the CD-ROM. In lesson09/complete/catalog, you will find catalog1.fla and catalog2.fla. If you are having any problems with the code you have typed in, you can find a copy of it in this file on the main Timeline.

In the next lesson, you start out by loading in all the SWF files you created in this lesson and earlier lessons. Then you test and debug the Tech Bookstore site and add a progress bar (the ProgressBar component) for each of the sections in the application.

What You Have Learned

In this lesson, you have:

- Learned about ActionScript 2.0 (page 242)
- Learned how to use objects, methods, and properties (pages 242–245)
- Found out how to use strict typing with variables (page 245)
- Used code hinting to speed up writing ActionScript (pages 246–248)
- Used functions and conditional statements (pages 248–250)
- Learned about scope and variables (pages 250–252)
- Found out about using _root, _parent, and levels in your ActionScript (pages 252–254)
- Extensively used the LoadVars object (pages 254–256)
- Created the Reviews page (pages 257–263)
- Added events, event handlers, and listeners to your code (pages 264–267)
- Incorporated CSS to format text that's loaded into a document (pages 268–270)
- Created the Catalog, News, and Home pages (pages 271–288)
- Added code so the Tech Bookstore's menu could animate (pages 288–295)
- Added ActionScript so the Tech Bookstore menu works (pages 295–298)

10 Loading and Optimizing Flash Content

It's time to start putting things together. So far, throughout this book, you have been creating a FLA file that will ultimately house the content of the Tech Bookstore website. The content for the website has been broken down into smaller little pieces that will load into the interface only when someone clicks a button. This is the most sensible approach to building any kind of Macromedia Flash application because it keeps the initial SWF file to download as small as possible.

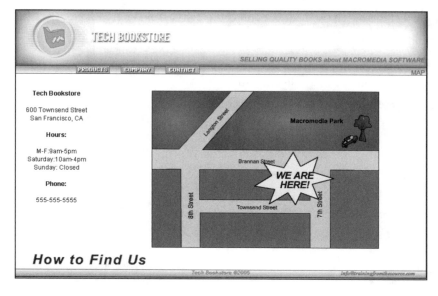

Loading content into the Tech Bookstore

There are other advantages to breaking the website content into smaller pieces. They are a little more subtle, but no less important: End users aren't forced to wait for content that they aren't interested in to download, and more than one person developing the project can work on it. If you did everything in one Flash file, you'd have a very long download time, and you'd be the only person able to work on the project.

In this lesson, you will complete the functional aspect of the website, saving publishing for Lesson 11. You'll start to gather the smaller SWF files you produced, and learn how to make your Flash application as efficient as you can make it. When you're finished, you'll test and debug the application to make sure that everything is working correctly *before* you publish it and post it to the web (or your local web server, in this case). You wouldn't put a half-eaten banana up for sale; likewise, putting a half-working Flash application on the web is very, very naughty. Shame on you for even thinking about it.

What You Will Learn

In this lesson, you will:

- Learn how to optimize websites
- Learn how to organize Flash projects
- Use runtime bitmap caching for playback performance enhancement
- Load SWF files into a Loader component instance
- Use a dynamic text field with event handlers to indicate load progress
- Use a dynamic text field with the LoadVars object to display text
- Load content into the Home, Catalog, Reviews, Tour, and News pages
- Send data out of Flash
- Add progress bars to content that is loading in
- Use MovieClipLoader to load in the Tech Bookstore
- Test and debug the Tech Bookstore

Approximate Time

This lesson takes approximately two hours to complete.

Lesson Files

Media Files:

lesson10/assets/video1.swf
lesson10/assets/video2.swf
lesson10/assets/video3.swf
lesson10/assets/sectionText.txt

Starting Files:

lesson10/start/tour_start.fla
lesson10/start/bookstore13.fla
lesson10/start/map.fla

Completed Files:

lesson10/complete/bookstore14.fla
lesson10/complete/loader.fla
lesson10/complete/map.fla
lesson10/complete/techBookstore.fla
lesson10/complete/tour.fla

Optimizing Flash Documents

Optimization is a wonderful term that means making-things-go. Seriously. The whole process has to do with making the file sizes of your SWF files small and fast to download, splitting your SWFs into smaller content-specific SWF files so that users of your application aren't forced to wait until retirement for your application to download before it can be used, and (the most-often forgotten step) making your SWF files gentle on the end user's computer. That is to say, making sure it doesn't eat up all the available CPU and memory that it can find on the end user's system. Nobody likes a glutton (except for maybe the ancient Romans), so you want to make sure that your SWF file isn't gobbling up the technological buffet.

A well-organized, well-planned Flash application rarely needs much in the way of post-development optimization, although you will always have some minor tweaking to do. In some ways, the concepts of this lesson really ought to come first, but the idea of optimization without a context to display it in doesn't carry over well, so it is next-to-last in the book. That being said, take the lessons you learn here to heart, love them, nourish them, and they will serve you very well. When you embark upon a Flash project of your own, you must consider the lessons of optimization up front, in your planning, storyboarding, development process, and all through your testing. It's as important to your Flash work as skin is to your body.

So far, you have been following many of the best practices for building Flash applications without perhaps fully understanding why. For instance, you produced much of your content (news, home, and so on) in separate and smaller SWF files. You avoided using alpha tweens and overusing animation. You loaded in external image files. Now, let's start talking about why you did all that.

Organizing Applications and Using Good Practices

There are many different kinds of websites when it comes to the way information is arranged. Some people might build a Flash site in which all the information downloaded by the users is contained in one mammoth file. The entire FLA file and everything associated with it (including JPEG images, sounds, and so forth) is contained in one SWF file that is progressively downloaded from beginning to end. Then the visitors can click through each page. Whether the user looks at all the content or not doesn't determine how much he or she has to download. Visitors download the entire website regardless of what they want to see. This is *not* a best practice unless you have a very, very small website.

Why, you ask. Well, for starters, why should your end users be forced to wait for content that they'll never look at to download before they can even use your site? Heck, why should users be forced to wait for an extensively long download time, period? People on the web have short attention spans, and if they have to wait for a long time for something to happen, they're likely to move along down the road and find a similar resource that doesn't make them wait for things to happen. Granted, you can mitigate this situation somewhat with progress bars or some other type of progress indication, but even then, people won't wait when they can get the same information or products faster and elsewhere.

Instead of creating a FLA file that contains all the content of your site in one large file, you should create a site that dynamically loads most of the content at runtime (when the SWF file plays in Flash Player). This is mostly how the Tech Bookstore is working, albeit with some exceptions for the purpose of learning. There are many ways to externalize data, such as hooking it up to a database or extensive use of XML text files, Flash Remoting, or Web Services. You can load JPEGs, PNGs, GIFs, MP3s, text, and other SWF files into your document on the fly. All these ways mean that you are working with dynamic content and improving the way your Flash documents work while loading only relevant information at the appropriate time.

Understanding Usability

Usability is a simple concept: Can people get around in your website without having to read a manual? If the answer is "yes," you've met the acid test for usability. You have to consider the usability of your Flash file and consider how easy it is for visitors to navigate your site. Is the size of your text large enough to read? Is the font legible? Does the visitor have the font installed, or are you embedding it? Are the buttons big enough, easy to find, and easy to understand as buttons? Is your site easy to navigate between each of the different sections? Sometimes you might create an "artistic" site where you specifically want the visitor to not really know how to navigate right off the bat. "Weird" navigation can be perfectly acceptable in limited situations (see http://cmart.design.ru for an excellent example), but just make sure you have considered who your intended audience is and what a member of that audience can expect to find at your site. If you were creating a shopping cart application for a business to sell its pet supplies, you wouldn't want to have three tiny + symbols at the bottom-right corner of the Stage for the main navigation! This is fine for an experimental Flash site, but not usable for a mainstream business application.

Once upon a time, Flash sites had "intros." These were often ponderous, superfluous animations that played obnoxious music and lasted forever. At one point, they were cool. And then a week went by and nobody cared any more. Seen it, we get it, you can use Flash, whoopdeedo. Where's the "skip" button?

You won't see as many Flash intros any more, thank goodness, partly because of the backlash against them. Many people hate intros and share that information with anyone who will listen. This said, many clients and individuals still love intros and create them for their websites, so they haven't completely disappeared yet. In some circumstances, intros can even be a good idea—for example, an intro that plays while a Flash game is loading into the browser cache. A best practice to follow is to "always do what the paying client wants you to do, but if you're going to make an intro, provide a skip intro button." What this skip intro phenomenon has taught us is how important usability and following good or standardized practices are when you create websites. The button immediately moves the user onto the main part of the website and stops the intro from downloading and consuming more bandwidth. Which means you'll get much less hate mail in your inbox.

Tip | *What you should take away from the skip intro idea is to always remember to give your visitor control. If the visitors don't want to download something, allow them to stop it and move on. If they don't want to hear your music, give them the option to turn it off. And it is always a bad idea to take over the visitor's computer by changing the site to full screen! Dynamically load your bandwidth heavy content whenever possible, giving your visitors the control over whether they want to download the information in the first place.*

Optimizing Animation

You already learned some of the pitfalls of animation. By way of review, those were alpha tweens (fade in and fade out) and shape tweens, both of which are processor-intensive. Brightness and tint tweens can also consume file size. But here's one you may not have considered: Animating vectors can consume CPU as if it's the last slice of cheesecake at a sweet-tooth convention. Here's why.

Vector graphics have to be completely redrawn from frame to frame. If you are motion tweening a vector graphic, each vector object that makes up the image has to be completely redrawn in its new position. Add to that vector background graphics in a different layer just sitting there while the animation occurs above it having to be redrawn for every frame, and you have an over-tasked CPU. A frame rate of 12 fps (frames per second) will begin to look more like 12 fpy (frames per year). So what to do?

- For graphics that are simply motion tweening, convert vector art to bitmap art where possible. This process might have to be done in an external editor.
- For complex vector backgrounds or other static vector graphics, convert the vectors to a movie clip object; then select runtime-bitmap caching on the Property inspector.

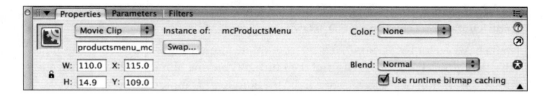

Runtime bitmap caching will treat movie clips, buttons, and even components as bitmap images after they've downloaded to the browser cache. This is a more efficient usage because the computer then has to turn pixels on and off only when a cached button or movie clip is moving, or even remaining stationary, rather than redraw each object of which the graphic is made.

Note *You should not use runtime bitmap caching on movie clips that contain animation or on buttons that contain animated movie clips.*

Sometimes it is quicker to create an animation using ActionScript than it is to painstakingly motion tween and animate movie clips on the Timeline. Using ActionScript sometimes (but not always) decreases the file size and workload when you have to animate something; however, your ActionScript might use up much more CPU than an animation tween in a Timeline. Most ActionScript-based animations use either an interval or a movie clip enterFrame event, both of which must be explicitly deleted when the animation is over. Neither setInterval nor enterFrame can stop on its own and will continue to run, even though the animation is over, eating up CPU. You have to delete them to make them stop. setInterval and enterFrame are beyond the scope of this book, but you should be aware of their pitfalls just the same.

Different processor speeds can also affect the playback of a SWF file. Older processors might play the SWF file back at a snail's place compared with a fast modern processor. The best ways to control for that are to test the SWF file on several different computers and examine how the SWF file runs on each machine. Some older computers have a difficult time playing a SWF file regardless of whether you use ActionScript or tweening to create animations. Something fading in or moving might play back very slowly and choppily on these machines. If you have a firm understanding of your target audience, you can produce your application for the lowest common denominator, as painful as that might be.

Making a Background More Efficient with Runtime Bitmap Caching

In this exercise, you will use runtime bitmap caching to boost playback performance in an animation. You'll be working with map.fla for this exercise.

1. Open map.fla from your TechBookstore folder on your hard drive, or from lesson10/start on this book's CD_ROM.

map.fla has a vector background that spans multiple frames. You will convert the graphics in this background to a movie clip and then turn on runtime bitmap caching so that the vector graphics don't have to be redrawn by the end user's computer in every frame.

2. Select your map layer, Right- or Control-click it, and choose Lock Others from the context menu.

You only want to select the graphics in the background layer, and nothing else. By locking the other layers, you avoid selecting anything but the graphics you want.

3. With the map layer selected, choose Edit › Select all, and then use the keyboard shortcut F8 to place all the selected graphics into a movie clip.

You can also draw a selection box around the whole Stage with the Selection tool; choosing Edit > Select makes sure that nothing gets left behind, though.

When all the graphics and text in the background layer are selected, press the keyboard shortcut F8 to convert the graphics to one big movie clip symbol. Call the symbol **mcBackground** and give it a movie clip behavior. Press OK.

4. Select the Movie Clip on the Stage and turn on runtime bitmap caching.

Runtime bitmap caching is turned on in the Property inspector and is available only for Flash Player 8 and above. Select the movie clip on the Stage and select the Use Runtime Bitmap Caching check box.

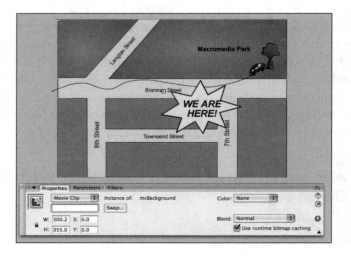

5. Save the file and choose Control › Test movie to see the animation.

When you test the movie, you'll see no real difference in the animation. However, runtime bitmap caching ensures a better playback performance when the end user's computer is overtasked with other programs.

Understanding Bandwidth and File Size

Bandwidth refers to the amount of information that is transferred between client computers and a web server. For example, a busy website might use five gigabytes of bandwidth in a month. Every time visitors arrive at your website, some bandwidth is consumed when they download the pages and media from it. Depending on the number of visitors you have and how big your website is, bandwidth quickly adds up over time on a site with some traffic, which can slow things down. It's like adding cornstarch to boiling water…the more you add, the more gooey and bogged-down everything gets. Although this is good for things like stews and pies, it is definitely not good for network traffic. This can be bad for another reason: some ISPs charge based on monthly bandwidth consumption. Therefore, you want to try and minimize how much information your visitors download on each page! Limiting bandwidth consumption affects the way you build your FLA file in many different ways that are outlined in the following sections. You want your visitors to download only the information they need and limit the surplus information they might not be interested in.

The first thing you can do to minimize bandwidth is to go through all your vector drawings, bitmap images, and sound files, and check their publish settings for when the SWF file is generated. For your vector drawings you can select Modify > Shape > Optimize to optimize the vector drawing. This can reduce (or smooth out) the vectors in the shape. If you have a lot of ragged edges, optimizing the shape reduces the number of calculations that are required by Flash to render the drawing. This in turn reduces overall file size and even improves the performance of the SWF file. You can Right-click (or Control-click) on the asset and choose Properties just as you did in earlier lessons for other media assets in the library (such as sound and images). You can change properties in the Publish Settings dialog box, too. Finally, you can use the Bandwidth Profiler in Flash to analyze and work on minimizing the file size and manage how the SWF file is downloaded to the visitor. The Bandwidth Profiler is discussed later in this lesson, and you will learn about the Publish Settings dialog box in the next lesson.

Considering User Platforms

SWF files are handled differently by different computers. Operating systems such as Windows and OS X and browsers such as Firefox and Internet Explorer each may handle an SWF file a little differently than others. For the most part, regardless of the platform or browser, your SWF file will play the same way for everyone viewing and using the application. The differences are infinitesimally small compared with something like an HTML page with style sheets, JavaScript, and so forth. However, there are small inconsistencies that are important to be aware of. A Mac will play your SWF file back a little bit more slowly than on a Windows-based machine. This has to do with the operating system and the Flash Player; however, it has been greatly improved with Flash Player 8, so the differences are quite insignificant if this Player is what your visitor has installed.

Note *A Mac and a PC handle colors differently. Graphics produced on a Mac and viewed on a Windows-based machine will appear darker than on the Mac. The opposite is true of graphics produced on Windows and viewed on a Mac. This has nothing to do with the SWF file itself; it has to do with gamma-correction differences between the machines. This inconsistency occurs no matter what you are using to create your website. When possible, use less-subtle tones and more contrasting colors to control for that difference.*

Loading External Content

You already learned how to load external content in Lessons 6 and 9. You saw that you can load JPEG, PNG, GIF, and SWF files into either movie clips or a loader component. What you haven't done yet is to let someone know that content is in fact loading, or, what's more, switched out what content goes into a Loader or movie clip instances based on a user interaction. You're about to do that in this next exercise.

Here's the rationale: You *could* have a separate Loader component instance or movie clip instance in some other keyframe in a Timeline; when a user clicks a button, you go to that keyframe with the new instance and load the new content in the interface at that point. This is overcomplicated and an inefficient use of end user resources. Every instance of a Loader component or movie clip that you make creates a new object in the end user's memory, which consumes resources. It makes more sense then to reuse a single object as often as possible, which is the goal of this next exercise.

Before we get started, you will be using two dynamic text fields to display information: One will display the download progress of the file being loaded into a Loader component instance; the other will display information about a section of the website, depending on which button was clicked. All this will happen in a one-frame Timeline and will be controlled with ActionScript. You already added Loader components to the Stage, drawn graphics, and made or used Button components, so the foundation of the file has already been created for you to save a little work and time. This leaves you free to focus on dynamic text fields and the ActionScript you have to write.

1. Open lesson10/start/tour_start.fla from this book's CD-ROM and save it as **tour.fla** in your TechBookstore folder on your hard drive.

Take a moment to look at the construction of this file: You have an empty actions layer, which you'll add ActionScript to in a few moments. You have a loaderdisplay layer, in which you will create a dynamic text field to display the progress of download of any file going into the Loader component instance on the Stage. The components layer contains three buttons with the instance names btnReviews, btnCompany, and btnContact, respectively. It also contains the Loader component instance that you will load SWFs into. The frame layer just contains a graphic the same size as the Stage and another the same size as the Loader component instance on the Stage. The text fields layer contains some static text right at the moment, but you will also add a multi-line dynamic text field, which will display information retrieved from a text file using the LoadVars class.

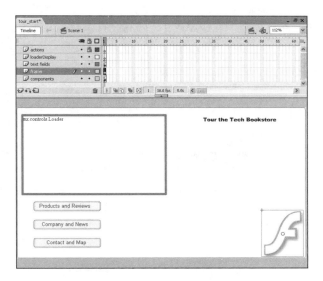

2. If you do not already have them in your TechBookstore directory, copy video1.swf, video2.swf, and video3.swf from the lesson10/assets directory into your TechBookstore folder on your hard drive. Also copy sectionText.txt into your Tech Bookstore directory from lesson10/assets.

These are the SWF files that you will be loading. If you look up their properties in Windows Explorer or do a quick Get Info on the Mac, you'll see that they're 1.8 megabytes each.

That's embedded video for you! Because we can't really "stream" these files, we'll need to indicate information about their download progress to try and mitigate the file size with user expectation. While they're downloading, you'll give your users some text to read to keep occupied. Sneaky, but effective.

3. Create a dynamic text field on the loaderDisplay layer, a multi-line dynamic text field on the text fields layer.

The loaderDisplay text field will indicate download progress. The text field in the text fields layer will display instructional text about how to use the website, loaded from a text file.

Select the Text tool and press and drag a fixed-width text field over top of the Loader component instance in the loaderDisplay layer. Set the text type to Dynamic. Set the font, font size, and justification to whatever you like; the solution file uses Arial Black, 12 pt, left-justified. Give the text field the instance name **percentLoaded**. Lock the loaderDisplay layer when you finish adjusting and positioning the text field.

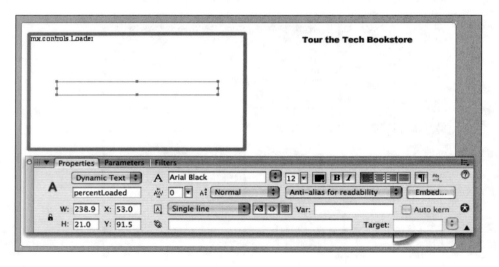

Select the text fields layer and unlock it. Drag a large dynamic text field about **270** pixels wide by **280** pixels tall (it doesn't have to be exact). In the Property inspector, select Multiline from the Line Type drop-down list. Press the Render Text as HTML button so that it is highlighted. Give the text field the instance name **displaySection**. Reposition the text field so that it appears similar to the one in the following figure.

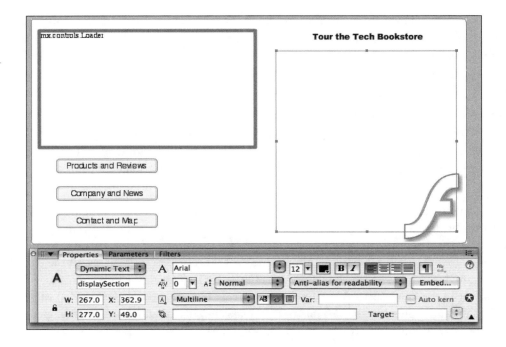

4. Select frame 1 of the actions layer and open the Actions panel.

There are a number of steps to do in the ActionScript. First, you have to create a reusable function that will handle SWF file loading. Then you have to create an object that handles what should happen when a file is loading, and what should happen when it's done. You also have to make a LoadVars object to load information from a text file, which is nothing new to you by now, and event handlers for buttons—also nothing new. Consider it practice.

5. Create a new function to load SWF files into the Loader component on the Stage. Name it **loadVideo**.

If Script Assist mode is on, turn it off now. At the top of the Actions pane, type the following ActionScript:

```
//loads the video embedded in SWF files using the loader component
function loadVideo(pathToFile:String,textToLoad:String):Void
{
    videoLoader.contentPath="";
    videoLoader.contentPath=pathToFile;
    displaySection.htmlText=loadSectionText[textToLoad];
}
```

First, you start with a comment that describes the purpose of the function. Next, you create a new function named loadVideo that accepts two arguments. The first argument, pathToFile, represents the path to the external file on the hard drive or server when it is deployed. The second argument, textToLoad, represents a string of text that will be stored in the LoadVars object when you create it.

Next, videoLoader.contentPath="" is a way of clearing out any content that may already be in the Loader component instance on the Stage. The Loader component on the Stage has the instance name videoLoader, and here you are using ActionScript instead of the Property inspector to say what content should load into the component instance. The next line assigns the path to the file on the hard drive or server when the function is called.

The final line instructs the text field displaySection to treat the text coming into it as HTML-formatted, and then gets its information from the LoadVars object. The assignment loadSection[textToLoad] might look a little strange to you because of the square braces. The square braces tell Flash to fill in the value for textToLoad before the rest of the line is executed, so it's read correctly that way. Otherwise, Flash would be looking for a property in the LoadVars object literally named textToLoad, and not its intended value. When the function runs, the variable textToLoad is populated with its value, the open square brace is converted to a ".", and the close square brace vaporizes. Flash then sees loadSection.productsAndReviews, for example. This process, which is called *dynamic evaluation*, is a way of saying, "Do this first; then worry about the rest of the line." And you thought you'd never use algebra.

6. Disable the button instances by default.

Underneath all your current code, type the following ActionScript:

```
//set initial button states
btnReviews.enabled=false;
btnCompany.enabled=false;
btnContact.enabled=false;
```

Again, you start out with an explanatory comment. Buttons and Button components have a property called enabled, which has a true or false value. When enabled is set to false, a user cannot click on the button; if it is a Button component, it is dimmed. In this case, we want to disable the buttons until the LoadVars object we will create has fully loaded its text file. Otherwise, people will click the buttons and not see the text if it hasn't loaded yet. This is an example of usability.

7. Assign default text to the displaySection text field.

Underneath all your current code, type the following lines of ActionScript:

```
//makes some default text
displaySection.htmlText="<p>Press a button below to view more information ¬
  about a section of the website</p>";
```

This assigns HTML-formatted text to the displaySection text field that tells a user what to do next. If you save and test your file at this point, you will see the text appear in the text field, and your buttons will be dimmed.

8. Create a LoadVars object, load a text file, and enable the buttons when the text file is fully loaded.

Underneath all your current script, type the following:

```
//creates the load vars object for loading the section text
var loadSectionText:LoadVars=new LoadVars();
loadSectionText.load("sectionText.txt");
loadSectionText.onLoad=function()
{
     btnReviews.enabled=true;
     btnCompany.enabled=true;
     btnContact.enabled=true;
}
```

You have worked with the LoadVars object before. The only thing really different here is instead of using it to display text right away, you are using it to make your buttons clickable again. Pretty clever, huh?

Again, this is an example of usability. When users click a button, they expect something to happen. By turning off the buttons until the information fully loads, you're preventing users from getting frustrated when they click something and the application just sits there.

9. Create a listener object that responds to progress and complete events. Add the listener object to the Loader component instance.

You were briefly introduced to the idea of listener objects in Lesson 9. Here, you want single object to handle two tasks. It has to listen for someone to tell it a file is loading; that's the progress event. The "someone" is the Loader instance. We'll get to that in a second. Also, you want it to do something when a file has finished loading. That's the complete event.

Lastly, the listener object barely cares who talks to it, as long as someone addresses it directly. Kind of like a New Yorker. People can scream and whoop and holler all around New Yorkers, and they couldn't care less. However, if someone comes right up to them and says, "Can you tell me the way to Times Square?" they can point you in the right direction if they're of a mind to (but don't trust the young ones, they always get you turned around). In

ActionScript, you'll have to tell the Loader component to let your listener object know when it is loading a file or when a file is finished loading, so it won't be ignored.

Underneath all your code, write the following lines of ActionScript:

```
//creates a listener object to handle progress indication and
//clears the progress indication when the video is fully loaded.
var myLoadIt:Object=new Object();

myLoadIt.progress=function()
{
    percentLoaded.autosize="left";
    percentLoaded.text=Math.round(videoLoader.percentLoaded)+"% of the ¬
        video has loaded";
}
myLoadIt.complete=function()
{
    percentLoaded.text="";
}

videoLoader.addEventListener("progress",myLoadIt);
videoLoader.addEventListener("complete",myLoadIt);
```

Be proud of yourself! You're doing very well so far.

As always, you start off with a comment. Then you create a generic object called `myLoadIt` from the Object class. The Object class is THE class in Flash, because everything is based from it. It's kind of dumb, however, because it doesn't really have its own properties or methods to speak of, which is what makes it great for a listener object. Think of it as modeling clay: Once you have it, you can shape it into anything you want.

After you have the object built, you tell it to respond to anything that tells it a file load is in progress. When it knows that's what's happening, it looks at the percent of data loaded into the `videoLoader` component instance on the Stage, rounds the number, and then displays that number n the `percentLoaded` text field you create earlier. You use concatenation (remember, the ActionScript glue stick) to add an extra piece of text to the information displaying in the text field so the end user understands what's happening.

The last two lines use the `addEventListener` method of the Loader component to tell `videoLoader` to let your listener object know when it's loading or finished loading a file.

Whew! One last thing to do and then you can test it.

10. Create event handlers for your buttons to load different SWF files containing embedded video.

Underneath all your current script, type the following lines of ActionScript:

```
//buttons cause video and text to display

btnReviews.onRelease=function()
{
    loadVideo("video1.swf","productsAndReviews");
}
btnCompany.onRelease=function()
{
    loadVideo("video2.swf","companyAndNews");
}
btnContact.onRelease=function()
{
    loadVideo("video3.swf","contactAndMap");
}
```

You already created event handlers for buttons. What's different with these event handlers is that you are calling your `loadVideo` function, and passing to the function the path to the video and the text to display from the LoadVars object you created. Also, you're loading each SWF file into a single Loader component instance, replacing current content with new.

Note *If the Loader component is already loading content when a new button is selected, the current download will be stopped in favor of the new download.*

11. Save and test your file. Simulate a download to see the progress indication.

Save tour.fla and select Control > Test Movie. If the Bandwidth Profiler is not turned on, select View > Bandwidth Profiler in the Test Movie Environment.

When you test a movie and it loads information in from the hard drive, it appears as if the content is loading quickly, but this gives you a false sense of security. To simulate a download, select View Download Settings, and then choose an option. Then select View > Simulate Download. Your progress indicator should show the percentages of each SWF file loaded when you click a video, and the download begins. When the download is finished, the text field displaying the percentage loaded is purged.

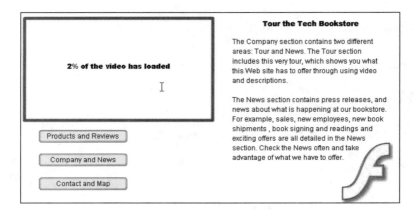

12. Save and close tour.fla.

In the next set of exercises, you will be loading content into the main Tech Bookstore website. You'll be using techniques similar to what you just learned, with a few slight modifications.

Loading Content into the Main Application

Throughout this book, you have created content that will ultimately load into the Tech Bookstore site at different points— some when a user first clicks a button, and some when the application first loads up. This decreases the amount of information you have to store in the main Flash SWF file, particularly some of the components that can quickly bulk up the size of your SWF file. So let's add the rest of the content into the Tech Bookstore.

1. Open bookstore13.fla if it isn't already open, and save a new version of the file by selecting File > Save As. Save the new document as **bookstore14.fla.**

Make sure that this file is saved in the TechBookstore folder on your hard drive. You can also find a copy of bookstore13.fla on the book's CD-ROM if you would rather begin with that file instead.

When you are placing the content in this exercise on the Stage, make sure that you leave enough room for the menus to drop down. Drag a horizontal guide to approximately **140** pixels on the vertical ruler. Place all new content below this guide.

2. Add a Loader component instance on the home layer. Resize the component instance to **580** by **345** and give it an instance name.

The home layer is in the pages layer folder. The Loader component instance is to load in the content for the Home page, which is in an external SWF file.

Expand the Components panel and drag an instance of the Loader component onto Frame 1 of the home layer, which is within the pages folder. Give the component an instance name of **home_ldr** and position it on the left side of the Stage under the navigation.

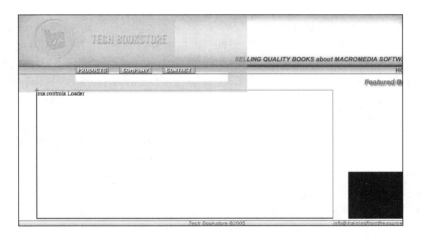

Resize the component to the size of the home.swf document (which is 580w by 345h) that the component will load in. Remember, you produced home.swf in Lesson 9.

Note *You can leave the component at its default size and let Flash resize the instance when the content loads in. It is often easier to size the component manually because it allows you to see where the content will load in relation to the other instances on the Stage. Also make sure that* scaleContent *is set to* false. *If it is set to* true, *your content will resize and this can end up distorting it. Text can look horrible after it is scaled.*

Set the contentPath for the Loader component to home.swf in either the Parameters tab of the Property inspector. This is the URL of the content you want to load into the component.

There are three properties you can change for the Loader component using the Property inspector:

- **autoLoad:** Determines whether or not the content should load automatically when the frame is loaded (true). If not, you have to explicitly call the load function (false).

- **contentPath:** The URL pointing to the content that should be loaded. This field accepts both relative and absolute URLs.
- **scaleContent:** Boolean (`true` or `false`) value that determines whether the Loader component should resize itself to fit the content being loaded (`false`) or whether the content should be scaled to fit the size of the existing Loader component (`true`).

For each of the sections in the website, you want to make sure that the `autoLoad` is set to `true` and the `scaleContent` is set to `false`.

3. Insert a new layer called **catalog**. Add a Loader component instance to the Catalog page. Resize the instance, set the `contentPath`, and position it on the Stage.

Insert a new layer directly below the home layer. Rename the new layer **catalog**. Insert a new keyframe on Frame 10, and delete all the frames on the layer after Frame 19 by highlighting them with the mouse, Right-clicking (or Control-clicking), and selecting Remove Frames from the contextual menu.

Click Frame 10 of the catalog layer in the Timeline and drag an instance of the Loader component onto the Stage. Give the component an instance name of **catalog_ldr**. Expand the Property inspector and set the `contentPath` to **catalog.swf** and then set the `scaleContent` property to **false**. Resize the component to the same dimensions as the catalog.swf document, which you produced in Lesson 9 and is **720** (width) by **345** (height).

Position the component so it is roughly in the center of the main content area, as seen in the following graphic.

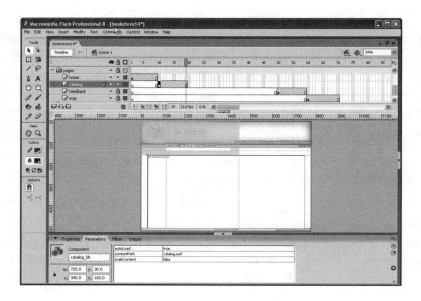

4. Insert a new layer called **reviews**. Add a Loader instance on the Reviews page to load in reviews.swf. Resize and position the component as well as change its parameters.

Insert a new layer directly below the catalog layer. Then insert a new keyframe on Frame 20 of the layer by pressing F6 and delete all the frames greater than Frame 30 on the layer. Highlight the frames with the cursor, Right-click (or Control-click), and select Remove Frames from the context menu.

Click on Frame 20 of the reviews layer and drag an instance of the Loader component onto the Stage. In the Property inspector, set the instance name to **reviews_ldr** and set the contentPath property to **reviews.swf**. Then set the scaleContent property to **false**. Resize the component to **720** by **360** and position it in the middle of the Stage.

5. Insert a new layer called **tour**. Add a Loader instance on the tour page to load in tour.swf. Resize and position the component and change its parameters.

Insert a new layer directly below the reviews layer. Then insert a new keyframe on Frame 30 of the layer by pressing F6 and delete all the frames greater than Frame 40 on the layer. Highlight the frames with the cursor, Right-click (or Control-click), and select Remove Frames from the context menu.

Click on Frame 30 of the tour layer and drag an instance of the Loader component on to the Stage. In the Property inspector, set the instance name to **tour_ldr** and set the contentPath property to **tour.swf**. Then set the scaleContent property to **false**. Resize the component to **720** by **360** and position it in the middle of the Stage.

6. Insert a new layer called **news** and add a Loader instance to the Stage. Give the instance an instance name and then resize and position it on the Stage.

Insert a new layer, rename it to **news**, and make sure that it is directly below the tour layer. Click Frame 40, insert a new keyframe by pressing F6, and then remove all the frames on the layer that are greater than 49.

Click Frame 40 of the news layer and add a Loader component. Give the component an instance name of **news_ldr**, set the contentPath to **news.swf**, and set scaleContent to **false**. Resize the Loader instance so it is **635** wide by **345** high and place it in the horizontal center of the News page.

When you are finished, the Timeline should look similar to the following figure.

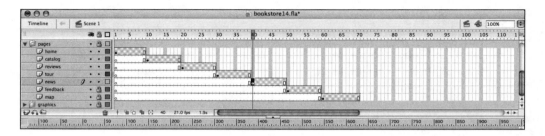

7. Give the Loader instance already on the map layer a new instance name.

The Map page already has a Loader component on the Stage from a previous lesson. Click the instance, and in the Property inspector give it an instance name of **map_ldr** and set the scaleContent property to **false**.

8. Add any additional graphics or text to the Tech Bookstore site.

Before you finish up, you might want to add some static text on some of the individual pages just to dress things up a little bit. Of course, this step is completely optional.

9. Clean up the library. Then test and save the changes that you made to the FLA file.

Move any of the new graphics or symbols you might have created, and the new components into their respective folders in the library.

At this point, you can test the entire Tech Bookstore application. Press Ctrl+Enter or Cmd+Enter to test the SWF file in the testing environment or in a web browser window by pressing F12. Each of the sections should now have content load when you click one of the menu buttons to navigate to each page.

If one of the SWF files does not load, make sure that it is saved in the TechBookstore directory, and that the SWF file's filename is entered correctly (without typos) into the Property inspector for the particular Loader instance.

Sending Data Out of Flash

At this point, you're getting down to the last few steps that you need to take to complete this application. One of the last tasks for you to complete is to send information out of Flash using the forms you created in Lesson 8. That's the subject of the next exercise. After that, you'll create a simple progress bar to let users know that Tech Bookstore website is loading when they first come to the page. First things first, though, and that's submitting data.

In Flash 8 Basic, there are several ways to send information out of Flash, all of which require some level of ActionScript. You can use the LoadVars object to send information out of Flash (and you will in this exercise), getURL, XML, and for more complex applications, Flash Remoting. Which method you choose depends on the application you are building, but all of them have one thing in common: There must be some technology on a web server somewhere that is waiting for the data you're sending out, and what's more, *understands* the data and what to do with it. This back-end work is really outside of the scope of this book because it requires an understanding of technologies that are much different from Flash. If you're a designer, it might make sense to team up with a developer who can help you develop the back-end technology to receive and process data for the projects you'll be working on in real life.

Sending Data Out of the Feedback Form

In the next exercise, you'll create a LoadVars object that will collect information from your form and then send it to a server. The server already understands what to do with the information, but that's really not our concern at this point. What we care about is getting the information *out*. You will be submitting information to your e-mail address using a script pre-created on an actual web server. You should still be working with bookstore14.fla in this lesson.

1. Select Frame 50 of the feedback layer.

You will place the ActionScript that collects and send the data out of Flash inside each movie clip Timeline. Frame 50 is where your mcQuestionForm and mcFeedbackForm movie clips are located.

2. Double-click mcFeedbackFrom. Add a hidden TextInput instance on the Stage to hold a value for the e-mail address that you will send the data to.

You are double-clicking mcFeedbackForm on the Stage to enter the movie clip's Timeline, in which you will place ActionScript and a hidden form element. You'll need to make sure that the feedback layer in the main document Timeline is unlocked so that you can edit the mcFeedbackForm movie clip.

Drag an instance of the TextInput component onto the Stage in the form layer. Using the Property inspector, set the text parameter to the e-mail address that you want to e-mail the feedback to, such as you@yourdomain.com. Enter your own e-mail address (or an account you can actually check) here.

Open the Component inspector panel by choosing Window > Component Inspector, and select the parameters tab. Set the visible parameter to **false** to hide the instance on the Stage. The visible parameter is not available on the Property inspector, which is why you are using the Component inspector panel to change its value. Assign an instance name of **tiEmailTo** to the TextInput instance using the Property inspector.

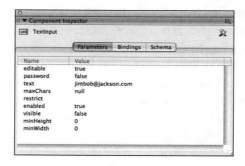

3. Add the following ActionScript into the Actions panel on Frame 1 of the actions layer in the `mcFeedbackForm` movie clip Timeline.

Select Frame 1 of the actions layer, still inside the mcFeedbackForm Timeline, and type in the following code into the Actions panel. This ActionScript is used to send data entered into the form to an e-mail address. An explanation of what this code does follows the listing.

```
//Sends the information out of Flash
bSend.onRelease = function() {
    var targetLoadVars:LoadVars = new LoadVars();
    var myLoadVars:LoadVars = new LoadVars();
    myLoadVars.emailFrom = tiEmail.text;
    myLoadVars.emailTo = tiEmailTo.text;
    myLoadVars.subject = tiSubject.text;
    myLoadVars.message = taMessage.text;
    myLoadVars.sendAndLoad ("http://www.flash-mx.com/ws/ ¬
        submit_feedback.cfm", targetLoadVars, "POST");
    targetLoadVars.onLoad = function() {
        trace(this.success);
    };
    gotoAndStop("thankyou");
};
```

The script you just typed might look a little intimidating, but it really isn't so bad once you know what it means. Ultimately, you're gathering information, storing it in sort of a programming version of an expand-a-file folder, and sending it out. You start with adding a comment, for reasons you've already learned. Commenting is your friend, so don't forget about it.

The next step is to add an `onRelease` event handler for your send button. This handler is called when a user clicks on the bSend Button instance. Then you create two LoadVars objects to send the data out. The first LoadVars object is used to hold the variables that the server-side script will return after it is done executing. The second LoadVars object holds all the variables that are sent to the server-side script.

After the LoadVars objects are created, the code copies the four text field values (`tiEmail`, `tiEmailTo`, `tiSubject`, and `taMessage`) into the `myLoadVars` variable. When the `myLoadVars` object is sent to a URL, all these variables are included. Then a server-side script can be used to process the variables. A server-side script is code written using a language such as PHP, ColdFusion, or ASP. The script interacts with web pages and is used to perform a particular task. The script sits on a server and can be used to load data, interact with a database, and perform other similar tasks—depending on what the code is written to do.

The following line of code is where Flash posts the values within the myLoadVars object to your server-side script:

```
myLoadVars.sendAndLoad("http://www.flash-mx.com/ws/ submit_feedback.cfm", ¬
    targetLoadVars, "POST");
```

The values in the LoadVars object are sent to http://www.flash-mx.com/ws/submit_feedback.cfm. Any results sent from the server-side script will be saved into the targetLoadVars object. The final parameter in the sendAndLoad() function is POST. POST tells Flash how to send the data to the server-side script. When sending the LoadVars object using the POST method, all fields are sent to the server-side script as form variables. Form variables are variables that are sent in the HTTP header, which is not visible to the visitor. This is suitable for long sets of variables, and more importantly, is necessary, because that's how the script is expecting data to come.

Note *The other option for the method is GET instead of POST. The GET method sends the values to your server-side script as URL variables along the query string. The query string, which is the part of the URL in the browser's address bar after the question mark, is suitable for sending short variables. For example, in the URL http://www.TrainingFromTheSource.com/index.cfm?name=jdehaan, the query string is name=jdehaan.*

The final section of ActionScript from the code block you typed in is used for debugging in the testing environment only. The trace statement appears in the Output panel when the data has been sent from Flash to the server-side script. This lets you know that Flash has sent the data when you are working in the testing environment. The trace statements are used only for development and testing purposes, and should be removed before you publish the file and upload it to a server for a website (sometimes known as the production environment).

Finally, you see the following code:

```
targetLoadVars.onLoad = function() {
    trace(this.success);
};
```

This code is triggered when Flash *receives* a reply from the server-side script, which sometimes takes a short period of time before it's executed as Flash waits for a reply. Currently, the server returns a string value of success or failure, which will be displayed in the Output panel (again, for testing purposes). You will be able to test this form after you have the buttons and menus working for the Tech Bookstore at the end of this lesson. In the real world, you would redirect a user to the "thank you" page only if the data were successfully submitted and generated error messages for the user if it were not. In this application, you don't provide feedback for the end user if there is an error. The success page, however, is targeted in the line: `gotoAndStop("thankyou");` which directs the playhead to the thankyou frame label.

4. Save the changes you made to bookstore14.fla.

Save your file and test it by selecting Control > Test Movie. Go to the feedback section of the site and fill out the feedback form. Press the send button, and if you specified your own e-mail address in Step 2, you should see an e-mail in your inbox sent from Flash.

Note *If your back button for some reason does not work, go to the "thankyou" frame, select it, and open the Actions panel. You added an ActionScript using Script Assist in Lesson 8. If you are in Script Assist mode, toggle it off, and change line 2 to read* **this._parent.gotoAndStop("form"),** *which tells the button to control the playhead in the movie clip Timeline a little bit more specifically.* This *refers to the button;* parent *refers to the movie clip Timeline.*

If everything works, save the file and leave it open. You will send data out of the Questionnaire form next.

Sending Data Out of the Questionnaire Form

In this exercise, you will use LoadVars to send values to a server, similar to the way you send information out of the feedback form you completed in the previous exercise. The questionnaire is more complex than the feedback form because you are not only dealing with text fields this time. The form has a NumericStepper component, List component, TextArea component, and two CheckBox components for which you have to get the values.

In this exercise, you will use ActionScript to send the variables to a server-side script, which then processes the results so they can be computed later.

1. In bookstore14.fla, make sure you are in Frame 50 of the main document Timeline. Double-click `mcQuestionForm` to open it in symbol-editing mode. Enter instance names for the component instances that are on the Stage.

Open bookstore14.fla from the TechBookstore folder on your hard drive that you worked on earlier in this lesson, if it is not already open. Make sure you are in Frame 50 of the feedback layer. Double-click `mcQuestionForm` to open the instance in symbol-editing mode. Lock the actions layer to prevent accidentally adding any symbols to that layer.

You first need to give instance names to the components that are on the Stage. Give the NumericStepper an instance name of **nsNumYears**, and the ComboBox an instance name of **cbNavigation**. Assign an instance name of **taBooks** to the TextArea component. Then assign the Designer CheckBox an instance name of **chDesigner** and the Developer CheckBox instance an instance name of **chDeveloper**. Finally, give the Send button an instance name of **bSend** if it is not already named.

2. Add ActionScript code to Frame 1 of the actions layer using the Actions panel.

Select Frame 1 of the actions layer in the mcQuestionForm instance and open or expand the Actions panel (F9). Type in the following code:

```
//sends questionnaire data out and to the server
bSend.onRelease = function(){
    var targetLoadVars:LoadVars = new LoadVars();
    var myLoadVars:LoadVars = new LoadVars();
    myLoadVars.surveyExperience = nsNumYears.value;
    myLoadVars.surveyNavigation = cbNavigation.selectedItem.label;
    myLoadVars.surveyBooks = taBooks.text;
    myLoadVars.surveyDesigner = chDesigner.selected;
    myLoadVars.surveyDeveloper = chDeveloper.selected;
    myLoadVars.sendAndLoad("http://www.flash-mx.com/ws/submit_survey.cfm", ¬
        targetLoadVars, "POST");
    trace("send");
    targetLoadVars.onLoad = function() {
        trace(this.success);
    };
    gotoAndStop("thankyou");
};
```

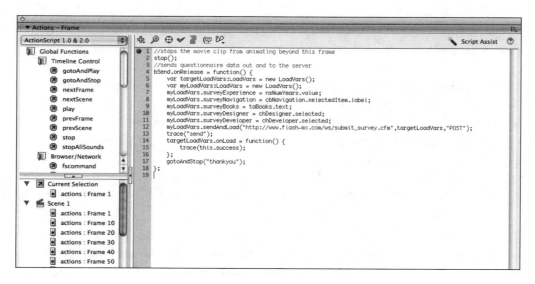

This code is similar to the previous exercise, in which you used LoadVars to send the feedback to the server-side script. There are a couple of major differences between the two scripts. Because the questionnaire uses several different component types instead of the TextInput and TextArea, grabbing the values from the component and adding them to the LoadVars object is slightly more complicated.

Each component is different, so they each have a different way to access the value of the component. For example, the TextArea and TextInput components store the current value in text, whereas the CheckBox component doesn't have a value, but instead has a Boolean (Yes/No) parameter called selected and denotes whether the component is checked or not. You access the current value of the NumericStepper component by accessing its value parameter.

The List component uses the parameter selectedItem, which is actually an object within itself and has two values: data and labels. You defined the labels and data values earlier in Lesson 8 after you dragged the List component onto the Stage. The value for labels is simply the label for the currently selected item, and the value for data is the value you defined in the Property inspector or Component inspector panel for the currently selected instance.

So how do you know all this stuff? The hardest part of ActionScript is knowing what does what, and learning how to manipulate information with prebuilt things such as components and movie clips and buttons. Aside from the volumes and references written about ActionScript 2.0, you have documentation right in Flash that explains what does what. The Help menu can be pulled up with the keyboard shortcut F1, or you can go to Help > Flash Help. There are gobs of entries about components all by themselves, where you can look up and learn more about how they work. Don't forget about help. It's a real lifesaver.

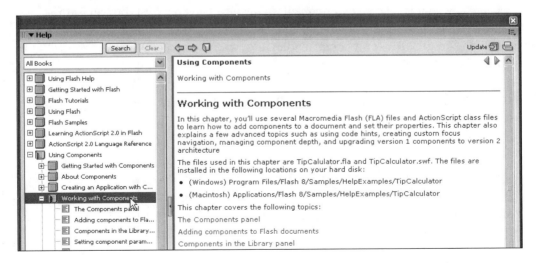

Just like the feedback form, you also have `trace` statements in the code to notify you when the request was sent to the server, and when the server responds, it will return success. These two `trace` statements can be safely removed when you are convinced that the application is working properly.

3. Save the changes to the FLA file.

After you have finished, choose File > Save to save your modifications to the file. Test your file with Control > Test movie and fill out the questionnaire. When you click Send, the values from each of the components are stored in a LoadVars object and are sent to a ColdFusion page.

Adding the ProgressBar Component

Progress bars are an important part of many larger Flash documents, particularly ones using video, audio, or complete sites built using Flash. In this case, you're dealing with all of the above! When you load in content, it is important to display indication onscreen that loading is taking place. You might have visitors using dial-up phone modems to view the website, or you might have a large video file that even visitors on the fastest broadband connections have to wait to start viewing. In these cases, a progress bar tells the visitor that content is in progress of loading. If you do not use a progress bar or preload content, your users might think something is wrong with the site because they do not see anything happening. A visual indication is quite important to let them know to hold on a second while the SWF file loads.

Earlier in this lesson, you used a dynamic text field to indicate the load progress of a SWF file being loaded into a Loader component. In the next two exercises, you will use a progress bar to do much the same thing, only without adding a text field of your own because the ProgressBar component handles it for you. Pretty nice of it, huh? You will still be using bookstore14.fla.

1. Open bookstore14.fla from the TechBookstore folder on your hard drive if it is not already open.

You are still working with the same FLA file you used for the previous exercise.

2. Select Frame 1 of the home layer. Expand the Components panel and drag an instance of the ProgressBar component onto the Stage.

Position the progress bar over the middle of the Loader component and give it an instance name of **pbHome**.

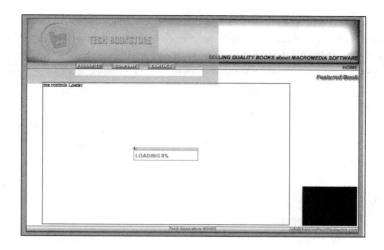

In the Property inspector's Parameters tab, set the mode to **polled** and set the source to the
instance name of the Loader component: **home_ldr**. The polled mode lets you use the
progress bar with anything that can use two ActionScript methods called getBytesLoaded()
and getBytesTotal(), which are used to monitor progress. Previously in the lesson, you
indicated progress with the progress event—not getBytesLoaded() and getBytesTotal()—
and placed that information in a text field. Movie clips don't have a progress event, so if
you want to reuse this Loader instance with a movie clip, you're out of luck if it is in event
mode (which works with only progress and complete events). Because you're working
with a Loader component, either event or polled mode works just fine.

3. Add the event listener Object ActionScript. Add this code on Frame 1 of the
actions layer.

When the content displays in the Loader component, the ProgressBar remains visible and
stays at 100%. You need to create an event listener that waits for content to finish loading
and then hides the ProgressBar component.

Select Frame 1 on the actions layer and add the following ActionScript below the existing
code in the Actions panel:

```
var pbListener:Object = new Object();
pbListener.progress = function(evt) {
    evt.target._visible = true;
};
pbListener.complete = function(evt) {
    evt.target._visible = false;
};
```

You've seen this ActionScript before: you're creating an object that will listen for progress and complete events; this time, however, these events will be relayed by the ProgressBar. The ProgressBar in this situation is sort of acting as an intermediary. It's watching the Loader's progress and complete events and matching it with its own progress and complete events. The progress indication happens without any ActionScript having to be written by you as a result. Your ActionScript is making sure that the ProgressBar is visible only when a file is loading and making it invisible when the file is finished. That's what the evt is all about. The evt option is the *broadcaster*, or the component talking to the listener object, which in this case, is the ProgressBar component.

You use the progress and complete events to toggle the visibility of the ProgressBar component. When the external SWF file is actively being loaded into the Loader component, the ProgressBar is visible on the Stage. It displays what percentage of the file has been loaded. When the complete event is caught, the content is fully loaded, and the ProgressBar component can be hidden on the Stage because the Loader instance already displays the loaded content.

4. **Create an event listener for the pbHome ProgressBar component to hide the ProgressBar instance.**

To hide the pbHome progress bar on the Stage when the content in the Loader component has finished loading, you need to add the following ActionScript code to the bottom of the actions layer. Add this code below the ActionScript you entered in Step 3:

```
pbHome.addEventListener("progress", pbListener);
pbHome.addEventListener("complete", pbListener);
```

This ActionScript adds two event listeners to the pbHome instance on the Stage. Now when the pbHome ProgressBar receives the progress event, it lets pbListener know; then pbListener executes the instructions in its progress event handler.

When the complete event is triggered by Flash, the pbListener event handler sets the visibility of the target component (the component that generates the event—which in this case is pbHome) to false. The event hides the symbol on the Stage. You can substitute evt.target with pbHome in the code in Step 3, and the code would work the same way. One drawback to *hard coding* (setting a definite single value instead of a variable that could change the value) pbHome into the function is that the function works only with that one component instance. By keeping the function dynamic and using the evt.target, you can reuse that same ProgressBar listener object on each of the ProgressBars instances throughout the entire FLA.

5. Add new ProgressBar instances for the remaining SWF files that need to be dynamically loaded into the site. Give each new instance a new instance name.

Repeat the process of adding ProgressBar components onto the Stage for the Loader component instances that load in the Reviews, News, Catalog, Tour, and Map sections. Give each new ProgressBar component instance a unique instance name. Make sure that you also change the source parameter for each new instance of the ProgressBar component to the Loader component instance it will be monitoring (news_ldr, map_ldr, etc).

Tip *Make sure that you add each ProgressBar to the layer for each page these Loader instances are on (map, news, reviews). If you choose a layer that spans multiple pages, your ProgressBar instance is visible on pages where it doesn't belong.*

6. Add an event listener to every page containing a ProgressBar component. Add the code onto the actions layer. Change the instance name in the code to match the instance name of the ProgressBar instance on that particular page.

You'll also need to add the two lines of event listener code from Step 5 to each frame in the actions layer with the ProgressBar components. Each listener can reuse the same pbListener event handler object defined on Frame 1 of the FLA file, but the listeners must be added to the same frame as the component instances because they won't "exist" until the playhead encounters them. For example, in the code on the frame labeled news (Frame 40), you would need to add the following code on the actions layer, assuming that your ProgressBar component had an instance name of pbNews:

```
pbNews.addEventListener("progress", pbListener);
pbNews.addEventListener("complete", pbListener);
```

As mentioned, ActionScript needs to be added to each frame that has a ProgressBar. There are already keyframes with the stop action on each page. You want to add this code following each stop action, and remember to modify the instance name in the code with the instance name of the particular ProgressBar component on that particular page.

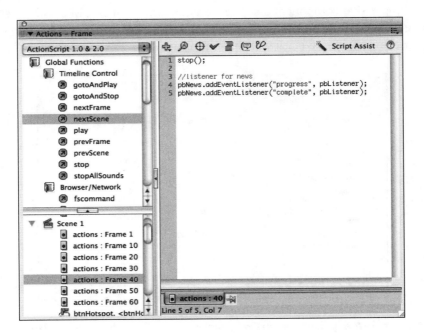

7. Save and test your file.

Make sure your ProgressBar components are doing what they're supposed to do. Choose Control > Test movie. As you navigate through each one of your pages, the ProgressBar component should become visible for a fraction of a second and then disappear from the page, telling you that the complete event is in fact doing what it should—making the component invisible after all the information has loaded into the Loader component instance on each page.

To see the ProgressBar component indicating progress, select View > Simulate Download and navigate through your site. You can change the download speeds in View > Download Settings.

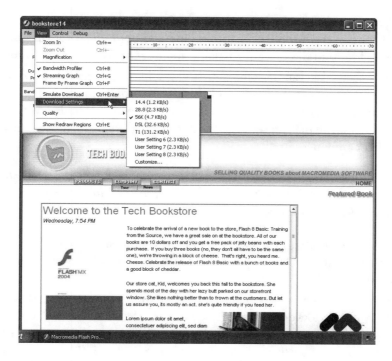

Note *If your ProgressBar components are not working, check the instances names of all your Loader components, the ProgressBar components, and their appropriate references in the ActionScript. You want to make sure your casing is correct and that each reference to a component is consistent.*

Loading the Tech Bookstore

The Tech Bookstore is not a massive file because a lot of its content is being loaded into Loader movie clips. However, it would take too long to load on phone modems not to have a progress bar for the entire site itself. Therefore, you will create a special SWF file that loads in the entire Tech Bookstore. This is not the only way to handle this process, but it is probably one of the easiest ways and, more importantly, it shows you how the MovieClipLoader class works to load in external content into a movie clip. You will find the MovieClipLoader class quite useful for this purpose and other sites that you build in the future.

The MovieClipLoader class is an ActionScript class that comes with Flash 8 Basic. Its purpose is to initiate, monitor, and complete loading of SWF files as well as JPG, PNG, and GIF images. Because it doesn't have a visual component associated with it, it's well suited for applications in which you plan to create your own progress bar, or something like it, to indicated download progress. In this next exercise, that is precisely what you are going to do.

1. Create a new FLA file called **loader.fla** and save it in the TechBookstore folder. This file will load in the Tech Bookstore online and contain a progress bar that you create yourself to load the bookstore using the new `MovieClipLoader` class.

The `MovieClipLoader` class can track the successful loading of content into movie clips, such as images and SWF files like the many bookstore.fla files you have created. Because the ProgressBar component adds about 30K in its own right, you will build a very lightweight SWF file so visitors with dial-up connections don't see a blank SWF file while waiting for the ProgressBar component itself to load in.

> **Note** *You might want to add a small graphic or small animation to entertain visitors while they wait. Now, you won't want to make the animation too intensive or else the visitor will have to wait for that to load as well!*

2. Change the fps speed of the new FLA file to **21** fps and the dimensions to **780** (width) by **520** (height). Rename Layer 1 to **progress**. Add a new layer above it and name it **actions**.

These dimensions and the frame rate match those of the Tech Bookstore. This means that your SWF file will not slow down after it is loaded into the loader.swf file. Why would it slow down, you ask? Because when you load one SWF file into another, it inherits the parent SWF file's frame rate, like it or not. Sort of like a "When in Rome…" for Flash.

You will place ActionScript in the actions layer to handle file loading; the progress layer will contain graphics that will visually indicate download progress.

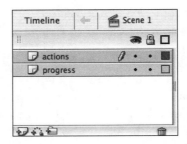

3. Create a rectangle on the Stage in the Merge Drawing model with a fill color of your choice. Resize the rectangle to approximately **150** pixels wide and a height of about **10** pixels.

The rectangle serves as a progress bar like the component you used earlier on. You can make the rectangle a different size, but try to maintain the same ratio and shape.

The fill color will be the actual progress bar that grows in size as the SWF file loads, and the stroke around the edge will contain the progress bar, showing visitors a depiction of how much more data the SWF file has to load in.

Switch to the Rectangle tool in your Tools panel. Choose any stroke and fill color that you like, make sure that you are in the Merge Drawing model, and draw a rectangle of any shape or size on the Stage.

4. Select the fill itself and convert it into a movie clip. Give this clip an instance name of **bar_mc**. Then select the stroke, convert it to a graphic symbol, and select Modify › Arrange › Bring to Front.

Select the fill on the Stage and press F8 to convert it into a movie clip. Open the Property inspector and type **bar_mc** into the <Instance Name> field.

When you convert the fill into a movie clip, it overlaps the stroke that surrounds that movie clip. Therefore, you need to select the entire stroke (double-click the stroke to select all the segments) and press F8 to convert it into a graphic symbol. Select the Graphic radio button, name the symbol **graphic_gr** and click OK. You won't be doing anything with the stroke itself, so it's converted to a graphic symbol simply to conserve file size. Remember, a movie clip adds more weight. Then when the stroke is a symbol and still selected, choose Modify > Arrange > Bring to Front, which changes the location of the symbol so it is visible in front of the bar_mc again.

5. Create a dynamic text field on the Stage and enter the text loading. Set the text to black 12 pt Arial font, and select the Alias text button. Set the justification for the text field to right, and resize the text field so there is leading space. Then position the field near the rectangle and give it an instance name of **pctLoaded_txt**.

Type **loading** into the text field. The text will display the percentage of the loaded SWF file in addition to this text and change as the percentage of loaded content updates because it is set to be a dynamic text field. Change the justification of the field to right so you can align the text to the right of the progress bar if you want. Because the text on the left side changes and the "loading" text remains stationary, the text field looks better when the SWF file loads.

You need to add some leading space so the text that is dynamically entered into the text field has some room to change size because of the dimensions of text as the numbers change in the text field. As you can see in the previous figure, this means making the text field quite large so it can hold all the text you are assigning to the text field. Double-click the text field so you see a white square in the lower-right corner. Click and drag the square to resize the text field.

Then make sure that you add an instance name of **pctLoaded_txt** using the Property inspector to assign a text value to it using ActionScript.

6. Select the rectangle and the text field and then convert them into a new movie clip by pressing F8. Give it an instance name of loader_mc.

Select both instances by pressing Shift while you click each one. Then press F8 and select the Movie Clip radio button. Enter **loader_mc** as the symbol name for the new movie clip and click OK. Then select the instance on the Stage and open the Property inspector. Enter **loader_mc** into the Property inspector as the instance name of the movie clip.

7. Add the ActionScript for the `MovieClipLoader` class into Frame 1 of the actions layer.

Select Frame 1 of the actions layer, and open the Actions panel. Enter the following code into the Script pane. A description of this ActionScript follows the code listing.

```
loader_mc.bar_mc._xscale = 0;
var myLoader_mcl:MovieClipLoader = new MovieClipLoader();
var mclListener:Object = new Object();
mclListener.onLoadProgress = function(target_mc:MovieClip) {
    var prog:Object = myLoader_mcl.getProgress(target_mc);
    var pctLoaded:Number = ¬
        Math.round((prog.bytesLoaded/prog.bytesTotal)*100);
    loader_mc.bar_mc._xscale = pctLoaded;
    loader_mc.pctLoaded_txt.text = pctLoaded+"% loaded";
};
myLoader_mcl.addListener(mclListener);
myLoader_mcl.loadClip("bookstore14.swf", this.createEmptyMovieClip("holder", ¬
    2));
```

This ActionScript is a little bit different from what you have been working with so far, but not by much. There are a few new things, though. The `MovieClipLoader` class is used to find out the progress and status of files being loaded into a movie clip. You create a new instance of the MovieClipLoader object and a new listener object to listen for events generated by the MovieClipLoader. You add a new listener for the mclListener object using the addListener method and then load the SWF file using the loadClip method. The loadClip method works as follows:

```
MovieClipLoader.loadClip("url", clip);
```

The URL path (either relative or absolute) is to the file you are loading in, and the clip is the movie clip instance (Loader instance, or level) into which you are loading the file. This works the same way as the MovieClip.loadMovie method.

The onLoadProgress listener is invoked when new content is downloaded onto the visitor's computer, so it is used to show the progress of the download (and helps you use the bar_mc to display that progress). The MovieClipLoader class has a getProgress method that takes a parameter that is the target movie clip into which you are loading the SWF file. This returns an object that we are calling prog, which has two properties: bytesLoaded and bytesTotal. Then you are rounding it and multiplying by 100 to get the percentage that the clip has loaded. You are saving the percentage loaded in a variable called pctLoaded.

You are scaling the bar_mc movie clip using the _xscale MovieClip property by the percentage that is loaded using the pctLoaded variable. _xscale refers to the scaling (resizing) of an instance along the *x* axis, which is horizontal. Then you are setting the value of the dynamic text field to display that percentage as well, and adding (or appending) on a bit of text as well (the % loaded text).

Because your SWF file is loading into level 0, it will "kick out" or discard any existing content there. So as soon as the SWF file has completed loading, the loader SWF file (including the progress bar) disappears. If you are loading content into a movie clip, you can use the following few lines of ActionScript in your FLA file:

```
mclListener.onLoadComplete = function(evt) {
    loader_mc._visible = false;
};
```

You can place these lines directly above myLoader_mcl.addListener(mclListener); when the onLoadComplete listener is invoked, the file has completely downloaded. So when this happens, the visibility of the loader_mc (the progress bar) is set to false so it doesn't sit there behind the loaded Tech Bookstore, which would look pretty bad, of course.

8. Test the FLA file.

When you test the FLA document, you might not be able to see the file loading because it is loading so fast off of your hard drive. You will probably notice quite a difference as soon as you put the files online and test the loader. In the next exercise, you will test all of the files to make sure they work correctly.

9. If everything works as expected, change the final line of ActionScript. Then save the changes you made to the file.

Because you won't be loading bookstore14.fla into the final version of the file, you need to change that final line, in which you are loading in the current version of the Tech Bookstore FLA file. Change the final line of the code on the actions layer to the following:

```
myLoader_mc1.loadClip("TechBookstore.swf", 0);
```

You will instead load in TechBookstore.swf, which will be the final version of the Tech Bookstore FLA file. The TechBookstore.swf file overwrites any of the existing contents because it is loading into level 0. If you are using a Linux or Unix server, the file will be case sensitive, so make sure you enter the correct case.

Testing and Debugging the Tech Bookstore

At this point, the Tech Bookstore should look somewhat complete. You can navigate between each page with your menus and buttons, thanks to the ActionScripts you added through the last two lessons. The content loads into each page because of the Loader components you added in the previous exercises, and you even have preloaders for the content that's loading (even if you don't see the progress because your hard drive is too fast!). Now it's time to test each of the areas and make sure that your content loads in and the ProgressBar component instances work correctly. You've been testing from time to time, just to make sure things work, but here you'll go over testing in just a little more detail.

At this point, you might have some modifications to make if things don't work exactly as you expect them to or if something is not loading in. The first thing you want to do is ensure that all your files are in the correct place in the TechBookstore folder and any other folders that you created within. You might have added new folders yourself and need to modify where the URLs point or you chose not to create folders at all and have everything in the TechBookstore folder (a bit messier, but easier when you're just starting out, which is why we chose to do it this way).

The *Bandwidth Profiler* allows you to determine the download performance of your SWF file by simulating what the SWF file will look like when it's loaded in using different bandwidth settings (such as phone modems and so forth).

Note *When your file is cached, sometimes it appears to load in more quickly than the bandwidth profile you have set. You might also run into problems with the SWF file not showing up if you choose to simulate a download (by pressing Ctrl+Enter or Cmd+Enter a second time), which occurs intermittently.*

The Profiler shows you the amount of data stored on each frame in the SWF file. This shows you how much information you should preload before displaying the content of the SWF file. If a SWF file is "streaming," it might stall out at a frame with more content than the others. This causes the playback to not be as smooth as you might want it to be. Remember that your content is always progressively downloading from the server instead of truly streaming. You will find out more about the Bandwidth Profiler later in this exercise.

1. Open bookstore14.fla and check the SWF file in the Bandwidth Profiler.

The Bandwidth Profiler can be accessed while testing the SWF file in the testing environment. Select Control > Test Movie or press Ctrl+Enter, and when you're in the testing environment you can select View > Bandwidth Profiler from the main menu or press Ctrl+B.

The Bandwidth Profiler displays lots of useful information, such as the dimensions of the Stage, the current frame rate, the size of the SWF file in kilobytes (as well as bytes), the number of frames in the SWF file, and the number of seconds it takes to play the SWF file back to a visitor.

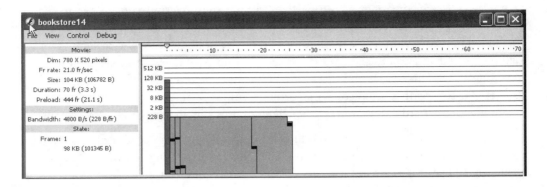

The Bandwidth Profiler also includes a graph that shows how much data is being sent by each frame, which helps you optimize the SWF file. If one frame has too much information and ends up slowing down the playback, you might want to move some of that data onto another frame that contains much less. Another feature closely tied to the Bandwidth Profiler is the ability to simulate download times within the Flash testing environment. By using View > Simulate Download, you can simulate the playback of your Flash SWF file when a visitor is using a slower modem. This helps you see how the SWF file plays back at on computers with slower Internet connections (such as dial-up access) and determines how long it takes before users can see content.

2. Choose to simulate a download setting; then test all your menu buttons to verify one last time that your progress bars are all working and your buttons are also all working.

You can modify the speeds at which you want to simulate playback by selecting a setting from the View > Download Settings menu. Speeds range greatly, from 14.4 dial-up access at 1.2 K per second to a significantly faster T1 connection at 131.2 K per second. If there are specific speeds you want to test at that aren't present in the list, you have the option of adding up to three custom download settings that you can set the number of bytes per second to test at. Testing your SWF file at several different speeds is always a good idea because it gives you a general concept of how long it takes before the visitor sees content. This can greatly affect the general website "experience," and as Macromedia says, "Experience Matters." If users have to wait for a long time for your SWF file to load, often they will give up and leave the site before even seeing any of your Flash content at all.

Make sure you test every menu option and every button you have. Fill out the feedback and questionnaire forms and make sure that they are working as well. Ensure that all your images and SWF files are loading into the interface. Try to find errors and fix any that you find.

3. **Save a new version of the bookstore14.fla file as techBookstore.fla.**

That's right, a new filename to complete all those bookstore files. Indeed, you are finished building the Tech Bookstore FLA files and all of its many associated and assorted SWF files. The only thing that's left to do is go through publishing the files and then putting them online. The hard part is over, and you should be really proud of all the assorted things that you've learned so far.

What You Have Learned

In this lesson, you have:

- Learned about website optimization (pages 302–305)
- Boosted playback performance with runtime bitmap caching (pages 305–307)
- Considered platforms (pages 307–308)
- Loaded external SWF files into a Loader component instance and indicated download progress (pages 308–316)
- Loaded SWF files for each of the remaining pages in the Tech Bookstore (pages 316–321)
- Sent data out of Flash using the LoadVars object (pages 321–328)
- Added instances of the ProgressBar to view content loading into the site (pages 328–333)
- Used the MovieClipLoader class to load in a SWF file (pages 333–338)
- Tested and debugged the Tech Bookstore (pages 339–341)

11 Publishing Flash Documents

Macromedia Flash 8 Basic can be used to produce many kinds of applications. The most popular use of Flash is for applications that will be deployed over the web, although it is by no means limited to that use. Flash is finding its way to handheld devices such as cell phones and PDAs, onto public kiosks, and broadcast, and pretty much anywhere an application can be found. For Flash 8 applications to be used on any kind of platform, though, they must first be published.

You've been working the authoring environment for Flash in the last 10 lessons. In this lesson, you will publish from the authoring file into a format that can be understood by Flash Player, which is the SWF format. You'll also publish HTML along with your SWF file as well, and add metadata to your SWF files so that search engines have an easier time finding them and listing you higher on search hits.

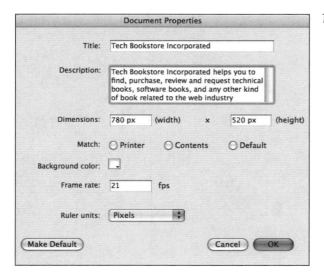

Tech Bookstore embedded in an HTML page

What You Will learn

In this lesson, you will:

- Add metadata to a file
- Create a new publish profile
- Learn how to change your publish settings
- Detect a visitor's Flash Player and redirect it as necessary
- Learn how to embed a SWF file
- Create an HTML page for the Tech Bookstore
- Upload your files to a server and view the bookstore online

Approximate Time

This lesson takes approximately 1 hour to complete.

Lesson Files

Media Files:

lesson11/assets/tile.gif

Starting Files:

lesson11/start/techBookstore.fla
lesson11/start/loader.fla

Completed Files:

Lesson11/complete/TechBookstore/(all files)

Adding Metadata and Publishing SWF Files

In Macromedia Flash 8 Basic (and Professional), designers and developers are able to include metadata into a SWF file so that search engines can find them, index them, and rank them higher in the results of a search. You've already seen where metadata is added when you modified document properties such as Stage size and ruler units.

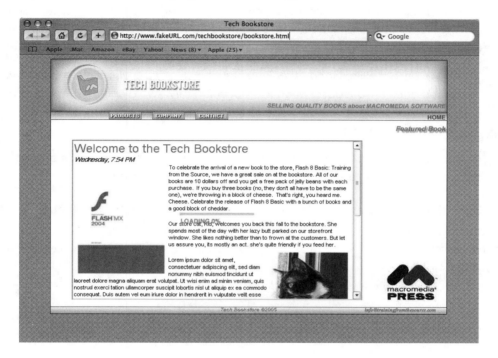

To put a Flash document on the web, you have to start by publishing a SWF file. You have already published SWF files when you embedded video in Lesson 7 and every time you tested your application with Control > Test Movie. This is why you can view your entire Tech Bookstore web application. However, for your Tech Bookstore application to be visible on the web, you have to embed at least the main SWF file, which in this case is the TechBookstore.swf (and loader.swf) into an HTML document. Fortunately, Flash can produce the HTML document for you and the HTML tags that embed the SWF file into it in the Publish Settings dialog box.

In this lesson, you will publish the Tech Bookstore and loader.swf with particular settings and loader SWF file and then embed the documents into a web page.

1. Open the techBookstore.fla file that you created in Lesson 10. Choose Modify ›
Document to add metadata.

You can also enter the Document Properties dialog box by pressing the size button on the
Property inspector.

In the Document Properties dialog box, enter a descriptive title in the Title field; in the
Description field, enter a brief description of what the Tech Bookstore website is, does, and
offers. Refer to the previous figure if you're stumped on what to write. Press OK when you
are finished.

> **Tip** *To increase the likelihood of ranking higher in search results, repeat significant
> keywords often in your description without being silly. Avoid common words and
> conjunctions. For the Tech Bookstore, repeating "books" or "software" throughout
> the description would make sense.*

> **Note** *In a normal setting, you would add metadata to all your Flash files prior to
> publishing. Here, we are just focusing on the main application itself.*

2. Open the Publish Settings dialog box by choosing File › Publish settings.

Additionally you can open techBookstore.fla from lesson11/start on this book's CD-ROM.
There are tabs in the Publish Settings dialog box that allow you to control the files that are
generated by Flash.

You used the Formats tab in several lessons to deselect the HTML option so the document
is not published along with the SWF file (because you don't need it). This tab allows you
to add additional file formats to publish as well, including an EXE or an HQX, which is
usually known as a Flash projector file. These files are useful for creating CD-ROMs and

kiosk presentations. Flash Player is embedded right into the executable file, so there is no need to worry about whether your end user has the latest Flash Player. Other file formats include image file formats and even the MOV video format.

3. Click the Create New Profile button at the top of the Publish Settings dialog box. Enter a name for the Publish profile and click OK.

A Publish profile saves a file on your hard drive that contains information about the publish settings you specify prior to creating the profile. This is handy if you always use the same settings to publish for many documents (such as all the SWF files you are loading into the Tech Bookstore file). You don't necessarily need a Publish profile for this document, but at least you know how to make one now. You will use this profile in the next exercise, but you will modify it to fit the necessary publish settings for loader.fla.

After you click the Create New Profile button, the Create New Profile dialog box opens. Enter **Tech Bookstore** or something similar into the text field as the new name for the Publish profile and click OK when you are finished.

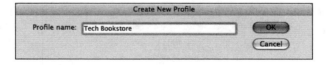

The new name is added to the Current profile drop-down list when you return to the Publish Settings dialog box. Now you can modify the settings of the Publish profile as required. These settings are saved into the profile.

4. Make sure that the HTML format is still deselected, and that the SWF file format is selected.

You are loading the TechBookstore.swf file into the loader.swf file so there is a progress bar for the site; therefore, you don't need an HTML page for the bookstore and you can deselect this check box. You will need the HTML page for the loader SWF file, which you will amend in the next exercise.

5. Click the Flash Tab and make sure the document is set to Flash Player 8, Bottom up Load order, and ActionScript 2.0 as the ActionScript version. Then make sure the Compress movie check box is selected. Select the Protect From Import and Omit Trace Actions check boxes.

All these settings are shown in the following figure. The Flash tab enables you to modify what version of Flash Player you are publishing the file to. You can change the version of ActionScript you are using (this includes the default components, which use ActionScript 2.0). Leave the document at the default ActionScript 2.0 setting for the document.

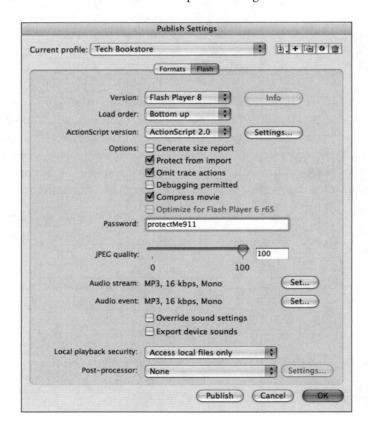

The player version must be determined based on the content of the Flash document. If you have ActionScript that does not work with the version of the player you have selected, errors are shown either in the Output panel or an error message appears when you try to save the file. When you use certain components that require Flash Player 8, you need to set the player version to Flash Player 8 (and ActionScript 2.0) in order for them to work. Other components can be set to Flash Player 6 or 7 and use ActionScript 2.0.

Tip *If you are unsure about which Flash Player or ActionScript version you need, you can try testing the SWF file by pressing Ctrl+Enter and viewing the results in the player. If you don't see the element in your SWF file, you know you have to modify the settings.*

Tip *ActionScript not supported by your selected player version will have a yellow highlight in the Actions panel.*

Load order specifies the order that the layers in your FLA files load into the Flash Player at runtime. If you choose Bottom up (default setting), the layers load from the lowest to highest. This is evident when someone with a slow Internet connection views your site because the items on the Stage appear in the layer order that you specify. It also can affect your ActionScript as well because the actions on lower layers (if you have them there) will be loaded before those on higher layers, if you use this particular setting. The Load order affects only the first frame of your SWF file.

There are many additional options available to you in this tab. Generate Size Report means the Output panel shows the amount of data in the final SWF file, broken down into content: frames, symbols, text characters, actions, and bitmaps. If you Omit Trace Actions, you won't see anything traced to the Output panel when you test the SWF file; however, when you publish for the final version of your SWF file and you have used ActionScript with trace actions, this setting is a must. When this is selected, Flash removes the trace actions from your ActionScript—both to reduce final file size and for a performance increase a little bit. An end user doesn't have an Output window in the browser, but that won't stop Flash Player from trying to execute trace actions!

When you protect a FLA file from import (using the Protect From Import option), the setting prevents other people from importing your SWF file into their own FLA documents, unless they have the password, which you type into the password field. SWF files import as a series of frames, bitmaps, and graphic symbols. Importing an SWF file does not preserve any ActionScript, layers, or components. If you lose a FLA file, importing the SWF file doesn't "get your FLA file back." It does help you get the images, but you'll have to reconstruct other aspects of the FLA file over again. But then again, this is why you back your files up, right?

Note *You should be aware that even if you do protect your SWF file from import, there are tools available online that can undo this option. There are also tools to open your SWF files and see the ActionScript that you use. Never, ever place sensitive information (such as passwords or similar) in a SWF file.*

If you select Debugging Permitted, you can remotely debug the SWF file. You can access the file when it is online and enter a password when prompted, which also helps protect the SWF file. If someone downloads the SWF file, they must use the password when they import it into Flash.

And finally, the Compress Movie option allows you to compress the SWF file so it's a smaller size. This works only for the Flash Player 6 r65 and greater (r65 refers to a minor release of Flash Player 6), so your visitors must have at least this version of player installed on their systems to view the SWF file. This is fine because you are creating a SWF file for Flash Player 8.

6. Set the JPEG quality setting to **100** and select the Override Sound Settings check box. Leave the default Audio Stream and Audio Event settings at their default settings.

The JPEG quality compresses the bitmap images in your FLA file as JPEGs with whatever quality you have specified with this slider. A higher value on the slider means a better-quality image because the JPEG is not compressed as much. If you set the quality too low, the SWF file size is smaller, but the images might end up distorted. If you will deploy over the web, optimize your images in a tool such as Macromedia Fireworks or Adobe ImageReady, and set this slider to **100**! You have greater control over your image quality versus your image file size in these other tools, and it is a horrible idea to compress images that have already been compressed. Because your images have already been optimized for the web, you are setting your quality to 100 to prevent any further compression from happening.

Select the Override Sound Settings check box. Whatever properties for each sound that you individually set using the library and Properties dialog box in the authoring environment are overridden by these settings for the entire SWF file, which helps decrease the overall file size of the SWF file when it's published. You can change the compression, the sample rate, and whether the sound is an event or streamed sound if you click the Set buttons. The default settings (MP3 with a bit rate of 16Kbps and Mono) is adequate for the Tech Bookstore. Of course, if you compressed sound in the Sound Properties from the Library panel, you were probably doing that for a very good reason. In that circumstance, you would *not* choose to override those settings.

To publish a file in one step, all you need to do is choose File > Publish from the main menu. This process automatically publishes the FLA file using whatever the current or default Publish Settings are. The files are created in whichever directory the current FLA file resides.

For the Local Playback Security option, leave the default selected, which is Access Local Files Only. When you are playing an SWF file locally, your SWF file can interact with different resources on your local computer or from a network that you may be connected to. For instance, you can store a JPEG or PNG image in a directory on your computer or on your network, which can be loaded dynamically when the SWF runs. It won't, however, be able to retrieve information from a different domain or an Internet resource, like Amazon.com or Petco.com. If you select Access Network Only, resources such as your LoadVars text files can be accessed only from a network, not locally.

7. Click the Publish button to publish the file. Then click the Import/Export Profile button and choose Export from the menu that appears to export the Publish profile you just created.

After you click Publish, techBookstore.swf is generated into the TechBookstore folder. Now you need to export the Publish profile to use it in other FLA files. The profile is saved as an XML document on your hard drive. The XML file contains your settings, which can then be imported into the Publish Settings dialog box when you create another FLA file where you need the profile.

Choose Export from the drop-down list that opens when you click the Import/Export Profile button. The Export Profile dialog box opens, in which you can type in a filename to save the profile as (or leave it as) **Tech Bookstore**. Click Save to export the Publish profile. Now you can import the profile into other FLA files that you create.

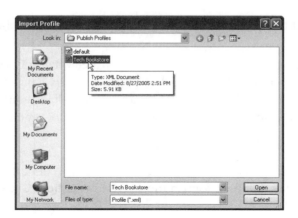

8. Click OK to close the Publish Settings dialog box. Save the changes you made to the Tech Bookstore by selecting File › Save.

After you have published the bookstore SWF file and exported the Publish profile, you are finished with the bookstore.

Detecting Flash Player

When visitors arrive at your site, you don't necessarily know which version of Flash Player is installed on their systems, or whether they have Flash Player installed at all (although the likelihood that they have some version installed is very, very high). The Tech Bookstore requires that visitors have the correct version of Flash Player to see the content of the SWF files that are loading into the Tech Bookstore (such as the tour) and the bookstore itself, which is Flash Player 8. Detecting Flash Player is a complex task to do well because it ultimately requires JavaScript written in to an HTML page. However, you can let the Flash publishing process do the hard work for you by creating a player-detection system instantly when you publish the file. Here's how.

1. Open loader.fla and open the Publish Settings dialog box by choosing File › Publish Settings. Import the Publish profile you just created in the previous exercise.

Import the Publish profile that you created in the previous exercise called Tech Bookstore. Click the Import/Export Profile button and select Import from the drop-down list. The Import Profile dialog box opens, in which you can choose a profile to import. Click TechBookstore.xml and then click the Open button.

Now the Tech Bookstore profile is available in the Current Profile menu. Select the Tech Bookstore profile. The profile maintains the same settings that you used for the previous SWF file that you modify in a few areas in the following steps.

2. Make sure that the Flash and HTML check boxes are both selected on the Formats tab.

Selecting this option means that the HTML page is created when you select the check box. You need to publish both HTML pages and a SWF document. Change the name of the HTML file in the HTML field to **bookstore.html**. This file will be modified later in this lesson. You do not need to modify any settings on the Flash tab—you can leave the default settings from the Publish profile you made earlier.

3. Select the HTML tab. Select the Detect Flash Version check box, and deselect the Loop and Display menu options in the Playback section. Click the OK button when you're finished.

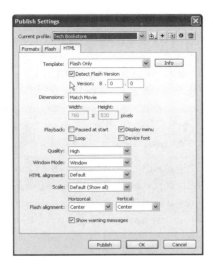

You need to make some changes on the HTML tab. Select the Detect Flash Version check box to create a Flash Player detection system. When you select this option, Flash will add the JavaScript that detects for the Flash Player version you specified in the Flash tab (Flash Player 8, in this case). If users don't have Flash Player installed, they are automatically redirected to `http://www.macromedia.com/go/getFlash/`, where they can then download and install Flash Player or the Flash Player version they need to see the Flash content on your web page.

When you are finished making edits, click the OK button to return to the Publish Settings dialog box. Make sure that you have deselected the Loop option under the HTML tab, and click the Publish button when you are finished.

Note *You can use Flash Player detection only if you publish to Flash Player 4 or greater.*

The other settings that were available under the HTML tab do not need to be modified, but here is a brief breakdown of what the settings under the HTML tab are used for:

Template: This setting specifies a kind of template to use for publishing the HTML portion of the movie. Click the Info button next to this setting to find out more about each kind that is available.

Dimensions: You can set the dimensions for the Flash SWF file that will be embedded in the document. The default Match Movie size is the current dimensions of the Stage, although you can set a different size, measured either in pixels or a percentage.

Playback: The playback options control how the SWF file plays at runtime. Loop means the SWF file returns to Frame 1 and plays again after it reaches the final frame on the Timeline. You can pause the SWF file when it begins using the Paused At Start option, and control the playback manually or use the contextual menu. You can choose whether to display a contextual menu in the running SWF file by selecting or deselecting the Display menu option. You can also choose whether to use device fonts in the SWF file (as were defined in Lesson 3 on using text). Select the Device Font option to use device fonts with static text. Note that the static text must be specifically set to use device fonts.

Quality: You can set the SWF file quality from Low to Best in this menu. Low doesn't use anti-aliasing and affords the fastest playback. However, Auto-Low will attempt to use better quality when possible, but also attempts to play back the SWF file quickly. High is the default that we use and always use anti-aliasing, but if there is animation, bitmaps are not smoothed (smoothing looks better but slows down the SWF file playback).

Window Mode: You can control the wmode attribute in the HTML file using this option. The Transparent Windowless option sets the background of Flash documents to transparent and removes the browser window around it (including the title bar). For example, you would use this mode if you were making one of those ads that appear to float over an HTML page. Opaque Windowless leaves the background in the Flash document, but still removes the browser around it. Always remember to offer some kind of button to close the SWF file somewhere in the SWF file. Window is the normal default mode where the Flash document appears in a normal browser window.

Note *Not all browsers support windowless mode. As for major browsers, recent Netscape browsers now support the windowless mode (NS 7+), as do Internet Explorer 5 (Windows) and Internet Explorer 5.1 (Mac) and above.*

HTML Alignment: Helps position the SWF file in the HTML page to the various sides of the browser window.

Scale: This option scales the SWF file if you changed the dimensions of the file in the Dimensions setting. Default maintains the aspect ratio of the original SWF file, whereas Exact Fit displays the document without keeping the aspect ratio, but will fill the dimensions you set. No Border scales the SWF file while keeping the aspect ratio, but it crops the Stage if necessary. No Scale stops the SWF file from scaling when the user resizes the browser window.

Flash Alignment: This option aligns the SWF file in the browser window and determines cropping if it is necessary. This affects your SWF file in particular when you choose different dimensions and the Stage is cropped.

4. Save the changes you made to the FLA file. You can close the FLA file, and Flash for that matter, when you are finished.

You are finished publishing the file. All you have left to do now is edit the HTML files that were generated and put all of the files online (or in a single place, so you can locally test the website).

Embedding an SWF File in an HTML Page

When you place SWF files online, you typically embed them in an HTML page. You do not have to learn HTML to do so because Flash generates the code for you. However, in this exercise, you will slightly customize the HTML document that Flash creates so you can add a background tile and center the SWF file on the page. When Flash produces an HTML file, the SWF file is already embedded.

You will create an HTML page in this exercise, embedding the Tech Bookstore SWF file within it. SWF files are embedded into an HTML page using the `<object>` and `<embed>` tags.

1. Open bookstore.html in an HTML editor or the text editor of your choice.

It doesn't matter if you are using a fully featured editor such as Macromedia Dreamweaver 8 or a simple text editor such as Notepad or TextEdit for this exercise. The changes you will make are very minimal to the file that already exists, so you don't need anything fancy to make your modifications.

2. Change the text in-between the title tags in order to name the site.

This name appears within the title bar of the web browser. You can rename this title to whatever you want the site to be called in the title bar. We have chosen Tech Bookstore, so this line is written as:

```
<title>Tech Bookstore</title>
```

3. Delete bgcolor="#ffffff" from the body tag. Change this attribute to background="tile.gif".

Underneath the title and head tags is the body tag. The bgcolor attribute sets the background color of the HTML page. However, instead of a background color, you might want to set a background image. On the CD-ROM is a file called tile.gif, and you can find it in the lesson11/assets folder. Copy this file into the TechBookstore folder and then change the `<body>` tag to the following:

```
<body background="tile.gif">
```

Adding a background image means that the image will tile over the entire background of the website, which will appear "behind" the SWF file. This particular GIF file is small and unobtrusive, creating a subtle pattern in the background.

```
87          versionStr = JSGetSwfVer(i);
88
89      }
90      if (versionStr != 0) {
91          if(isIE && isWin && !isOpera) {
92              tempArray = versionStr.split(" ");
93              tempString = tempArray[1];
94              versionArray = tempString .split(",");
95
96              versionMajor = versionArray[0];
97              versionMinor   = versionArray[2];
98
99              versionString = versionMajor + "." + versionMinor;
100             versionNum = parseFloat(versionString);
101         } else {
102             versionNum = versionStr;
103         }
104         return (versionNum >= reqVer ? true : false );
105     }
106  }
107
108     return (reqVer ? false : 0.0);
109 }
110 // -->
111 </script>
112 </head>
113 <body background="tile.gif">
114 <!--url's used in the movie-->
115 <!--text used in the movie-->
116 <!--
117 loading
118 -->
119 <script language="JavaScript" type="text/javascript">
120 <!--
121 var hasRightVersion = DetectFlashVer(requiredMajorVersion, requiredMinorVersion);
122 if(hasRightVersion) {  // if we've detected an acceptable version
123     var oeTags = '<OBJECT CLASSID="clsid:D27CDB6E-AE6D-11cf-96B8-444553540000"'
124     + 'WIDTH="780" HEIGHT="520"'
125     + 'CODEBASE="http://download.macromedia.com/pub/shockwave/cabs/flash/swflash.cab">'
126     + '<param name="movie" value="loader.swf" /><param name="loop" value="false" /><param name="quality" value="high" /><param name="bgcolor" value="#f
127     + '<EMBED src="loader.swf" loop="false" quality="high" bgcolor="#ffffff" '
```

Tip As a best practice, backgrounds should be set using CSS and not HTML attributes. For this application, changing the HTML attribute is acceptable, but if you aren't using CSS these days, you're so 10-years-ago. Very nearly literally. Learn it, love it, live it.

4. Add a DIV tag to contain the Tech Bookstore and center it horizontally on the page.

Under the <body> tag, you sometimes see a lot of commented-out text. When the HTML document contains text like this, it is quite similar to the commented-out code you might have in a Flash file in that it can provide directions to coders and explain what the code does. The text that is commented-out in these generated HTML files contains the text that is found inside the SWF file, which helps index the content better for search engines.

Add the following lines below the `<body background="tile.gif">` tag:

```
<div align="center>
```

After these lines come the `<object>` and `<embed>` tags, plus all the code that embeds the SWF file so all browsers can see it. After all that code and just above the `</body>` tag, add the following, which will close the DIV tag and contain the Flash file:

```
</div>
```

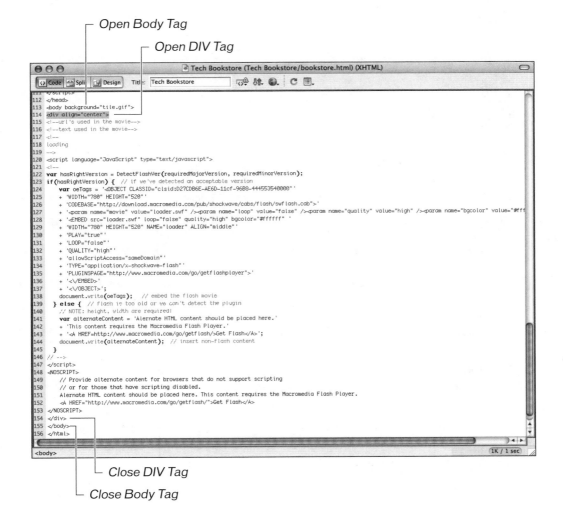

Open Body Tag

Open DIV Tag

Close DIV Tag

Close Body Tag

When you are completely finished, the entire HTML file for the bookstore_content.html page should look similar to the following figure.

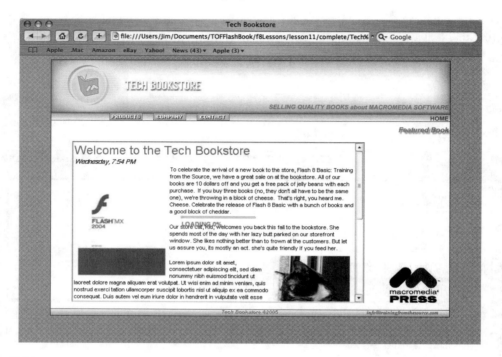

Tip *After you have finished editing the HTML file, make sure that you go back to the Publish Settings dialog box for the loader.fla file and deselect the HTML option under the Formats tab. This way you won't overwrite the changes to any of the HTML documents if you republish the FLA file.*

5. **Save the changes that you have made to the HTML file and then open the HTML page to view it in the default browser.**

Save the HTML file and then you can close the file. Find the file in the TechBookstore folder and double-click the bookstore.html file that was published to open the bookstore using the default web browser. If your computer defaults to a text editor instead, choose to open it in a browser instead. Click through the file and explore the different areas.

In the following exercise, you will upload all the files to a server or you will organize the ones you need neatly into a single folder.

Uploading the Tech Bookstore to the Web

If you have access to upload files to the web, the next step is to upload the Tech Bookstore so it can be viewed online. Because you do not need all the files you have created during the book for the website, you need to organize all the files specifically for the bookstore into a single folder and then upload them to the server. If you do not have web space, you should stop at the step that uploads the files and test the site locally off your hard drive. But if you want to put your site online, follow these simple steps right to the end.

1. Open the TechBookstore folder on your hard drive. Then create a new folder on your hard drive in which you will move (or copy) the files for the Tech Bookstore site.

Because you have been saving most of the files inside the TechBookstore folder, there are a lot of files stored in the folder, including ones that shouldn't be uploaded. You do not need to upload all the files because you do not need the FLA files or the imported images online for the website. You need to upload only some of them: the HTML files, SWF files, and files that you are dynamically loading or linking to the site.

The new folder you create can be called whatever you want, such as bookstore.

2. Move the following files into the folder you just created.

You need to move all the files that you need for the site into a single location. They include the SWF files and media files loading into the SWF files, as well as the HTML documents you published in this lesson. For your convenience, the files you need are in the following list:

bookstore.html	video1.swf
loader.swf	video2.swf
tile.gif	video3.swf
TechBookstore.swf	mmpresslogo.jpg
home.swf	home01.jpg
catalog.swf	home02.jpg
reviews.swf	styles.css
tour.swf	home.txt
news.swf	news.txt
map.swf	sectionText.txt

You also need to move the catalog folder and the reviews folder into this folder alongside these other files.

3. **After you moved all the files required for the Tech Bookstore into a single location, connect to the web server where you want to host the material, and upload the documents to the web.**

You are probably using FTP to connect to a web server or you might be using another file-transfer method (perhaps even hosting off of your own computer). At any rate, you need to transfer the files to a server so you can put them online. Transfer all the files that are inside the folder you created in the previous step. You don't need to transfer the folder as well, although it's likely you want to create a folder on the server to hold all of these files.

4. **Open the Tech Bookstore in a web browser.**

Type the location to the bookstore's index page into your browser of choice. Because you have Flash Player installed, bookstore.html will load with the SWF file content.

If your visitors do not have the correct Flash Player installed (perhaps it is older than Flash Player 8) or no Flash Player is installed at all, they will be directed to the www.macromedia.com/go/getFlash page that notifies them of this fact and tells them where the player can be downloaded from.

It's always easy to forget to publish a file or perhaps even save one in the wrong directory on your hard drive. If you are missing any SWF files from this list, open the FLA file again and publish the FLA file so a SWF file is saved in the TechBookstore folder. Then upload this new file to the server into the correct directory. You might also want to check that you have remembered to upload the catalog and review folders as well. Finally, you want to make sure that all the references to your external data are still valid after you have posted your files.

The complete published Tech Bookstore is in the lesson11/complete/TechBookstore folder on the CD-ROM. This folder contains the completed SWF files and HTML files for the website.

Wrapping It All Up

You have successfully completed the website (we hope)! It's important to go take a break and put your feet up after a major undertaking, so that's your final step in this book: Go take a break. Get some ice cream. Chocolate peanut butter even. You deserve it.

Hopefully, you have found out how much fun Flash can be, and just how easy it is to get started using the software. Obviously, it doesn't end here. But hopefully this is what you might call a firm foundation in Flash, and you will feel both confident and free to experiment and expand your base of knowledge. Now that you have created an entire website, you can start creating your own projects using Flash while continuing to learn new tips and tricks along the way.

Make sure you visit the forums for this book at `www.TrainingFromTheSource.com/forum`, in which there is a specific forum dedicated to getting help with the book, and information on add-ons. Unfortunately, it's usually not possible to write a perfect book or create perfect software, and from time to time there are updates to the software or to the player that might mean changes to the bookstore application must be made. If something like this occurs (or anything else), your questions can be answered on the forum. You might find an answer even faster by checking the errata, forum, and FAQ pages on the supporting website we've mentioned many times throughout the book: `www.TrainingFromTheSource.com`.

You will probably have questions left over about ActionScript because a tutorial format just doesn't allow a person to clarify everything you probably want to know about the ActionScript language (even what's included in the lessons). There is a lot of help in the community, which is one of the best parts of using Macromedia Flash 8. So thanks for reading, best of luck with your future projects, and we hope to see you out there!

What You Have Learned

In this lesson, you have:

- Added metadata to a file for search engine visibility (pages 345–346)
- Created a new Publish profile (page 347)
- Changed the publish settings (pages 348–352)
- Detected the Flash Player version (pages 352–355)
- Embedded a SWF file in an HTML page (pages 355–358)
- Put the Tech Bookstore online (pages 359–361)

A Installing Extensions

You can install extensions into Macromedia Flash that include components, effects, tools, screen types, behaviors, and commands. You can install extensions using Macromedia's Extension Manager or by manually placing the extensions within the Flash directory on your hard drive. You can also manage existing extensions that you have installed from a single interface when you use the Extension Manager. Download the latest Extension Manager from the following URL: `www.macromedia.com/exchange/em_download`.

Note *You need the Macromedia Extension Manager 1.7 (or greater) to install extensions for Flash 8 Basic. Extension Manager also allows you to install extensions for Dreamweaver 8 and Fireworks 8.*

After you close any Macromedia software you have running after downloading the Extension Manager, you can run the installer that you downloaded. After the Extension Manager installs, it will open like any other stand-alone program.

You can open the Extension Manager using the Start menu on Windows, in your Applications folder on the Mac. You can also access the Extension Manager right in Flash by choosing Help > Manage Extensions.

Installing Extensions and Components

Components are distributed by using MXP files, which are installed using the Extension Manager. You double-click the MXP file, which opens the Extension Manager that installs the extension, so it is available within Flash. Then you can access the extension directly in Flash. Other extensions might be distributed as EXE, SWC, or even FLA files. The SWC and FLA files have to be placed in the correct directory to work properly.

You might also encounter plug-ins, which are sometimes installed using EXE files. These extensions take you through an installation process, perhaps requiring you to enter a serial number. Where the extension appears in Flash depends on what the extension is for. For a Timeline effect extension, the extension is found alongside the other Timeline effects you have in Flash (Insert › Timeline Effects).

To install an extension on your computer, open the Extension Manager and then choose File > Install Extension to open the Extension to Install dialog box. You can also click the Install New Extension button. The Select Extension to Install dialog box opens, and you can select any MXP file on your hard drive that you want to install and then read and accept the disclaimer.

After the component installs, you see a message similar to the following, notifying you that it has successfully installed.

After extensions are installed on your system, they can be toggled, sorted, or removed by using the Extension Manager. Selecting an extension from the list enables you to see a brief description of the extension and as well as additional information by the author on the extension and how to use or access it in Flash. When you install an extension in a multiuser environment (Windows NT, 2000, XP, or Mac OS X), the Extension Manager installs components and extensions only for the logged-in user.

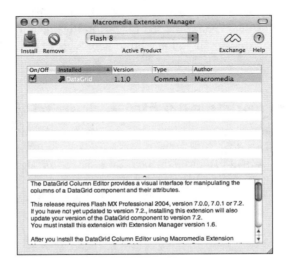

You can manually install components if you have a FLA or SWF file. On a Windows-based system, find the user configuration folder in the following folder: C:\Documents and Settings\<USERNAME>\Local Settings\Application Data\Macromedia\Flash 8\en\ Configuration\Extensions (or <username>\Library\Application Support\Macromedia\ Flash 8\en\Configuration on the Mac). The path is a bit different if you change the location of the Documents and Settings folder or your default settings.

Note To see all the folders listed previously on Windows, it might be necessary to modify your folder options so Windows Explorer displays hidden files. Do this by choosing Tools › Folder Options from Windows Explorer's main menu. Then click the View tab in the Folder Options dialog box; and in the Advanced settings pane, make sure that "Show hidden files and folders" is selected from the Hidden Files And Folders folder.

Many directories, including Behaviors, Components, Effects, Libraries, Panel Sets, and Templates are found in the Configuration folder. Do remember that if you install components by directly placing them in the user's folder, you can't manage them via the Extension Manager.

Note After you have installed new components or behaviors, you must choose Reload from the Components panel or you must restart Flash. The component is available in the Components panel.

Extensions might appear within the Components panel, Common Libraries, Commands menu, or the Behaviors panel. Extensions might be installed using the Extension Manager instead of an EXE file or require you to manually place it in a particular directory. If you installed the extension using an MXP and the Extension Manager, there will be an On/Off check box to disable the extension if you need to. There is also a File > Remove Extension option available.

Adding Commands and Behaviors to Flash

Commands are used to repeat tasks numerous times. You can download commands from the Flash Exchange or create them yourself by saving steps from the History panel. Commands and behaviors can be installed using the Extension Manager as well.

You can also create your own custom commands very easily by following these steps:

1. Open up the History panel.

Choose Window > Other Panels > History to open the History panel.

2. Do a common task in Flash.

A common task might be creating an actions layer. Do anything that is registered by the History panel and that you might want to repeat as some kind of task in Flash.

3. Select the steps that should be saved as the command in the History panel.

These steps will be reproduced when you choose to run the command.

4. Within the History panel, Right-click (or Control-click on the Mac) and choose Save As Command from the contextual menu.

A dialog box appears and prompts you for a name for this command.

5. Assign a name to the command.

You can replay the command after you have assigned a name to it. All you need to do is select the command name from the Commands menu or Commands > Run Command from the main menu. If you choose the latter, the Open dialog box pops open, and you need to select a specific command to run from the hard drive. Commands are saved as Flash JavaScript files and have a JSFL extension. If you create your own custom commands using the History panel, the JSFL file will most likely be saved to the following directory: C:\Documents and Settings\<USERNAME>\ Local Settings\Application Data\ Macromedia\Flash 8\en\Configuration\Commands (or <username>\Library\Application Support\Macromedia\Flash 8\en\ Configuration\Commands on a Mac).

Behaviors are used to make your SWF files more interactive without having to write ActionScript code yourself in the Flash authoring environment, and you have used many of them throughout the exercises in this book. You can install a behavior using the Extension Manager or place it directly in a folder on the hard drive. Place the behavior in the following folder: C:\Documents and Settings\<USERNAME>\Local Settings\ Application Data\Macromedia\Flash 8\en\Configuration\Behaviors (or <username>\ Library\Application Support\Macromedia\Flash 8\Configuration\ Behaviors on the Mac). After you put a behavior in the Behaviors folder, you need to restart Flash or choose Reload from the Options menu in the Behaviors panel. To delete a behavior, you need to delete the behavior's XML file from the user's folder above.

Where to Find Extensions

One of the best places (if not the best place) to find Flash extensions is at the Macromedia Exchange at `www.macromedia.com/go/flash_exchange`. Accessing the Exchange is easy. You can reach the site from Flash by selecting Help > Flash Exchange or by selecting Macromedia Flash Exchange from the Start page.

Extensions (including components, code snippets, or plug-ins) are created by Macromedia as well as members of the Flash community. Although many extensions are for sale, some are free. You will be are sometimes required to pay for extensions or components before you are allowed to download them, although this sometimes means that you get a higher-quality component or extension with some level of customer support as well. Some extensions are available from personal or commercial websites, blogs, or even forums.

Macromedia has published a list of companies that have created third-party extensions in the form of plug-ins for Flash 8 and earlier. A list of select companies offering plug-ins can be found at `www.macromedia.com/software/flash/extensions`. The extensions include plug-ins that create text effects, charts, image effects, and an extension that converts your 2D art and text into 3D animations.

> **Note** *You can find a more detailed list of where to find third-party tools and extensions in Appendix B.*

You can also find more commands on the Flash Exchange by choosing Commands > Get More Commands from the Command menu in Flash.

B Resources

As of this writing, most resources available for Macromedia Flash are specific to Flash MX 2004. However, because the Flash community is very good at keeping pace with new versions, the resources listed in this appendix will undoubtedly update to include Macromedia Flash 8 in no time at all.

Online resources are extensive and useful when it comes to answering very specific needs to your Flash-related queries. Forums, e-mail lists, weblogs (blogs), and tutorial-based websites are important parts of the Flash community. In recent years, the Flash-related blogs have popped up everywhere. These web pages journal the experiments and learning of many great Flash minds in the community. Searching the Flash blogs is a great way to find out about others who are going down the same path you are and learn a bit more each day. Most of them even allow you to comment on each entry that is made.

Macromedia.com

There are many great resources on Macromedia.com just waiting to be found. Here are some useful links from the site that will help you when working with this book—and even more so when you're finished with it.

Download Software: www.macromedia.com/downloads

Download trial versions or purchase software from this location.

Developer Center for Flash: www.macromedia.com/devnet/flash/

The Flash Developer Center offers many great articles and resources for you each and every week. From articles to tutorials, to papers and sample applications, you will never run out of great things to read and try for yourself.

Tech Notes (Flash): www.macromedia.com/support/flash/technotes.html

The Tech Notes are a great resource if you're running into problems or want to find out some tips and tricks for Flash. Think of the Tech Notes like a great big FAQ in a way. If you have "issues" with Flash, this is the place to go for some support.

Macromedia Exchange: www.macromedia.com/cfusion/exchange/index.cfm

The Macromedia exchange is where you can either upload your own components and extensions, or find them for download. Although many are free, some are for purchase.

Third-Party Extensions: www.macromedia.com/software/flash/extensions/

This is a list of Macromedia's latest third-party extensions. This page links to extensions you might want to try installing or purchasing. Macromedia teams up with companies that develop useful extensions that help you get more out of Flash.

Wish List: www.macromedia.com/software/flash/contact/wishlist/

The Wish List is where you can go to either report bugs or send a note saying what you most want to see added to Flash. If you have great ideas for the software—or find a bug to report—fill out this form, which is sent to the Flash team for examination.

User Groups: www.macromedia.com/cfusion/usergroups/

User groups are a great way to meet other people developing content using the Macromedia product line. Find a group in your local area or start your own.

MX News Aggregator (MSNA): www.markme.com/mxna

MX News Aggregator for Macromedia and community blogs. Start here for the extensive Flash blog circuit and find the latest news on everything Macromedia-related.

Tutorial and Resource Sites

Although tutorial and resource sites are plentiful, you will probably have to do a bit of searching to find what you are looking for. That said, there is a lot of opportunity to become involved in the Flash community. Surf around and find your "spot." Many friendly people out there are more than willing to help you as you learn the ropes. Many of these sites also offer forums and a related community.

Flash MX: www.flash-mx.com

This website is dedicated to Flash-based tutorials, news, and book and software reviews.

Macromedia Developer Center: www.macromedia.com/devnet

The Developer Center (also known as DevNet) contains resources for all of Macromedia's product line. Each product has an area devoted to resources on development using the software.

Informit Network: www.informit.com

This is a large resource site for web designers and developers. It contains a section devoted to Flash.

ActionScript.com: www.actionscript.com

Flash reference and online community. This site even offers a growing reference of the ActionScript language that you can contribute to using a commenting system. The ActionScript Reference is like a nonofficial Macromedia LiveDocs system.

ActionScript.org: www.actionscript.org

An extensive reference and tutorial site.

Studiowhiz: www.studiowhiz.com

Studiowhiz offers tutorials, reviews, and a forum on everything to do with web design and development. This website includes a lot of content on Macromedia Flash.

UltraShock: www.ultrashock.com

An online community for Flash that includes resources for learning the software.

Flash Zone: www.flzone.net

Resources and information about Macromedia Flash, including tutorials, extensions, and news.

Tip of the Day: www.flash2004.com/tipoday

A Flash (or Studio MX) tip of the day provided daily by numerous members of the Macromedia online community.

Flash Enabled: www.flashenabled.com

Information on creating Flash content for mobile devices.

SwiftDev: www.swiftdev.com

Online community and resources for those working with Swift.

Person 13: www.person13.com

Includes articles and information primarily on Flash Remoting and ActionScript 2.0, written by the jovial Joey Lott.

Lionbich Studios: http://www.lionbichstudios.com/flash_tutorials_01.htm

Tutorials on the Macromedia Studio suite, including beginner to advanced tutorials on Flash.

FullAsAGoog: www.fullasagoog.com

An excellent Flash blog aggregator.

MX Developers Journal: www.sys-con.com/mx

A magazine devoted to the MX product family.

Forums

Forums are plentiful out there. Flash forums exist in many languages and many sizes. There are high traffic forums and smaller ones where you can get to know the regulars. Whatever you're looking for, you'll probably find it.

Flash MX 2004 Forums: www.flashmx2004.com/forums

These forums are exclusively dedicated to working with Macromedia Flash.

Were Here Forums: www.were-here.com

A busy online community (forums) for Flash designers and developers.

Macromedia Web Forums (Flash): http://webforums.macromedia.com/flash/

Official Macromedia web forums. Also available in newsgroup format (news://forums.macromedia.com).

Flash Move: www.flashmove.com/board/index.php

An online community for Flash.

FlashKit: www.flashkit.com

One of the biggest and the oldest, this established community is also probably the busiest.

Flash MX Files: www.flashmxfiles.com/phpBB2/

Busy forum with a wide range of Flash-related subjects.

E-mail Lists

If you aren't partial to forums, perhaps you want to join some e-mail–based lists. These e-mail lists range from high-traffic to moderate- and low-traffic lists. There are many out there to join, and sometimes you happen across the best ones by chance. This list contains some of the more common (public) ones, although there are many more.

Flashcoders: `http://chattyfig.figleaf.com/mailman/listinfo/flashcoders`

An advanced list discussing the finer aspects of coding ActionScript. Discussion is limited to intermediate to advanced topics involving ActionScript. This is a high-traffic list.

Flash Newbie: `http://chattyfig.figleaf.com/mailman/listinfo/flashnewbie`

Flash novice list run by the fine people who bring you Flashcoders.

Flash Lounge: `http://chattyfig.figleaf.com /mailman/listinfo/flashlounge`

A great "on-topic and clothing-optional" list run by the fine people who bring you Flashcoders.

Flasher: `www.chinwag.com/flasher`

General Flash discussion.

DevMX: `www.devmx.com/mailing_list.cfm`

Mailing list that focuses on discussing dynamic flash.

Extensions and Fonts

Third-party extensions might include components, plug-ins, behaviors, and commands. The following websites offer free extensions for the community. See the following section on Macromedia links for extensions available on the Macromedia website. At the time of writing, there were not many tools online making use of the extensibility layer in Flash. Go to `www.TrainingFromTheSource.com/resources` for the latest links available.

> **Tip** *Remember that the extensions you find in these sites might not be compatible with the components found in Flash 8. If the components you download are built using ActionScript 1.0 (for Flash MX), they might not work with the ActionScript or components you use in your Flash sites.*

Flash Component.com: `www.flashcomponent.com`

This is a great exchange site for Flash components. The components here are free, and you can provide or read feedback on each one. At the time of writing, content available was for Flash MX and MX 2004.

Flash Components.net: www.flashcomponents.net

You can download free components from this site. You can preview components and use the tutorials on the site describing how to build and use components in Flash. At the time of writing, available content was for Flash MX 2004.

Ghostwire component set: www.ghostwire.com

An excellent set of version 1 components that serve as an alternative to the default set of components that come with Flash. Lightweight and extremely useful, these components are currently compatible with Flash MX and MX2004, and will work within Flash 8 as well.

Flash DB Components: www.flash-db.com/Components

Component libraries available for download.

Flash Components.com: www.flashcomponents.com

A subscription-based service. A monthly fee allows you to download components from this site.

Miniml: www.miniml.com

Long-time, respected source for pixel fonts.

Fonts for Flash: www.fontsforflash.com

Many interesting and unique pixel fonts are available from this source.

Third-Party Tools and Integration

Third-party tools are very important for exploring different ways to integrate special content, such as 3D or video. Explore some of your options through downloading trial versions. These third-party tools are built specifically with integrating with Flash in mind. Also, integrating server-side software is sometimes necessary depending on what you need to get done. The following links include some good reference sites for application server software.

Toon Boom Studio: www.toonboom.com

Professional animation and drawing tool primarily used by animators and then directly imported into Flash.

Swift 3D: www.swift3d.com or www.erain.com

A stand-alone 3D program that is used to create content that can be imported into Flash. You can also use an exporter to save SWF files from 3D Studio Max.

Sorenson Squeeze: www.sorenson.com

Software that's used to compress media that can be imported into Flash. You can output as video, SWF files, or FLV files (among others) that can then be used in your Flash applications.

Wildform Flix: www.wildform.com

Flix compresses your video so it can be imported into Flash. Much like Squeeze, Flix can be used to create many different kinds of video files, including SWF and FLV files. There are several different versions of this software available. Wildform also offers other tools that can be used in conjunction with Flash.

SWiSH: www.swishzone.com

Create animations and more, easily and without having to create a FLA file in Flash. Many interesting effects are available from the website.

ActionScript Viewer (ASV): www.buraks.com/asv

This software is incredibly useful if you have ever lost a FLA file. ASV allows you to view inside a Flash document and view the code that is used to make it work. You can also view Timeline placement of instances and grab graphics from inside of the SWF file. It does not re-create the FLA file for you (this is simply not possible).

Flash Jester: www.flashjester.com

Tools used to extend the capabilities of Flash.

SWF Studio: www.northcode.com

Tool used to extend the capabilities of Flash Projector files.

Ming: http://ming.sourceforge.net/

This is a C library for generating SWF files and is a series of wrappers for Python, C++, PHP, and more.

Flash Remoting: www.macromedia.com/software/flashremoting

The official word on Flash Remoting MX. Remoting components that you can install with Flash MX 2004 are included in this area of the site. Flash Remoting includes support for ColdFusion MX (included with the server), .NET, and Java. Flash Remoting for .NET and JAVA is not free.

AMFPHP: www.amfphp.org

Official Site for Flash Remoting with PHP. This third-party tool is not supported by Macromedia, although it is free.

Flash Communication Server: www.macromedia.com/software/flashcom/

The official part of Macromedia's site for the Flashcom server.

ColdFusion MX 7: www.macromedia.com/software/coldfusion/

The official word on ColdFusion MX 7: an application server that works very well with Flash. The server script you send your form information to was written using CFML, the markup language for ColdFusion.

ASP.NET: www.microsoft.com/net

Get started learning ASP.NET. This site is a good jumping point for learning how to use this server-side language.

PHP: www.php.net

The place to start learning or using PHP for your work that integrates with a server.

Related Macromedia Press Books

Other Macromedia Press books that might interest you as you continue to learn Flash 8 include the following:

ActionScript for Macromedia Flash 8: Training from the Source, by Francis Cheng; Jen deHaan; Robert L. Dixon; and Shimul Rahim (ISBN 0-321-33619-4)

Developing Extensions for Macromedia Flash 8, by Barbara Snyder (ISBN 0-321-39416-X)

Learning Actionscript 2.0 for Macromedia Flash 8, by Jen deHaan and Peter deHaan (ISBN 0-321-39415-1)

Macromedia Flash 8: A Tutorial Guide, by Jan Armstrong and Jen deHaan (ISBN 0-321-39414-3)

Macromedia Flash MX 2004 ActionScript: Training from the Source, by Derek Franklin and Jobe Makar (ISBN 0-321-21343-2)

Macromedia Flash MX Professional 2004 Application Development: Training from the Source, by Jeanette Stallons (ISBN 0-321-23834-6)

Object-Oriented Programming with ActionScript 2, by James Talbot (ISBN 0-735-71380-4)

Studio MX 2004: Training from the Source, by Jeffrey Bardzell (ISBN 0-321-24158-4)

Using ActionScript Components with Macromedia Flash 8, by Bob Berry, Jen deHaan, Peter deHaan, David Jacowitz, and Wade Pickett (ISBN 0-321-39539-5)

Macromedia Flash 8 Professional: Training from the Source, by Tom Green and Jordan Chilcott (ISBN 0-321-38403-2)

C Keyboard Shortcuts

This appendix includes tables listing the shortcut keystrokes available to perform commands on the Macromedia Flash 8 menus. Both the Windows and Mac shortcuts are shown for each command. The menu tables are in the same order in which they appear on the Flash 8 menu.

File Menu

Command	Windows Shortcut	Mac Shortcut
New	Ctrl+N	Cmd+N
Open	Ctrl+O	Cmd+O
Close	Ctrl+W	Cmd+W
Save	Ctrl+S	Cmd+S
Save As	Ctrl+Shift+S	Cmd+Shift+S
Publish Settings	Ctrl+Shift+F12	Option+Shift+F12
Publish	Ctrl+F12	Shift+F12
Print	Ctrl+P	Cmd+P
Exit	Ctrl+Q	Cmd+Q
Import to Stage	Ctrl+R	Cmd+R
Open External Library	Ctrl+Shift+O	Cmd+O
Export Movie	Ctrl+Alt+Shift+S	Cmd+Option+Shift+S
Default Publish Preview (HTML)	F12	F12

Edit Menu

Command	Windows Shortcut	Mac Shortcut
Undo	Ctrl+Z	Cmd+Z
Redo	Ctrl+Y	Cmd+Y
Cut	Ctrl+X	Cmd+X
Copy	Ctrl+C	Cmd+C
Paste in Center	Ctrl+V	Cmd+V
Paste in Place	Ctrl+Shift+V	Cmd+Shift+V
Clear	Backspace	Delete
Duplicate	Ctrl+D	Cmd+D
Select All	Ctrl+A	Cmd+A
Deselect All	Ctrl+Shift+A	Cmd+Shift+A
Find and Replace	Ctrl+F	Cmd+F
Find Next	F3	F3
Edit Symbols	Ctrl+E	Cmd+E
Cut Frames	Ctrl+Alt+X	Cmd+Option+X
Copy Frames	Ctrl+Alt+C	Cmd+Option+C
Paste Frames	Ctrl+Alt+V	Cmd+Option+V
Clear Frames	Alt+Backspace	Option+Delete
Remove Frames	Shift+F5	Shift+F5
Select All Frames	Ctrl+Alt+A	Cmd+Option+A
Preferences	Ctrl+U	Flash > Preferences

View Menu

Command	Windows Shortcut	Mac Shortcut
Go to First	Home	Home
Go to Previous	Page Up	Page Up
Go to Next	Page Down	Page Down
Go to Last	End	End
Zoom In	Ctrl+=	Cmd+=
Zoom Out	Ctrl+-	Cmd+-
Magnification: 100%	Ctrl+1	Cmd+1
Magnification: 400%	Ctrl+4	Cmd+4
Magnification: 800%	Ctrl+8	Cmd+8
Show Frame	Ctrl+2	Cmd+2
Show All	Ctrl+3	Cmd+3
Outlines	Ctrl+Alt+Shift+O	Cmd+Option+Shift+O
Fast	Ctrl+Alt+Shift+F	Cmd+Option+Shift+F
Anti-alias	Ctrl+Alt+Shift+A	Cmd+Option+Shift+A
Anti-alias Text	Ctrl+Alt+Shift+T	Cmd+Option+Shift+T
Work Area	Ctrl+Shift+W	Cmd+Shift+W
Rulers	Ctrl+Alt+Shift+R	Cmd+Option+Shift+R
Show Grid	Ctrl+'	Cmd+'
Edit Grid	Ctrl+Alt+G	Cmd+Option+G
Show Guides	Ctrl+;	Cmd+;
Lock Guides	Ctrl+Shift+;	Cmd+Shift+;
Edit Guides	Ctrl+Alt+Shift+G	Cmd+Option+Shift+G
Snap to Grid	Ctrl+Shift+'	Cmd+Shift+'
Snap to Guides	Ctrl+Shift+;	Cmd+Shift+;
Snap to Objects	Ctrl+Shift+/	Cmd+Shift+/
Hide Edges	Ctrl+H	Cmd+Shift+E
Show Shape Hints	Ctrl+Alt+H	Cmd+Option+H

Insert Menu

Command	Windows Shortcut	Mac Shortcut
New Symbol	Ctrl+F8	Cmd+F8
Frame	F5	F5

Modify Menu

Command	Windows Shortcut	Mac Shortcut
Document	Ctrl+J	Cmd+J
Convert to Symbol	F8	F8
Break Apart	Ctrl+B	Cmd+B
Optimize	Ctrl+Alt+Shift+C	Cmd+Option+Shift+C
Add Shape Hint	Ctrl+Shift+H	Cmd+Shift+H
Distribute to Layers	Ctrl+Shift+D	Cmd+Shift+D
Convert to Keyframes	F6	F6
Clear Keyframe	Shift+F6	Shift+F6
Convert to Blank Keyframes	F7	F7
Rotate 90 degrees CW	Ctrl+Shift+9	Cmd+Shift+9
Rotate 90 degrees CCW	Ctrl+Shift+7	Cmd+Shift+7
Remove Transform	Ctrl+Shift+Z	Cmd+Shift+Z
Bring to Front	Ctrl+Shift+Up	Option+Shift+Up
Bring Forward	Ctrl+Up	Cmd+Up
Send Backward	Ctrl+Down	Cmd+Down
Send to Back	Ctrl+Shift+Down	Option+Shift+Down
Lock	Ctrl+Alt+L	Cmd+Option+L
Unlock All	Ctrl+Alt+Shift+L	Cmd+Option+Shift+L
Align Left	Ctrl+Alt+1	Cmd+Option+1
Align Horizontal Center	Ctrl+Alt+2	Cmd+Option+2
Align Right	Ctrl+Alt+3	Cmd+Option+3
Align Top	Ctrl+Alt+4	Cmd+Option+4
Align Vertical Center	Ctrl+Alt+5	Cmd+Option+5
Align Bottom	Ctrl+Alt+6	Cmd+Option+6
Distribute Widths	Ctrl+Alt+7	Cmd+Option+7
Distribute Heights	Ctrl+Alt+9	Cmd+Option+9
Make Same Width	Ctrl+Alt+Shift+7	Cmd+Option+Shift+7
Make Same Height	Ctrl+Alt+Shift+9	Cmd+Option+Shift+9
To Stage	Ctrl+Alt+8	Cmd+Option+8
Group	Ctrl+G	Cmd+G
Ungroup	Ctrl+Shift+G	Cmd+Shift+G

Text Menu

Command	Windows Shortcut	Mac Shortcut
Plain	Ctrl+Shift+P	Cmd+Shift+B
Bold	Ctrl+Shift+B	Cmd+Shift+P
Italic	Ctrl+Shift+I	Cmd+Shift+I
Align Left	Ctrl+Shift+L	Cmd+Shift+L
Align Center	Ctrl+Shift+C	Cmd+Shift+C
Align Right	Ctrl+Shift+R	Cmd+Shift+R
Justify	Ctrl+Shift+J	Cmd+Shift+J
Tracking Increase	Ctrl+Alt+Right	Cmd+Option+Right
Tracking Decrease	Ctrl+Alt+Left	Cmd+Option+Left
Tracking Reset	Ctrl+Alt+Up	Cmd+Option+Up

Control Menu

Command	Windows Shortcut	Mac Shortcut
Play	Enter	Enter/Return
Rewind	Ctrl+Alt+R	Cmd+Option+R
Step Forward One Frame	.	.
Step Backward One Frame	,	,
Test Movie	Ctrl+Enter	Cmd+Enter
Debug Movie	Ctrl+Shift+Enter	Cmd+Shift+Enter
Test Scene	Ctrl+Alt+Enter	Cmd+Option+Enter
Test Project	Ctrl+Alt+P	Cmd+Option+P
Enable Simple Buttons	Ctrl+Alt+B	Cmd+Option+B

Window Menu

Command	Windows Shortcut	Mac Shortcut
New Window	Ctrl+Alt+K	Cmd+Option+K
Project	Shift+F8	Shift+F8
Properties	Ctrl+F3	Cmd+F3
Timeline	Ctrl+Alt+T	Cmd+Option+T
Tools	Ctrl+F2	Cmd+F2
Library	Ctrl+L or F11	Cmd+L or F11
Align	Ctrl+K	Cmd+K
Color Mixer	Shift+F9	Shift+F9
Color Swatches	Ctrl+F9	Cmd+F9
Info	Ctrl+I	Cmd+I
Scene	Shift+F2	Shift+F2
Transform	Ctrl+T	Cmd+T
Actions	F9	Option+F9
Behaviors	Shift+F3	Shift+F3
Components	Ctrl+F7	Cmd+F7
Component Inspector	Alt+F7	Option+F7
Debugger	Shift+F4	Shift+F4
Output	F2	F2
Web Services	Ctrl+Shift+F10	Cmd+Shift+F10
Accessibility	Alt+F2	Option+F2
History	Ctrl+F10	Cmd+F10
Movie Explorer	Alt+F3	Option+F3
Strings	Ctrl+F11	Cmd+F11
Hide Panels	F4	F4

Help Menu

Command	Windows Shortcut	Mac Shortcut
Help	F1	F1

Actions Panel

Command	Windows Shortcut	Mac Shortcut
Pin Script	Ctrl+=	Cmd+=
Close Script	Ctrl+-	Cmd+-
Close All Scripts	Ctrl+Shift+-	Cmd+Shift+-
Go to Line	Ctrl+G	Cmd+,
Find	Ctrl+F	Cmd+F
Find Again	F3	Cmd+G
Replace	Ctrl+H	Cmd+Shift+H
Auto Format	Ctrl+Shift+F	Cmd+Shift+F
Check Syntax	Ctrl+T	Cmd+T
Show Code Hint	Ctrl+Spacebar	Cmd+Spacebar
Import Script	Ctrl+Shift+I	Cmd+Shift+I
Export Script	Ctrl+Shift+X	Cmd+Shift+X
View line Numbers	Ctrl+Shift+L	Cmd+Shift+L
Word Wrap	Ctrl+Shift+W	Cmd+Shift+W
Preferences	Ctrl+U	Cmd+U (only in Actions)

Debugger Panel

Command	Windows Shortcut	Mac Shortcut
Continue	F10	F10
Stop Debugging	F11	F11
Step In	F6	F6
Step Over	F7	F7
Step Out	F8	F8

Output Panel

Command	Windows Shortcut	Mac Shortcut
Copy	Ctrl+C	Cmd+C
Find	Ctrl+F	Cmd+F
Find Again	F3	F3

Index

alpha levels/controls
  color, 68
  keyframes, 148
  motion tweens, 137, 138–139
    versus brightness tweens, 136, 304
  opacity, 40
anchor frame labels, 20
  file sizes, 307
Angular blending, 143
animations/animating. *See also*
    frame-by-frame animations;
    motion tweens/tweening;
    shape tweens/tweening
  actions, stopping, 129–132
  creating, inside movie clips, 128
  edit-in-place mode, 129
  menus, 288–295
  Movie Clip button, 140–141
  nesting, 98
  optimizing, 304–305
    runtime bitmap caching, 305–307
  overview, 127
  paths, 149–155
  scrubbing, 136–137
  synchronizing with sound, 196
  using ActionScript, 127, 305
  using movie clips, 127
anti-aliasing
  bitmap graphics, 57
  Bitmap Text option, 84
  device fonts not supported, 72
  text, 74, 77
asynchronous communication, 264
audio. *See* sound(s)
authoring environment. *See* workspace

B

backgrounds
  color, 9
  runtime bitmap caching, 305–307
bandwidth, 307
Bandwidth Profiler, 307, 315, 339–340
behaviors
  interactive FLA documents, 159
  loading JPEGs, 160–164
  opening web pages, 164–166

third-party behaviors, 160
  website resources, 373–374
Behaviors panel, 159
  Action lists, 165
    modifying actions, 166
  adding behaviors
    Add Behavior button, 163, 164
    object instances, 160
  Event lists, 165
beveled joins, strokes, 51
bit rates, 193
bitmap caching, runtime, 305–307
bitmap fills, Color Mixer, 61
bitmap graphics
  anti-aliasing, 57
  compression, 57, 58
  importing, optimization settings, 57
  scaling, 56
    disadvantages, 37
Bitmap Properties dialog box
  anti-aliasing, 57
  compression, 57–58
Bitmap Text option, anti-aliasing, 84
blending options, shape tweens, 143
bounding boxes, 64
built-in components, text, 71
Button class, 243, 244
Button component, 12, 215, 223–228, 231, 276
  adding, 26
  versus button symbols, 228
  deleting from libraries, 54
  linkage identifiers, 224–226
  triggering events, 228
buttons. *See also* text buttons
  aligning, 12, 103
  animating, 140–141
  versus Button component, 228
  creating, 100–102
  duplicating, 173
  events, 99
  file sizes, *versus* movie clips or graphic
    symbols file sizes, 111
  hit area, 101–102
  instances, behaviors, 160, 161, 163
  invisible buttons, 106–107, 109–110
  menus, 295–298

Training from the Source

Macromedia's *Training from the Source* series is one of the best-selling series on the market. This series offers you a unique self-paced approach that introduces you to the major features of the software and guides you step by step through the development of real-world projects.

Each book is divided into a series of lessons. Each lesson begins with an overview of the lesson's content and learning objectives and is divided into short tasks that break the skills into bite-size units. All the files you need for the lessons are included on the CD that comes with the book.

**Macromedia Flash 8:
Training from the Source**
ISBN 0-321-33629-1

**Macromedia Flash
Professional 8: Training
from the Source**
ISBN 0-321-38403-2

**Macromedia Flash 8
ActionScript: Training
from the Source**
ISBN 0-321-33619-4

**Macromedia Studio 8:
Training from the Source**
ISBN 0-321-33620-8

**Macromedia Dreamweaver 8:
Training from the Source**
ISBN 0-321-33626-7

**Macromedia Dreamweaver 8
with ASP, PHP and ColdFusion:
Training from the Source**
ISBN 0-321-33625-9

**Macromedia Fireworks 8:
Training from the Source**
ISBN 0-321-33591-0

macromedia®
PRESS